The Institute of World Politics
1521 16th Street, NW
Washington, DC 20036

The International Politics of
Post-Conflict Reconstruction
in Guatemala

The International Politics of Post-Conflict Reconstruction in Guatemala

Nicola Short

First published in 2007 by
PALGRAVE MACMILLAN™
175 Fifth Avenue, New York, N.Y. 10010 and
Houndmills, Basingstoke, Hampshire, England RG21 6XS
Companies and representatives throughout the world.

PALGRAVE MACMILLAN is the global academic imprint of the Palgrave Macmillan division of St. Martin's Press, LLC and of Palgrave Macmillan Ltd. Macmillan® is a registered trademark in the United States, United Kingdom and other countries. Palgrave is a registered trademark in the European Union and other countries.

ISBN-13: 978–0–230–60051–5
ISBN-10: 0–230–60051–4

Library of Congress Cataloging-in-Publication Data is available from the Library of Congress.

A catalogue record for this book is available from the British Library.

Design by Newgen Imaging Systems (P) Ltd., Chennai, India.

First edition: December 2007

10 9 8 7 6 5 4 3 2 1

Printed in the United States of America.

Contents

List of Figures, Graphs, and Tables   vii

1   Introduction   1
2   Reading Gramscian Politics   9
3   The Ensemble of Social Relations in Guatemala   31
4   The Peace Process   63
5   The Post-Conflict State   91

Appendix 1: Political Chronology of Guatemala   111
Appendix 2: Text of the Socio-Economic Accord   115
Notes   151
Bibliography   171
Index   185

List of Figures, Graphs, and Tables

Figures

3.1 The Current Economic Regions and
   Roads of Guatemala   35
3.2 The Insurgent Regions of Guatemala over Time   47
5.1 Outline of the Socio-Economic Accord   93

Graphs

3.1 Composition of U.S. Foreign Direct Investment   45
3.2 Nontraditional Agricultural Exports in
   Millions of US$ 58
3.3 Guatemalan Maquila Exports in Millions of US$ 58
3.4 Guatemalan Tourism Earnings in Millions of US$ 59
4.1 Bilateral Aid 1980–1990 in US$ Millions   67
4.2 Bilateral Aid 1991–2000 in US$ Millions   67
4.3 Multilateral Aid 1980–1990 in US$ Millions   67
4.4 Multilateral Aid 1991–2000 in US$ Millions   68

Tables

3.1 Guatemalan Coffee Exports by Nationality of
   Exporter, 1938–1939   36
5.1 Outline of the Socio-Economic Accord   105

I

Introduction

The peace process in Guatemala has the potential to become one of the standard-setting achievements of the second half of the twentieth century, in the same class as the Camp David Agreement between Egypt and Israel, the peace settlement in Namibia, the Paris Accords on Cambodia, and the peaceful transitions that took place in Czechoslovakia, Germany, Hungary, and Poland after the collapse of communism in the Soviet Union. It is an ambitious attempt, by visionary Guatemalans and the international community as a whole, to end an ostensibly internal conflict that has torn a country apart for almost two generations.

—Sir Marrack Goulding, former UN under secretary general[1]

The Guatemalan peace process has been considered a success in academic and policymaking circles. It involved polarized groups in dialogue, which seemed impossible during several decades of war. It provided a development program to modernize the economy and national infrastructure that had the support of international organizations and both sides of the negotiating table. The peace process appeared to involve widespread popular participation, and by extension reflect a significantly democratic process. In this reading, the peace process involved disenfranchised communities in national level politics, in principle enhancing both the quality of their representation and their capacity for participation.

Perhaps the greatest sense of success is associated with the perception that the peace agreements were able to address effectively the roots of the armed conflict, or the social bases of conflict (Pásara 2001: 12; Byrne 1997: 3; Goulding 2000: xv). In its strongest formulation, this position argues that the provisions for the post-conflict state in the agreements provide the sort of development necessary for a broadly redistributive project in a country with abysmal social indicators—levels of poverty, access to health care and education, and so on—in both absolute terms and relative to the size of the economy (Burgerman 2000: 81). This view particularly sees the Socio-Economic Accord as striking a balance between social and macroeconomic or structural adjustment concerns.

Another element of the sense of success regarding the Guatemalan peace process relates to the achievement of a robust statement of indigenous rights. Beyond representing an enormous accomplishment in the Guatemalan context, the far-reaching scope of indigenous rights in the agreements is seen as a model for such statements internationally. Christopher Chase-Dunn (2000) argues, for example, that "Guatemala's accord on Identity and Rights of Indigenous Peoples... is a conceptual breakthrough that many other countries should emulate" (109).

The peace process was similarly considered a success in terms of its effect on liberalizing domestic politics in Guatemala. This view, related to the successes of the Indigenous Rights Accord, suggests that the negotiations themselves promoted an opening for broader civic participation in national politics, particularly among center-left organizations and for the promotion of human rights (Armon et al. 1997: 5–6). Suzanne Jonas (2000) uses the metaphor of springtime "because new spaces were opening up within an exclusionary system for broader participation in politics, and indigenous and women's organizations were blossoming" (5). Indeed, the process is credited with cultivating a civil society "capable of playing a leadership role in monitoring and advising the civilian government" (Burgerman 2000: 64).

As Sir Marrack Goulding suggests in the quote at the outset, the accomplishments of the Guatemalan peace process are not seen to be limited to the domestic sphere alone: they are considered a success of the "international community" as well. The Guatemalan peace process is seen as a success for the UN on several issues. Perhaps most significantly, the UN mission for the verification of human rights in Guatemala, MINUGUA, is widely accepted as having reduced human rights abuses and created an atmosphere that allowed wider participation in the peace process than would have otherwise occurred. The UN's role as mediator was seen as both highly successful and an important development in the role of the secretary general in the promotion of peace internationally. Susan Burgerman (2000) describes the case of Guatemala as one of the "most illuminating examples" of "direct intervention in the settlement of civil conflict by the United Nations (UN) Secretary General" in part because the UN mediator's conduct "extended beyond the role of 'good offices' to initiating independent proposals, including recommendations for disarmament procedures, military restructuring, and judicial and constitutional reform measures" (63). Finally, the international community is seen as having succeeded in Guatemala in terms of its coordination on financial questions and its willingness to consider "peace conditionality" in policies vis-à-vis Guatemala. Guatemala provided an opportunity for the UN and the international financial institutions (IFIs) to address the criticism of working at cross-purposes, which had been particularly leveled against the Salvadoran peace process (de Soto and del Castillo 1994). The achievement of communication and coordination between the multilateral institutions constitutes part of the understanding of the peace process as a success of the international community.

To borrow a metaphor that Finn Stepputat (1999) uses for the post-conflict Guatemalan State, in many ways the peace process itself served as a laboratory for the UN and the IFIs to refine their understandings of peace negotiations and post-conflict reconstruction (54). These "trials" were considered positively conclusive: Jeremy Armon (1997) echoing the sentiments of many, has argued that the lesson of Guatemala is that "there is clearly a facilitatory role for the international community in bringing civil wars to an end, and nurturing the conditions for increased political tolerance and diversity" (7).

To the extent that there have been concerns about Guatemala since the peace process, significant levels of criminal violence, for example, for many the blame lies not with the peace process itself, but with the failure to implement the peace agreements fully. Roland Paris (2004), for example, argues that the failure to implement certain fiscal measures in the peace agreements has undermined the social spending-structural adjustment balance in the accords, threatening the prospects for peace (131–134).

The (re)construction of the post-conflict state implies the most profound questions of political theory: how are political institutions to be designed, under whose authority or consent, and how will economic production and distribution be organized? Yet as Paris has observed, these essential political-theoretical questions have largely been implicit in the peacebuilding discourses and practices since the end of the cold war (5). In the case of Guatemala, one might ask: how and on what grounds were the social bases of conflict addressed? On what foundation were indigenous rights established? What new understandings were explicitly or implicitly established to improve coordination between multilateral organizations that historically approached post-conflict reconstruction differently?

The atheoretical bias of much of the current policy-related research on peace processes and post-conflict societies reflects a general orientation toward "problem-solving" knowledge. Problem-solving theories "take the world as they see it" and aim to make "relationships and institutions work smoothly by dealing effectively with particular sources of trouble" (Cox 1981: 129). Such theories accept the dominant social scientific categories and social institutions as legitimate, "value-free" parameters of analysis implicitly adopting certain kinds of ahistoricity vis-à-vis the subjects they examine. Problem-solving theory is "value-bound" in that it accepts "the prevailing order as its own framework" and engages with a "continuing present" in the form of "the permanence of the institutions and power relations which constitute its parameters" (129).

By contrast, as captured in Robert Cox's famous dictum, "theory is always for someone and for some purpose," the purpose of a critical theoretical perspective is to uncover the interests behind dominant understandings of the status quo that problem-solving theories implicitly reproduce (128). Where problem-solving theories take social and political institutions as "given," critical theories seek to analyze them in terms of their histories, interrelationships, and processes of transformation. A critical perspective thus implies understanding how power is constructed historically and how power relationships become naturalized or obscured. Where problem-solving theory establishes narrow parameters on its analytical remit, critical theory seeks to establish a holistic understanding: "the critical approach leads towards the construction of a larger picture of the whole of which the initially contemplated part is just one component, and seeks to understand the processes of change in which both parts and whole are involved" (129).

This book suggests that a holistic method of analysis is necessary to understand peace processes in their full theoretical, historical, and international context and to evaluate fully the success claims made regarding the Guatemalan peace process.

Thus, the point of departure of this work is to construct a critical theoretical framework to evaluate peace processes in the post–cold war era (chapter 2). It does so by offering a reading of the work of the early twentieth-century Italian political theorist Antonio Gramsci. Gramsci's great theoretical contribution was written in prison in fascist Italy (1929–1935); his *Prison Notebooks* have become available to English-speaking audiences only gradually. In 1976 Herbert Reid and Ernest J. Yanarella (1976) suggested the value of using a Gramscian approach in Peace Research, a proposal that was not visibly taken up by the field. Indeed, as Lee-Anne Broadhead (1997) has noted, Peace Research largely missed this critical theoretical turn that greatly influence other, related fields of study, especially International Relations/International Political Economy (IR/IPE) through the work of Cox.[2]

Gramsci's method is historical materialist: it seeks to analyze the material foundations and historical construction of social institutions. His most notable theoretical contribution involves his particular attention to theorizing the role of cultural institutions and civil society in mediating power in society. In this sense his work is particularly suited to the study of conflict, because it provides a way of theorizing the history and materiality of identity. The emphasis in IR/IPE has been to use Gramsci's political theory, especially his conceptions of power, hegemony, and historical blocs, to examine the structural face of power established through the international economy and expressed through international relations. It is argued here that combining that tradition with a theorization of the question of difference through the lens of "articulation," as Stuart Hall has done in using Gramscian theory in Cultural Studies, provides a way of understanding social relations across a number of fields, within states and between them, including the different material and subject positions of "North" and "South" in different world orders.

A Gramscian analytical framework provides an important lens with which to understand the transformation of the "ensemble of social relations" in Guatemala over time, and the dense, mutually constitutive relationships between the material, the subjective, and conflict in that evolution (as discussed in chapter 3). Such a perspective, for example, illuminates the particular logic of the origins of the counterinsurgent state, which cannot be understood as a reaction to "communism"—as claimed by U.S. and Guatemalan elites—but as a reaction to the challenges to the "disarticulated" socioeconomic relations in Guatemala. The construction of the counterinsurgent state is not overdetermined by the logic of capitalism, but reflects modernization theory's subjective interpretation of capitalist accumulation in the postcolonial era in the South: a reiteration of the persistent question of how "liberalism" deals with its culturally embedded "Other." This legacy takes a violent, irrational guise, under the weight of the contradictions inaugurated by modernizing counterinsurgency; contradictions that lead to the impulse for a new, neoliberal order, one that does not supersede liberalism's challenges but rearticulates them with a new ethicopolitical rationale.

A Gramscian reading of the Guatemalan peace process shows the complex interaction between international and regional politics and the local politics over the course of many years of negotiations (chapter 4). The parameters for peace process in Guatemala were determined by a number of factors, including the regional and international context of the discussions, and the role of different international actors in supporting (or withdrawing support for) various Guatemalan State and civil society actors before and during the negotiations. While there were great efforts by international actors to engage civil society in the negotiations and to "liberalize" Guatemala's political culture, this did not democratize participation in the sense that economic factors still greatly determined the degree of influence of civil society actors. Furthermore, the structure and sequencing of the negotiations themselves relegated the most "essential" questions of the post-conflict state to the least democratic period of the negotiations. Overall, the peace negotiations can be understood as a "passive revolution" of elites, who were able to manage these key aspects of the post-conflict society in their interests while maintaining a coercive apparatus for the state.

Perhaps most interesting, however, is what a Gramscian reading of the peace accords themselves can illuminate about the post-conflict state: how this neoliberal raison d'etat addresses the particular contradictions of the genocidal modernizing, counterinsurgent state in Guatemala (analyzed in chapter 5). The "resolution" offered by the accords would not be fully implemented, though the implementation process and associated forms of international oversight—a consultative group of donors and the related peace conditionality—were consistent with neoliberal world order.

In sum, a Gramscian reading of the Guatemalan peace process offers a critical theoretical analysis of peace processes, one that challenges peace research to engage with the profound political-theoretical implications of peace processes and post-conflict reconstruction. It provides a basis for understanding the material and subjective dimensions of conflict in international and historical perspective, a method to illuminate the operation of power in "consensual" milieux such as   peace negotiations, and a means to link the blueprints for the post-conflict state embodied in peace agreements to world order. The chapters that follow provide the explanation for how this can be done, and the implications the Guatemalan case has in turn for understanding political theory and world order.

2

Reading Gramscian Politics

The political and social theory of Antonio Gramsci has had a significant influence among critical scholars in the social sciences.[1] Yet, perhaps more than the work of other theorists, Gramscian analysis is not self-evident and requires interpretation and exegesis: most significantly, Gramsci's greatest contributions to theory were written in prison, under the gaze of censors, circumstances under which he developed a number of euphemisms and codes for political figures and events. Compounding this, however, is the fact that Gramsci's prison note-books have become available to scholars only gradually, being published in a somewhat piecemeal manner, particularly in translation, making the task of interpretation more challenging.[2] These issues not-withstanding, Gramsci has often been subjected to partial readings that flatten his political theory to (a typically oversimplified understanding of) his conception of hegemony.

This chapter provides a reading of Gramsci's political and social theory, one that aims in particular to understand how his theories can be used to analyze peace processes. Gramsci's conception of power involves mutually constitutive ideational, subjective, and material components. These elements are manifest and operate across different levels of analysis: individual consciousness, group identity, and world order, where within different social and political formations, different perspectives are "articulated" to one another though both material and ideational relationships to constitute the whole. Gramscian analysis provides insight into how these structural and subjective faces of power condition the possibilities for social change, as well as a way to understand the material and subjective dimensions of group identity, constraints on progressive social change, and the operation of power across institutional boundaries (the state and civil society, the domestic and the international).

A Gramscian Conception of Power

No reading of Gramsci's work is complete without understanding his contribution to theorizing power, which, while heavily related to his conception of hegemony, cannot be reduced to it. Nevertheless, as the most "naturalized" condition of power, hegemony represents the foundation of Gramsci's most original and sophisticated contributions. It thus provides a fruitful point of departure for understanding Gramsci's conceptions of power, which involves the interplay between coercion and consent, where struggles for social dominance occur in the mutually constituted material and ideational realms.

Gramscian hegemony reflects a form of political power that operates predominantly through consent, yet with the ever-present possibility of coercion to protect the dominant order. Hegemony manifests itself as "spontaneous consent" for "the general direction imposed on social life by the dominant fundamental group." State coercion exists to guarantee this "natural" social condition: "The apparatus of state coercive power . . . 'legally' enforces discipline on those groups who do not 'consent' either actively or passively. This apparatus is, however, constituted for the whole of society in anticipation of moments of crisis of command and direction when spontaneous consent has failed" (Gramsci 1991: 12). Thus, the legitimacy of coercion is constructed around a specific social order. Force, "domination," is a resource held by the ruling groups but its legitimate use is a shared construction of dominant and subordinate groups.

Hegemony requires that a potentially dominant group express its narrow corporate interests in universal terms that appeal to the larger sociopolitical unit, which unifies different groups' social and political aims under an ideology that ultimately privileges the hegemonic group (181–182). The political purchase of hegemonic concepts comes from their ability to seem universal, in the interest of all. Thus, "the development and expansion of the particular group are conceived of, and presented as being the motor force of a universal expansion, of a development of all the 'national' energies" (181–182). Hegemony expresses the shared political understandings of dominant and subordinate groups. The dominant group controls the apparatuses of force in society; however, the social order is accepted and equally reproduced by subordinate groups. Hegemony is "ethicopolitical" in that cultural factors are as important as economic and political ones in its justification. Yet Gramsci qualifies this element by reiterating that "the philosophy of praxis [Marxism] . . . judges the reduction of history to ethico-political history alone as improper and arbitrary, but does not exclude the latter" (Forgacs 1988: 195).[3]

The universalization stage is the most "purely political phase" of hegemony, and the universal expression of the hegemon's interests may involve specific concessions to subaltern groups (Gramsci 1991: 181). The hegemonic group may need to modify implicitly its goals to accommodate those of other groups. Such compromises are of an "economic-corporate" kind, they do not "touch the essential," that is, the economic order at the root of a society. "[T]hough hegemony is ethico-political, it must also be economic, must necessarily be based on the decisive function exercised by the leading group in the decisive nucleus of economic activity" (161). The concessions inherent in the notion of consent in hegemony are made precisely to preserve the social order, not to empower marginalized groups. Though dynamic in its expression, ultimately hegemony protects a particular economic order.

Hegemony is a condition of power that does not require the direct exercise of force, although it does require the continuous leadership of a dominant group:

> A social group can, and indeed must, already exercise "leadership" before winning governmental power (this indeed is one of the principal conditions for the winning of such power); it subsequently becomes dominant when it exercises power, but even if it holds it firmly in its grasp, it must continue to "lead" as well. (57–58)

Hegemony must be continually renewed through the exercise of intellectual and moral leadership, and such leadership requires understanding and appealing to the interests of subordinate groups. The coercive threat underpinning the hegemonic group's dominance appears only when the system breaks down. Thus, as Cox (1993) puts it, "coercion is always latent but is only applied in marginal, deviant cases. Hegemony is enough to ensure conformity of behaviour in most people most of the time" (52). Not all ruling groups are hegemonic, they may rule through direct coercion; however, the consent implied in a hegemonic system is the most stable form of power. The construction of consent, then, through "intellectual and moral leadership" represents a significant dimension of attaining power.

There is little in the *Prison Notebooks* on the specifics of "intellectual and moral leadership" (Gramsci 1991: 57). Nonetheless, Gramsci argues that "All men are intellectuals... but not all men have in society the function of intellectuals" (9). Those that "function" as intellectuals reflect historically formed social groups that make up a social order (10). Intellectuals are socially situated: each group may produce its own "organic" intellectuals. However, intellectual activity is a complex exchange between the "common sense" of one's lived experience and "ideological superstructures" that shape society. The intellectual process is complex and " 'mediated' by the whole fabric of society and by the complex of superstructures" (12). Thus there is a dialectic between an intellectual's background and the attraction of intellectual activities of other groups. The more important social groups are able to promote "more extensive and more complex elaboration" of their positions (10). This power of attraction can end up "subjugating the intellectuals of other social groups...thereby creat[ing] a system of solidarity between all the intellectuals, with bonds of a psychological nature (vanity, etc.) and often of caste character (technico-juridical, corporate, etc.)" (60).

Knowledge is infused with the social categories of society and the power relationships that they imply. As Stephen Gill (1993a) notes, based on Cox's famous observation, "by linking a theory of knowledge to a theory of identity and interests, Gramsci was able to show how...theory is always for someone and for some purpose" (25). Intellectuals, although potentially counterhegemonic, more often serve as " 'deputies' exercising the subaltern functions of social hegemony and political government" for the dominant group, generating "spontaneous" consent and justifying state coercion (Gramsci 1991: 12). Indeed, Gramsci uses the term intellectual to mean anyone who actively articulates rationales for the political-social order, whose ranks have greatly expanded in the modern era. "The democratic-bureaucratic system has given rise to a great mass of functions which are not all justified by the social necessities of production, though they are justified by the political necessity of the dominant fundamental group" (13).

The role of intellectual elaboration as part of the exercise of power has rightly been the focus of much neo-Gramscian scholarship, for example, Gill's (1990) study of the Trilateral Commission and William I. Robinson's (1996b) discussion of the role of U.S. academe in defining democracy. Such studies engage with the "organic" intellectual activity of dominant groups. Yet intellectual and moral leadership occurs in more diffuse ways as well, as Cox (1979) has illustrated in his discussion of NGO networks dealing with North-South issues and the New International Economic Order, where within such multilateral fora the material demands of research dictate that "intellectual production is now organized like the production of goods or of other services"; incorporating other view points around basic orthodoxies.

For intellectual activity to have any leadership potential it must be compatible with the "common sense" of the groups to be influenced. Common sense captures "the conception of the world which is uncritically absorbed by the various social and cultural environments in which the moral individuality of the average man is developed" (Gramsci 1991: 419). This phenomenon reflects the accumulation of conventional wisdom over time: it is a reflection of dominant cultural and historical legacies in a society (325–326). Only philosophies that engage with common sense can become historically effective. As Stuart Hall (1996) puts it, "formal coherence cannot guarantee [an ideology's] organic historical effectivity. That can only be found when and where philosophical currents enter into, modify and transform the practical, everyday consciousness or popular thought of the masses" (431). This expression may come from a number of sources, including subordinated members of hegemonic institutions: for example, Gramsci (1991) observes that subaltern groups in the military demonstrate the most conspicuous allegiances to the hegemonic project (13, fn).[4]

Gramsci understands ideas as material forces that create political consciousness and political subjects (365). An individual may have competing political identities, but consciousness is also a collective phenomenon, "a consequence of the relationship between 'the self' and the ideological discourses which compose the cultural terrain of society" (Hall 1996: 433). Gramsci (1991) conceives of consciousness as grounded both in the actual, material circumstances of real life, as well as in one's socialization, which he describes as "two theoretical consciousnesses" (333).[5] This latter element, one's received understanding of the world, may be as powerful and meaningful as the former. This received conception of one's self creates collective identities and conditions one's propensity for political action (in potentially debilitating ways: "often powerfully enough to produce a state in which the contradictory state of consciousness does not permit any action...and produces a condition of moral and political passivity" [333]). Gramsci does see transformative potential in the critical understanding of oneself, which "takes place through a struggle of political 'hegemonies,'" but the outcome of this struggle may not be guaranteed (333). Hall (1996) argues, "this complex, fragmentary and contradictory conception of consciousness is a considerable advance over the explanation by way of 'false consciousness' more traditional to marxist theorizing but which is an explanation that depends on self-deception and which he rightly treats as inadequate" (433). Political identification occurs in terms that are salient to a specific collective sense of history and society, whose transformation—as it is constructed by both dominant and subaltern groups—is psychosocially complex.

Gramsci understands power as embedded in social practices and reinforced by the material and ideological structures of society. To take Steven Lukes' (1974) discussion of power as a guide, Gramsci's most approximates a three-dimensional view of power. In Lukes' schema, a one-dimensional view sees power only as expressed through overt conflict. A two-dimensional view sees power expressed through both conflict and the ability to set the public (or other relevant) agenda: "it allows for consideration of the ways in which *decisions* are prevented from being taken on *potential issues* over which there is an observable *conflict* of (subjective) *interests*…" (20, emphasis in original). The third view of power goes further to look at how power might act to create peoples' understanding of their own interests, and thus might operate beyond the realm of observable conflicts of interest.[6] Barry Hindess (1976) has rightly critiqued Lukes' conception for failing to include the social context of power in his emphasis on maintaining an empirical focus. As Gramsci's conception of power is quite explicitly embedded in the "ensemble of social relations," it moves beyond Lukes' third dimension.[7]

Gramsci's account of power is more vigorous and satisfying than definitions of power in mainstream IR. As Paul Hirst (1998) observes, the dominant understanding of power in IR involves a "capacity-outcome" model, where power is a "simple quantitative capacity" exercised in a zero-sum game, so "an actor's capacities can be judged essentially by outcomes—who 'has' power is who prevails" (133–134). He argues that this is not only true of realists, but of their critics as well, who fail in their critiques to offer coherent alternatives (134).[8] Gill (2003) has observed that, like realists, world systems analysts understand power as "power over"; he calls the two collectively, "the conventional wisdom on the American case" (74). The combination of world systems theory and Gramscian analysis, as has been attempted, for example, by Robinson, thus implies significant tensions with the reading of Gramsci offered here, as Robinson does not explicitly reconcile the relationship between these two conceptions of power.[9] (His analysis does provide a helpful reading of the nature of democracy promotion in U.S. foreign policy, including documenting some of the specific strategies used to marginalize popular elements in authoritarian-democratic transitions. This contribution, rather than representing a compelling alternative to neo-Gramscian IPE, would fit under the rubric of an elaboration of "intellectual and moral leadership" in the reading of Gramsci offered here.)

Although Gramsci's (1991) understanding of power and hegemony appear to operate in a "totalizing" manner, "a social form 'always' has marginal possibilities for further development and organizational improvement" (222). As hegemony is exercised through continuous leadership, it may also be challenged and replaced through a "war of position." A war of position is the strategy of creating the intellectual and moral leadership component of hegemony before holding the state's coercive power: it is the creation of a viable alternative hegemony in civil society before controlling the institutional "state." The war of position reflects the ideological-cultural battle to be waged, in contrast to the war of manoeuvre, the physical, military battle to control the state, of conventional revolutionary politics. Gramsci (1991) understood that in the modern political environment the war of position would increasingly replace the war of manoeuvre (206–275; Hall 1996: 427).

Nonetheless, conservative forces generally have the advantage vis-à-vis progressive forces in society. Gramsci (1991) describes conditions where the elite respond to a crisis in their leadership or power through a top-down reorganization of society in terms of a "passive revolution" (61).[10] In a passive revolution, the case for social change is co-opted by the dominant group; in the end, a degree of social change is achieved, but on terms favorable to the dominant group and without the participation of the majority. (Gramsci considered fascism in Italy to be an example of a passive revolution, unlike many Marxists of the day, who considered it the "last gasp of capitalism.") This co-optation may manifest itself in various strategies, such as the intellectual leadership inherent in successful hegemony, or the notion of direct co-optation that Gramsci (1991) terms *trasformismo*: the appropriation of leadership from, or the wholesale restructuring of, opposition parties or groups such that they lose their independent identity (58 fn6).

In sum, deconstructing Gramsci's conception of hegemony allows for an understanding of the constituent elements of his understanding of power: a phenomenon that operates through a combination of coercion and consent. The means of coercion are held by the socially dominant group; however, the legitimacy of its use must be constructed across society. This social construction of consent is material, in the sense that dominant groups have greater resources for the elaboration of "ethicopolitical" rationales for structuring society in their interests, a position that history favors as such perspectives become manifest in the "common sense" understandings of society and its traditions. However, the materiality of lived experiences also informs individuals' consciousnesses and may provide the grounds for an emancipatory critique, though this is by no means assured.

The multifaceted nature of power—material, ideational, subjective—is "institutionalized" and operates both through social structures and through subjectivity. For this reason, Gramsci emphasized the necessity of analyzing politics in full context, what he called the "ensemble of social relations."

The Ensemble of Social Relations

Gramsci's (1991) understanding of politics as informed by power operating through historically and materially constructed knowledge and subjectivity is reflected in a broad conception of the state. In his view, the "state = political society + civil society" (262–263).[11] This amplification of the notion of state reflects Gramsci's observation that at the time of the Russian Revolution "advanced" liberal states were very resilient to revolutionary social change. He (1978) argues that in these cases powerful interests did not need to control the state itself to exercise power over society: they could do so through the arena of civil society. Civil society reflects an "organizational reserve" of the ruling classes. As a result, "[t]he state apparatus is far more resistant than is often possible to believe, and it succeeds, in moments of crisis, in organizing greater forces loyal to the regime than the depth of the crisis might lead one to suppose" (409).

For Gramsci (1991), the idea of state includes the social structures of civil society that affect political consciousness: religious institutions, the education system, the press, and so on. The state is seen not merely as the monopoly of "legitimate" force but as an active agent in socializing the body politic. It is administrative and coercive, as well as educational and formative (258–259). Governance occurs through the state narrowly conceived, as well as through the institutions of civil society where the ideological structures of the dominant classes can be constructed and disseminated. It incorporates a combination of direct coercion, socialization, and the cultivation of consent embodied in the notion of hegemony.[12]

Luis Razeto Migliaro and Pasquale Misuraca (1982) suggest that Gramsci's understanding of the state is not "a fortress to be stormed, as a machine which can be operated differently by various political managements, or as an institutional apparatus which can be the property of a class," but rather "the organization of relations between leaders and led" (72, 73). Thus for Gramsci, rather than emphasis on the "character" of the state (capitalist, socialist, etc.) per se, the emphasis is on the "ensemble of social relations" and its implied strategies of governance (77).

Gramsci's understanding of civil society has been widely cited and often misinterpreted, particularly by those who maintain, consciously or not, a liberal ontology of the term, "unable to break free from the binary State/non-State opposition that resides at the heart of classical liberal theory" (Buttigieg 2005: 38). Thus, those associated with the *Global Civil Society Yearbook* among others, have claimed Gramsci's understanding of civil society was located in the realm of the " 'non-state *and* the non-economic area of social interaction'" (38). As Joseph A. Buttigieg (2005) shows, such claims misunderstand Gramsci's work, particularly his conception of the integral state, which challenges the liberal ontological division between the state and private interests. For Gramsci (1991), civil society—far from noneconomic—plays a mediating role between the economic structure and the state ("between the economic structure and the State with its legislation and its coercion stands civil society" [208]). His emphasis is less on an inviolable sphere protected from the state than on a cultural milieu that constructs the rationality and *homo economicus* necessary for production; as Hoare and Newell suggest, "civil society is in effect equated 'the mode of economic behaviour'" (209). Liberal ontology assumes civil society exists in opposition to the state: Gramsci's conception of the integral state directly challenges this idea. Gramsci did see civil society as the site for any potentially counterhegemonic politics; however, the emancipatory significance of such movements depends not on their location as part of "civil society" but on the content of their political program (as well as their ability to affect meaningful "intellectual and moral leadership").

The "historical bloc" provides a means of conceptualizing the institutionalization of the "ensemble of social relations" at a particular historical moment. The historical bloc is "the complex, contradictory and discordant *ensemble* of the superstructures is the reflection of the *ensemble* of the social relations of production" (366, emphasis in original). This conception is a feature of Gramsci's theory that is often considered to distinguish him most from orthodox Marxism (Smart 1983: 39; Forgacs 1988: 424). Yet Gramsci (1991) makes this claim specifically by appealing to Marx.

> [Marx's propositions tend] to reinforce the conception of *historical bloc* in which precisely material forces are the content and ideologies are the form, though this distinction between form and content has purely didactic value, since the material forces would be inconceivable historically without form and the ideologies would be individual fancies without the material forces. (377, emphasis in original)

Razeto and Misuraca suggest that the difference between Gramsci and (the later) Marx on this matter involves their different understandings of civil society. As Marx reduced civil society to economic relations devoid of mediating institutions of intellectual and moral leadership, he could not distinguish specific relations between base and superstructure, and as a result "the concrete ways in which the economy and society actually relate to the state escape analysis and subsequently are seen abstractly, by means of speculative concepts, such as determination, correspondence, reflection, conditioning, etc." (Razeto Migliaro and Misuraca 1982: 80). Gramsci's conception of civil society, by including the dimension of intellectual and moral leadership, allows for more precise and multidimensional analysis.[13] Gramsci's notion of a bloc involves the dimension of political subjectivity, rather than exclusively "objective" categories of some orthodox Marxisms (Boggs 1984: 228–229).[14]

The relationships between social groups within a historical bloc can be understood through the lens of articulation, as the work of Hall has shown. As he (1980) notes, the term articulation has two meanings in English: both "joining up" as in a structural form and "giving expression to," which capture elegantly the structural and subjective aspects of the concept (322). Hall argues that the idea of "articulation" can capture the relationship between race and other collective identities, "not by deserting the level of analysis of economic relations (i.e. mode of production) but by posing it in its correct, necessarily complex, form" (322). The concept of articulation underscores the necessity of demonstrating (rather than assuming), what the "nature and degree of 'correspondence' [between social groups] is, in any specific historical case" (330). Hall credits Gramsci with this raising the necessity of such historically specific (and contingent) analysis within the Marxian tradition. Gramsci's emphasis on the historical bloc as a "historically concrete articulation" of the specificity of the "structure-superstructure complex" reflects this ethos and allows for a "rigorously nonreductionist" conception of the relationship between the material and the social (332).

Hall (1996) argues,

> The ethnic and racial structuration of the labour force, like its gendered composition, may provide an inhibition to the rationalistically conceived "global" tendencies of capitalist development. And yet, these distinctions have been maintained, and indeed developed and refined, in the global expansion of the capitalist mode. (436)

With this perspective in mind, marginalized sectors in a social formation become sites for critical analysis. Hall reflects on practices of incorporating "backwards" sectors—for example, peasant economies in industrializing Latin American societies, Gramsci's Sardinia, or apartheid era "Bantustans"—into more "advanced" economic structures: "Theoretically what needs to be noticed is the persistent way in which *these* specific, differentiated forms of 'incorporation' have consistently been associated with the appearance of racist, ethnically segmentary and other similar social features" (1996: 437, emphasis in original). For Hall (1980), racism is not exclusively a problem of capitalism, nor do all capitalisms have the same issues of race: he argues, "one is required to show how thoroughly racism is reorganized and rearticulated with the relations of new modes of production" and "how and why racism has been specifically overdetermined by and articulated with certain capitalisms at different stages of their development" (337, 38–39).

The subjectivity of marginalized groups must be given an autonomous voice in strategies for progressive social change. In his discussions of the "Southern question" in Italy (the uneven development of the South in relation to the North), Gramsci (1978) noted that the Southern peasants had been oppressed and exploited "in yet more odious and bestial ways" than the Northern workers (445). Obstacles to a mutual alliance existed on both sides: Northern workers internalized Northern bourgeois attitudes that viewed the South as an impediment to the North and Southerners as biologically inferior (444). Southern peasants were likewise ill-served by Southern intellectuals (such as Benedetto Croce), whose affiliations lay with national and European society (460). The political challenge involved helping Southern peasants to see their true affiliation should be with

Northern workers rather than with the Southern gentry, a process in which Gramsci argued that the Turin workers should not ask for "guarantees of any kind: neither to the party, nor to a programme, nor to the discipline of the Socialist parliamentary group" but allow their Southern collaborators remain answerable to their own constituencies (446, 51).

Articulation extends the notion of integral state to an appreciation of how power not only operates across the "public/private" division of state-civil society, but through subjectivities and identities. Articulation illuminates how coercion and consent may vary in their specific expression vis-à-vis different elements in the "ensemble of social relations," and that these are naturalized through the production of different political subjects.

Although, as Gill (1993b) has argued, there is no single interpretation of Gramscian political theory as it applies to questions of IPE, scholars working in this tradition have applied the idea of the ensemble of social relations and the historical bloc to IR (2). Robinson (1996b) has charged that this tradition has failed to consider "hegemonic relations between dominant and subordinate classes in the core-periphery context" (30).[15] As discussed below, this accusation seems unfounded, although it is argued here that the idea of "articulation" is a useful lens for understanding the complex relationships between the material and the subjective between industrializing and developing countries in the global ensemble of social relations.

Cox's (1987) *Power, Production, and World Order* represents one of the most elaborated neo-Gramscian IPE studies of world order. In his framework, world orders, raisons d'etat, and the social forces of production are mutually constituting: states construct the possibilities for production, world orders affect the possibilities of different raisons d'etat, and changes in both states and world orders affect changes in production (105–109). His framework describes several world orders and associated raisons d'etat (of which there could be more than one for any particular world order). The period of liberal hegemony (1848–1870), constructed the liberal state in the core, but not in the periphery, though it exported the functions of the liberal state as widely as possible (145–146).[16] In non-European, penetrated regions, new social orders were constructed not on the basis of an internal liberalism, but on the basis of preserving the basis for the core's "liberal" production and exchange. Under the period of American hegemony that Cox identifies (the end of World War II until the end of the Breton Woods system), different raisons d'etat were likewise constructed in core and periphery (218–219). Cox suggests that hegemonic world orders do not produce a single raison d'etat, but they do tend "to limit forms of state to those that are compatible with the prevailing social structure of accumulation" while economic-productive structures are made compatible with the hegemonic order (209–210).

Cox does, then, examine the differential impact of world order on forms of state and production in the industrialized world and the non-industrialized world. However, his analysis remains predominantly concerned with the nature of world order, focusing on the degree of attachment to the dominant economic order more than the social implications of such differences. As he argues, in the liberal world order,

> The responsibility of the state and the state system was to ensure the conditions for this open world economy while refraining from interfering with the operations of these economic agents. This was the meaning of "liberal" as attached to the terms state or world order. Liberalism had a circumstantial connection with political pluralism and parliamentary government in the British case. Regimes in other countries proved capable of achieving the same balance between economy and politics under authoritarian auspices. Both were "liberal" in the sense discussed here. (127)

This emphasis on world order obscures the experience of noncore social formations vis-à-vis the hegemonic or dominant condition, subsuming them into the dominant logic.

However, posing the question of uneven development as a question of articulation brings attention to how the heterogeneous elements within the ensemble of social relations across North and South might be analyzed. Indeed, the issue of "articulation" as it pertains to race, for example, directly reflects the historical-materially structured nature of international production around the construction of subjective differences. The "norm against noticing" race in IR remains a challenge to the discipline that cannot be resolved here (Vitalis 2000: 333). Nonetheless, it can be argued that even if the end of colonial rule and the generalization of the state as the form of political administration across the globe appeared to "resolve" the question of race in mainstream international relations, from a Gramscian perspective, such a move at the formal, institutional level does not account for how power operates across numerous social fields in the ensemble of social relations. Articulation is a useful analytic tool to capture how politics differ within core countries vis-à-vis core-periphery relations within a single historical bloc. It also captures the politics of subjectivity that have so structured development discourse and practices.

Gramscian Politics and the Analysis of Peace Processes

Incorporating the idea of articulation to the analysis of IPE provides a broader framework for the analysis of world order. Cox (1987) describes the immediate post–World War II era outside the Soviet sphere as a world order historical bloc characterized by U.S. hegemony, based on the premise that the world economy was "a positive sum game in which some businesses and some national economies may benefit more than other but in which all have the opportunity to gain" (217). This order underwritten by U.S. military dominance, and reinforced by multilateral financial institutions (especially the IMF), which were able to use both incentives and sanctions to incorporate "more reluctant governments" and "disabled national economies" (217). The raison d'etat of core states under this hegemony involved a Keynesian/New Deal state that negotiated the concerns of labor vis-à-vis national factions of capital and between national capital and international markets (Cox 1987: 220; Gill 2003: 87). John Gerald Ruggie (1982) has described the intellectual and moral leadership of the United States in securing consent among industrialized states and the construction of international organizations to establish such an order as a form of "embedded liberalism." The essence of embedded liberalism was a compromise brokered by the United States with other industrialized states: "unlike the economic nationalism of the thirties, it would be multilateral in character; unlike the liberalism of the gold standard and free trade, its multilateralism would be predicated upon domestic interventionism" (393). As such, "embedded liberalism" reflected a consensual hegemony in Cox's schema; however, this hegemony was not global: it excluded the Soviet Bloc countries and the nonindustrialized South.

While relations in the West were governed by an embedded-liberal compact among industrialized states; the nonindustrialized states of the "global South" were articulated to this order differently. The West sought to incorporate the South into the broader liberal-capitalist bloc; however, the "development problematic" assumed different material and subjective conditions, which positioned the South differently in the postwar order.

The intellectual and moral leadership dominant in the West, and largely emanating from the United States, around development issues in this period is captured in the principles of modernization theory. The classic expression of modernization theory is W.W. Rostow's (1990) *The Stages of Economic Growth: A Non-communist Manifesto*, which posited a universal sequence of development through which all societies would pass, based on the Western experience with industrialization. For Rostow, the colonial experience was a necessary precursor to modernization, as non-Western societies were incapable of modernizing themselves: "Colonies were often established initially not to execute a major objective of national policy, nor even to exclude a rival economic power, but to fill a vacuum; that is, to organize a traditional society incapable of self-organization (or unwilling to organize itself) for modern import and export activity" (109). And, indeed, the implication of modernization theory was that "development" involved the continued viability of colonial economic relationships between industrialized and nonindustrialized countries.[17]

Modernization theory posited a hierarchy of cultural values: as Tariq Banuri (1990) puts it, "a linear scale on which industrialized countries were unequivocally ahead of the Third World and the 'modern' sector unequivocally ahead of the 'traditional' sector within the Third World" (42). Modernization theory stressed the necessity of promoting the transition from the "traditional" to the "modern," and to achieve this, a strong commitment to elites as agents of such change (Leys 1996: 10; Roxborough 1988: 755). (As a corollary, such research provoked consideration of the "rationality" of traditional societies [Banuri 1990: 41–44].[18])

In their preference for "modern" elites, modernization theories assumed the persistence of "disarticulated" social hierarchies, where sociological divisions between groups understood as "traditional" and "modern" allow for the persistence of coercive and exploitative practices. Wages can be kept below the minimum otherwise required to maintain and reproduce the labor force by having the subsistence economy provide part of people's sustenance, a system that functions economically because such peripheral economies produce for external markets: there is no need to maintain purchasing power among workers as in a center economy (de Janvry 1981: 36). "Disarticulation" reflects a mode of production "structured in dominance," although it may formally appear free. As Alain de Janvry explains (1981), "From the standpoint of the employer, labor is 'free' and fully proletarianized; labor is only semiproletarianized since part of the laborers" subsistence needs are derived from production for home consumption" (37). (Peasants may nonetheless participate to a certain extent "freely" in the disarticulated economy because they opt to maintain some control of their economic lives [84].[19]) Disarticulated economies rely on the state to assist private landlords in controlling labor (83).

Modernization theories securitized the development problematic, assuming that the modernization process was inherently destabilizing to non-Western societies and thus needed to be controlled by a strong state. The development of counterinsurgency theories accompanied modernization theories as an extension of the requirement of maintaining order in such conditions. To maintain the validity of hierarchical social order, counterinsurgency theories attribute instability not to objective conditions of exploitation, but to the vulnerability of engaging in "modernization" and outside agents who manipulate the marginalized. Traditional sectors of society—the peasantry and native peoples—are understood as apolitical, naive and easily manipulated by external agents of subversion (Shafer 1988: 106). Ultimately, counterinsurgency makes control of the population and its identity, rather than the conventional military question of control of territory, its central project (Blaufarb 1977: 288; McCuen 1966: 98; Stepputat 1999: 57). As with the obscured but necessary relationship between state coercion and private production in disarticulated economies, counterinsurgency also operates by shifting the boundary between public and private, operating through paramilitary, extra-legal warfare (McClintock, 1985: 272).

Modernization theory implied a completely different raison d'etat to the Keynesian embedded-liberal compact: one based on the preservation of social inequalities and elite rule through strong militaries to contain what were posited to be massive dislocations in the modernization process. Similarly, developing countries could not be considered part of a "hegemonic" bloc, to the extent that within states, modernization theory did not allow for meaningful consent, and between states, while there were alternative models of development—socialism, and later dependency theory–informed projects—the degree of autonomy that a developing country had in pursuing such models was strongly conditioned by its position in the cold war rivalry. Nonetheless, the idea of articulation provides a way of understanding how subaltern elements are incorporated into a world order: with particular raisons d'etat that fit within the dominant economic order, but are differentiated through both material conditions and the distinct, associated subject positions.

Understanding world order in these terms provides a way of theorizing the ontology of violent conflict during the cold war in holistic context: understanding how power operates across the international/domestic divide and public/private, appreciating the complex interplay between material and subjective in conflict (and resisting reductionism of, for example, the "greed or grievance" debate).

The Guatemalan conflict took place across two world orders—the "embedded-liberal"—modernization world order and the neoliberal world order, in which the peace process occurred. The transformation of world order affected the raison d'etat over the course of the war, as well as the relationship between internal and external actors associated with the conflict (the details of which are discussed in chapter 3). Furthermore, the world order historical context in which the Guatemalan peace process—as well as many others—took place (in the decade after the end of the cold war, the UN had engaged in four times the number of peace operations that it had in the course of the cold war [Paris 2004: 17]) structures the possibilities for the peace process itself and the post-conflict state.

The "embedded-liberal"—modernization world order began to change in the 1970s for both material and ideational reasons. The material dimension of this change was the breakdown of the economic logic of the Keynesian state with the rise of inflation in the 1970s in the North, and for the developing world, the related phenomenon of the debt crisis. The ideational dimension of this change was the adoption of neoliberal theories to analyze and address the crisis of the Keynesian state. The rise of neoliberalism as a dominant ideology resulted in new raisons d'etat and a new world order historical bloc, including new logics of development and rationalities of power.

As Cox (1987) suggests, the transformation of the global economy in the 1970s had much to do with the policies of the United States, which "international[ized] what otherwise were a series of domestically induced inflations" (275). Deficit spending in the United States contributed to inflation and higher interest rates internationally; servicing public debt became a costly expense for citizens of industrialized countries. "Stagflation" and widespread unemployment together undermined both the material basis of accumulation and the legitimacy of the system "as those who paid taxes were pitted against those who benefited from state revenues—private sector against state-sector workers, middle classes against welfare recipients" (281).

Neoliberalism was not the only possible response to the crisis of the postwar compact in the industrialized countries in the 1970s, though it was these conditions that allowed it to become historically effective through the intellectual and moral leadership of powerful actors. Neoliberalism has its intellectual origins in the early postwar period, where certain liberal intellectuals concerned with the increasing appeal of socialism assembled around such groups as the Mont Pélèrin Society (founded by Friedrich von Hayek, among others) and the German journal *Ordo*. As a response to the economic changes of the 1970s, certain states took a leading role in establishing neoliberalism and promoting it as international policy: in particular the United States under Ronald Reagan and the United Kingdom under Margaret Thatcher (although Chile was one of the first states to restructure along such lines under Pinochet in the early 1970s [Harvey 2005]).[20] The international consensus on such principles emerged from a process of intellectual and moral leadership associated with unofficial discussions, such as those in the Trilateral Commission and the Club of Rome, that became generalized through multilateral organizations.[21] Crucially, though such transformations led to the end of the U.S. role as guarantor of the international economic order, they reinforced rather than undermined international economic consensus. As Cox (1987) explains,

> When, during the 1970s, the explicit norms of Bretton Woods (fixed exchange rates and most favored nation treatment, for instance) were either totally or partially abandoned, the practice of policy harmonization became correspondingly more important to the maintenance of consensus. The habit of policy harmonization had been institutionalized during the two preceding decades and was, if anything, reinforced in the absence of clear norms. Ideology had to substitute for legal obligation. (259)

The end of the Soviet Union and communism in Europe not only led to the "collapse of an alternative social myth (to capitalism)," as Gill (2003) puts it, but also to the swift restructuring of the Russian economy by the IMF and other international forces (26, 72).[22]

The multilateral ideological consensus was particularly reinforced vis-à-vis the developing world through the issue of debt. Third world debt was generated not only by the oil shocks of the 1970s, but, among other factors, soaring global interest rates associated with the United States' deficit spending to fund military spending from the early 1980s under Reagan. With the move off of the gold standard in the 1970s, multilateral financial institutions changed focus from Europe to the third world: the IMF became focused on stabilizing developing economies with balance of payment problems and the World Bank became the multilateral agency for aid and development. The remits of the IMF and World Bank would increasingly converge around the logic of structural adjustment programs: programs designed to reconstruct debtor countries' economies to service their debt obligations through liberalization of exchange rates, trade, export promotion, the elimination of subsidies, balanced budgets, and privatization of public enterprise (Feinberg 1988). The term "Washington Consensus" emerged as a way of describing this neoliberal understanding shared by the Bretton Woods institutions, the U.S. government, and other networks of "intellectual and moral leadership" centered in Washington, DC.[23] This convergence reinforced the dominance of the Bretton Woods institutions vis-à-vis the UN system on questions of development policy (Bello 2002: 4).

Neoliberalism emphasizes the use of market-based mechanisms to organize economic, political and social affairs. It promotes economic policies designed to lower inflation, deficits and debt, and create "macroeconomic stability." In the service of smaller government expenditures and debt, it promotes the privatization of state assets and services, and the reduction in government spending on social services. Neoliberalism also promotes deregulation to reduce the government's direct role in the economy and to allow for market signals to function. The free mobility of capital—across sectors, regions, and countries—is considered essential to such market mechanisms, as is a strong regime of property rights (Harvey 2005: 65–66).[24] Thus, although neoliberalism centers around the virtues of market mechanisms to the exclusion of an explicit role for the state in most decision making, it does require the state to establish the institutional and legal foundations for such market mechanisms and to guarantee protections for capital, as the driving force behind the effectiveness of market mechanisms is the logic of (capitalist) accumulation. Gill (1995) has called the construction of such institutional and legal frameworks the "new constitutionalism."

Neoliberalism attempts to insulate market-based decision making from social forces. It thus places a great emphasis on "technocratic" expertise (that endorses an apolitical view of economic analysis) and constructs institutions that isolate economic policy from political forces (Harvey 2005: 66). In contrast to traditional notions of constitutionalism, which protect the rights of individuals, neoliberalism new constitutionalism "confers privileged rights of citizenship and representation to corporate capital" through the imposition of discipline on public institutions by insulating key aspects of the economy from democratic oversight and strengthening the surveillance mechanisms associated with access to international finance, such as the international financial institutions and private bond-rating agencies (Gill 2003: 132). For industrialized countries, discipline is exerted by the need to raise funds in globalized financial markets (136); for developing countries, discipline is exerted by the need to acquire finance through the IFIs and the conditionalities associated with their structural adjustment programs.

With the reduction of the role of the formal state government, and the normative value placed on the private sphere, neoliberals assume a large role for civil society as the preferred site for politics. As David Harvey (2005) observes, "The shift from government (state power on its own) to governance (a broader configuration of state and key elements in civil society) has therefore been marked under neoliberalism" (77).

Michel Foucault argued that neoliberalism theoretical novelty is that it abandons liberalism's assumption of the naturalness of market, and recognizes that the market can be constituted and maintained only through political intervention (Lemke 2001: 913).[25] He suggested that early neoliberals reversed the problematic of Keynesian capitalism: social policy "instead of lessening the anti-social consequences of competition...had to bloc the anti-competitive mechanisms which society can spawn" (195). More radically, the Chicago School took the problematic a step further, positing that the market was not an autonomous sphere to be protected, but in fact the field of the social, to the extent that rationality itself was understood in market terms.[26] For neoliberalism, government action is both justified and limited by the economy: "government itself becomes a sort of enterprise whose task it is to universalize competition and invent market-shaped systems of action for individuals, groups and institutions" (197).

As it redefines liberal assumptions about the relationship between government, the market, and society, neoliberalism similarly redefines liberal assumptions about economic rationality and political subjectivities. It no longer sees economic rationality as a natural characteristic, but one that can rightly be cultivated by the state. "Whereas in the classical liberal conception, *homo economicus* forms an external limit and the inviolable core of government action, in the neo-liberal thought of the Chicago School he becomes a behaviouristically manipulable being…" (200). The citizen is understood as a self-entrepreneur, subject to the responsibility of individual investment decisions involving areas of social services previously under the government's remit: illness, unemployment, poverty, move from being social problems to being individual problems of "self-care" (201–202).

Neoliberalism involves a particular ethicopolitical rationale, which justifies the construction of public institutions in such a way that they transmit market discipline to states, societies, and individuals. With the emphasis on markets as the only proper organizing principle for society, and the mistrust of public institutions as restrictive of liberty and discriminatory (captured or biased toward particular interests in society), neoliberals implicitly reframe the question of democratic participation from public institutions to markets. For neoliberals, democracy is not located in public institutions but in the "nondiscrimination" of market mechanisms. As the market constructs the possibilities for development—of states or individuals—the project becomes cultivating one's own competitiveness.

The neoliberal raison d'etat accepts the world market as "the ultimate determinant of development," and the role of the state, beyond constructing the appropriate frameworks for private property and the market, involves adopting a strategy for its own competitiveness (Cox 1987: 290).[27] This rationality can be found, for example, in works such as Michael Porter's (1990) *The Competitive Advantage of Nations*. Competitive advantage replaces the comparative advantage of classical trade theory under international economic conditions of "total competition"; the theory posits that the state is not naturally endowed with given factors of production but constructs them, while maintaining the logic of market mechanisms to govern the economy.

Similarly, for individuals, market discipline is also accompanied with a particular ethos of "possessive individualism." C.B. Macpherson coined the term to express the attitude of early liberals toward individuals, who were seen as "owners of their persons, capacities, and fruits of their capacities" (White 2003), though for early liberals, any such capacities were naturally endowed (Macpherson 1962). Neoliberalism understands the individual not only as an owner of the self, but as an entrepreneur of the self: analogous to the neoliberal state, the individual's capacities are not naturally given, but developed within the context of market rationality.[28] In this sense, the "self" as capital is both a field of investment and a potential commodity.

The neoliberal historical bloc, then, introduced a new emphasis on market discipline in world affairs, which constructs the conditions for new raisons d'etat and political-economic subjectivities, within a particular ethicopolitical rationale, which in a sense is more "universal" in its logic than the explicit double standards of the "embedded-liberal"-modernization world order it replaced. This, of course, is not to say that neoliberalism is more democratic than the previous order: as demonstrated above, it has numerous antidemocratic tendencies. Indeed, Harvey has shown (based on the analysis of Gérard Duménil and Dominque Lévy), neoliberalism fundamentally reflects a project to restore class power, and as such has had profound contradictions in practice, particularly vis-à-vis finance capital, which it seeks to deregulate, but then consistently bails out from the resulting financial instability (Harvey 2005: 16, 73–74). Gill (2003) puts it more bluntly, suggesting neoliberalism should rightly be described as "oligopolistic neoliberalism": "oligopoly and protection for the strong and a socialization of their risks, market discipline for the weak" (123).

In conclusion, how should peace processes in the neoliberal era be understood? A Gramscian perspective implies two dimensions of analysis embodied in the questions: to what degree do peace processes involve meaningful negotiation and contestation of the future state among different elements of the ensemble of social relations and/or to what degree do peace processes reflect the logics of the neoliberal historical bloc to reconstruct the state along such lines? From a Gramscian perspective, peace processes in principle could involve the potential to reconstruct the ensemble of social relations in a progressive manner, as they conclude violent conflicts, that is, potential wars of maneuvre, where there is sufficient military power on each side to require negotiations. However, given the structural power embodied in world order historical blocs, a Gramscian perspective is classically "intellectually pessimistic" about the possibility for progressive social change.[29] In the neoliberal era in particular, the role of the international community in peace processes becomes an important question: what role does it play in creating genuine possibilities for contestation in peace negotiations? How does it influence the post-conflict state, particularly through the provision of finance and associated conditionalities? These questions will be considered in the chapters that follow.

3

The Ensemble of Social Relations in Guatemala

This chapter considers the ensemble of social relations in Guatemala and its evolution over time before the peace process. In general, the Guatemalan raison d'etat can be understood as one that has significant points of correspondence to world order historical blocs: after 50 years of liberal/conservative debates following independence in 1821, liberals became dominant in the 1870s, parallel to the liberal world order historical bloc. In the 1930s, the "liberal" order was replaced by a dictatorship, which was challenged by a progressive reform movement in the mid-1940s. This "springtime" of progressive politics came to an abrupt end with a U.S.-assisted military coup in 1954, a move that inaugurated a counterinsurgent-modernizing state associated with the post–World War II, cold war/"Pax Americana" historical bloc. The neoliberal world order would transform the state further in the period before the peace process.

The ensemble of social relations in Guatemala involves elements of culture and "common sense" that are "rearticulated" as the material conditions of society change, conditioning the horizons for how such transformations are understood and socially manifest. Thus a racialized class hierarchy in Guatemala was established from the earliest colonial times, but it took a concrete "essentialized" form in the liberal period through the generalization of coffee plantation agriculture across the country. This inaugurated a form of "social disarticulation" in de Janvry's sense, upon which the Guatemalan economy was structured for a hundred years, though it did come under challenge in the 1940s and 1950s. The response to that challenge—the counterinsurgent-modernizing state—would paradoxically also generate the conditions associated with the emergence of a more neoliberal order, one that would challenge the logic of that basis of accumulation.

The Gramscian framework outlined in chapter 2 provides several helpful tools for the analysis of the Guatemalan case. It illuminates the dynamics behind the origins of conflict: the progressive movement in the 1940s and 1950s was nationalist-capitalist in orientation, but nonetheless provoked the intervention of the United States in support of U.S. capital and Guatemalan elites, a paradox that can be understood by appreciating the political economy of modernization theory and its reliance on social disarticulation. Furthermore, in Guatemala, the operation of power across public/private is particularly vivid: from the origins of the independent state, labor practices have involved the collusion of public authority with private interests and means of coercion, a condition intensified under the logic of the counterinsurgent state. Indeed, the U.S. intervention itself relied on private consulting firms and reinforced the role of private business associations in governance in Guatemala (anticipating a number of more recent practices in U.S. foreign policy). Furthermore, the Guatemalan case makes clear the necessity of an analytical framework that does not reify the boundary of "state" but can examine the specific articulation of forces across domestic and international.

In what follows, four historical moments in the ensemble of social relations are examined—the construction of the disarticulated state, its challenge during the reform decade, the reconstruction of the counterinsurgent state, and the challenges to the counterinsurgent state under the move toward neoliberalism—with particular attention to the relationship between the material and the subjective in the context of conflict and social change.

Disarticulation in Guatemala: Race, Force, and Economy

The Guatemalan economy can be understood through the lens of "disarticulation." As noted in chapter 2, "disarticulated" societies are based on production that relies on artificially low wages complimented by household subsistence production and enforced through the collusion of state and private landlord coercion. The marginalized elements of a disarticulated society participate in such arrangements in order to maintain some degree of autonomy from the dominant, discriminatory society: "Whereas the fully proletarianized worker loses both control of the production process and ownership of the means of production, the semiproletarianized worker maintains these two forms of control. Because semiproletarians seek to protect this control, they compete fiercely on the labor market and accept wages below the price of subsistence" (de Janvry 1981: 84).

Nonsubsistence production in Guatemala has been based on agricultural products grown in plantation conditions for export: first concineal, followed by indigo, then coffee and sugar cane, to which were added bananas, cotton, and cardamom in the twentieth century.[1] Coffee, however, was the first product that could be cultivated throughout the country, and is thus associated with the expansion of the plantation economy from the 1860s, and a liberal government from 1871, which, unlike its conservative predecessor, was prepared to engage the state actively in constructing the infrastructure for the promotion of exports (Smith 1990a).[2] Coffee cultivation required only large numbers of workers for four–six months of the year; this and the experience of a major peasant revolt in 1837, promoted the protection of indigenous communities as "labor reserves" for seasonal agriculture (McCreery 1986: 104).[3] Indigenous communities "could be allowed and even encouraged to survive...to reproduce and train an agricultural workforce and sustain these individuals in the off-season or when they became too ill or old for productive use in the export sector. Resources were manipulated so that villages had the minimum land necessary, 'depending on the size of the community' " (104).

Given the sense of labor shortages associated with the expansion of coffee, the liberal government reintroduced the colonial forced labor requirement, the *mandamiento*, in 1876 (103–105).[4] That such measures clearly conflicted with liberal principles of free labor went largely unacknowledged.

> The government was rarely willing even to acknowledge the existence of *mandamientos* and insisted instead that the indigenous population enjoyed the "precious guarantees of the constitution." which included freedom of contract. Indians, however, found themselves sent repeatedly against their will to the coast. Such hypocrisy initially confused even a few local officials: "It seems that Item 3 of your recent note calls for issuing *mandamientos*." They quickly caught on, however, and each year dispatched thousand of *mozos* from the highland coffee estates. (107)[5]

Mandamiento was constructed by the state for the benefit of the private sector. One way of being exempted from the *mandamiento* was to already be in debt peonage to a private finca. The forced labor system drove wages down for debt peons and "free" labor (111–112).

Carol Smith relates the evolution of race in Guatemala to the generalization of coffee cultivation. According to Smith, the term *ladino*—which today refers to the non-Indian/Latin population—originally referred to Indians who had lost their cultural ties to the indigenous lifestyle.[6] The introduction of coffee as a cash crop created (what is today) the racial distinction: *ladinos* became managerial agents for the white elite and transformed culturally and economically to be more "modern." As a result, they were perceived to be less indigenous. Smith (1990a) argues that race was more compelling than class difference because those of the same class (smallholding peasants) but of different "ethnicities" were spatially separated. (Figure 3.1 shows the economic regions of Guatemala.) "Ladinos (who at this point in time were presumed to have some white blood) filled the newly created class positions because, as 'partial' whites, they did not challenge traditional ideology of race hierarchy in taking the mediating role as agents between plantation owners and workers" (85). The exploitative power behind the racial hierarchy meant that "*ladinos*" participated in this arrangement, "not only because some of them benefited from the exploitation of Indians but because all of them benefited from being treated as non-Indians" (90).

Race hierarchy and the modernization project of the liberals were explicitly connected:

> Progressive Guatemalans, wanting to both "enlighten" and "whiten" their nation, attempted a vast overhaul of national institutions in imitation of Western models. They also attempted to encourage European migration in order to improve the local racial stock. While Guatemalan progressives blamed Spanish colonialism for Guatemala's backwardness, they had no program for development other than a dependent, imitative one. As they saw it, development required all of Guatemala to become as Europeanized (and, they hoped, as white) as the Creole elite. (76)

The period of liberalism associated with this move to coffee cultivation is marked both by the "radicalization" of class divisions along cultural lines and by the involvement of foreign investment in the economy. Coffee production particularly attracted foreign immigration in the 1880s and 1890s; such farmers "got away with a highhanded manner in part because Liberal ideology presumed the inherent

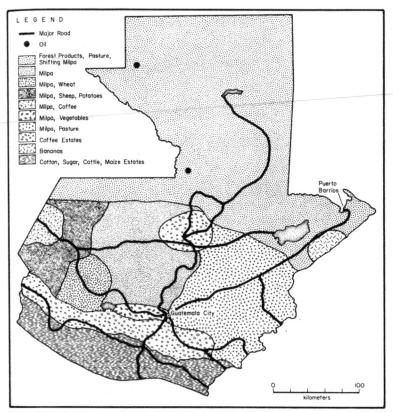

Figure 3.1   The Current Economic Regions and Roads of Guatemala

Source: Courtesy of the Teresa Lonzano Long Institute of Latin American Studies, University of Texas at Austin.

superiority of immigrants from the more developed countries" (McCreery 1994: 233). Germans were the largest and most prominent group of expatriate farmers; however, the presence of foreign investment in the economy was more widely spread, involving French and U.S. ownership of transport facilities and British and German control of marketing channels (Smith 1990a: 83–84). By the 1930s, foreign interests owned all six of the largest coffee companies in Guatemala (McCreery 1994: 234). McCreery provides data on the composition of the sector by 1938–1939, as reflected in table 3.1.

The racialized categories associated with the expansion of coffee in Guatemala were reinforced by international capital that, through its knowledge of civil engineering and access to the European markets, was able to reiterate the "superiority" of Europeans and whites.

Table 3.1   Guatemalan Coffee Exports by Nationality of Exporter,
1938–1939

Nationality	Exports (Quintales)	Value (Quetzals)
German	497,549	Q4,974,719
Dutch	218,975	2,214,590
U.S.	210,921	2,083,194
Guatemalan	67,474	696,924
Spanish	12,025	115,122
English	9,100	86,718
Total	1,016,044	Q10,171,267

Source: David McCreery, Rural Guatemala 1760–1940. Stanford: Stanford
University Press, 1994.

Liberalism in this context took a particular form in as much as it
attempted to replicate formally, culturally, and racially the
industrialized countries taken as models. This required a particular
intervention by the government that Frederick Stirton Weaver (1999)
has aptly observed is quite similar to the tenets of modernization
theory. He notes,

> Such vigorous, interventionist state policies might seem inconsistent
> with the discourse of nineteenth-century liberalism, but Guatemala
> Liberals recognized the logic of the analysis: the scale of needed change
> was so great that it required an agent independent of current social
> forces...This meant that a technocratic and authoritarian state, sup-
> posedly neutral and above politics, was necessary and appropriate to
> produce a more open, free, and prosperous Guatemala. (136)

The resolution of development and liberalism as understood in
Guatemala and later the United States thus invokes the use of "neutral, technocratic and authoritarian" techniques of government, which
require military guarantees. "The congruence with North American
modernization theory—with Huntington (1968) as the classic statement—is once again impressive" (Weaver 1999: 136).
    Of equal significance to foreign investment in coffee was the for-
eign investment in bananas, which was controlled by the U.S.-based
United Fruit Company (UFCO).[7] The most controversial aspect of the
UFCO's operations in Guatemala involves the degree to which its

expansion was associated with the construction of the commercial transportation infrastructure and thus the control it was able to exert over the economy more broadly, earning it the moniker "*El Pulpo*" (the Octopus). The company controlled the railways, ports, and telegraph system in Guatemala and dominated most of the shipping that its agricultural exports relied upon.

The UFCO's expansion occurred under the dictatorship of President General Jorge Ubico Casteñada (1931–1944) and the economic crisis of the 1930s.[8] Ubico's conception of modernization required international capital and the iron hand of the military to overcome Guatemala's developmental limitations (Grieb 1979: 32–33). Ubico's biographer, Kenneth Grieb (1979), suggests that despite the monopolistic practices of UFCO, "many Guatemalans, among them Ubico, exhibited a decided preference for investment from the United States and placed a high priority on the attraction of North American firms to the republic" (182). He explains:

> The Caudillo considered the Yankees shrewd businessmen, and felt that establishing ties with the hemisphere's great power and world financial center would prove beneficial to his nation, particularly since the relative proximity to the Northern Colossus offered the trading advantages that would serve to stimulate the development of the Guatemalan export sector. (182)

Nonetheless, Ubico's oppressive measures alienated the nascent urban middle class, which had only come into being under his administration (Dosal 1995: 78).

The nexus between modernization and militarization would be manifest in Ubico's "reform" of the labor laws wherein vagrancy laws replaced the debt peonage of the earlier order, expanding the militarized state into labor policy.[9] The difference was largely cosmetic, to the extent that in addition to "conventional" definitions, the Guatemalan law defined vagrancy in terms of how much land one possessed and cultivated (McCreery 1995: 220; Cambranes 1985: Chapter 8; Dunkerley 1988: 25–42). The labor required under such laws amounted to nearly half the year for many indigenous men (Handy 1984: 98; Forster 2001: 33). Racism underlay such policies. Ubico felt Indians were unsuited to politics (which should be left to the urban elite), and that the best way to incorporate them into national life was through military conscription: the indigenous "'come [to the military] rude, brutish, and with primitive origin, but they return learned, polished, with good manners and in condition to face life'" (Handy 1984: 99). This view of the indigenous was widespread, and echoed by a U.S. attaché who argued that as most Indians were illiterate, they had no idea what they were doing at the polls and should be disenfranchised (91).

The UFCO was imbued with assumptions about race and engaged in coercive labor practices as well. Beyond the harassment of smaller landowners to sell their property and "company store" practices that made laborers virtually indentured servants of the company (82–83, 89), the race hierarchy of the UFCO was pronounced.[10] Cindy Forster (2001) notes that "lynch law reigned with perfect impunity in the banana zone to silence workers' collective actions as well as individual outbursts of rage against white managers" (16). Indeed, according to Stephen Schlesinger and Stephen Kinzer (1983), the extent of the racism displayed by UFCO alarmed its own public relations advisor, whose memo on the subject earned him "company-wide silent treatment" (82).

Challenging Disarticulation: Reforms and Reaction

The reform period (1944–1954) unfolded across two governments, those of Juan José Arévalo and of Jacobo Arbenz, and involved a steady challenge to the primacy of locally and foreign-owned plantation agriculture. As this program unfolded it gradually began to be seen as threatening to dominant interests, culminating in a U.S.-backed coup. Although the reforms, particularly of Arbenz's administration, were framed in terms of a "communist" threat, in fact they were explicitly capitalist in orientation: they sought only to transform the "feudal" relationships of locally owned plantation agriculture and provide worker's rights to employees of internationally owned agribusiness. The true threat of these reforms to powerful interests had to do with attempting to transform the labor relations associated with social disarticulation.

Ubico lost support of the oligarchy and resigned. The military attempted to have the legislature install its preferred successor, a move that precipitated a revolt among young military officers, who had the integrity to allow for elections.[11] Juan José Arévalo, a university professor with a doctorate in Education from Argentina, won 85 percent of the vote (the enfranchised population then including only literate men [Gleijeses 1991: 36]).[12]

Arévalo's reform program involved two significant elements: a labor code and a social security scheme. The labor code of May 1947 affirmed the right to unionize, guaranteed the right to strike and protected workers from unfair dismissals, although agricultural unions were limited to farms employing over 500 workers and the right to strike was subject to a conciliation mechanism (Dunkerley 1988: 139–140; Gleijeses 1991: 41; Handy 1984: 107–108). The Guatemalan Institute of Social Security (IGSS) was created in January of 1948 and was soon considered one of the most incorrupt and effective elements of the Guatemalan government (Gleijeses 1991: 42). Arévalo's policies were accompanied by greater political freedoms to the urban population and less repression and a commitment to rural education to the countryside (43, 161). Yet the reforms of his administration were limited in their scope, explicitly stopping short of any land reform.[13]

Nonetheless, such social changes met with resistance from elites, who "soon branded these freedoms as intolerable excesses and began to reminisce about the times of Ubico, when 'social peace' had reigned supreme" (43).[14] Indeed, "'The conservative elements,' the U.S. military attaché reported, 'attribute labor unrest to communism, look with horror on social reforms and reflect that it was easier to do business, easier to make money, and easier and safer to live during the dictator era'" (48). Although the United States seemed content to allow Arévalo to remain in office, confident of the strength and unwavering anticommunism of the military as well as the prospect of a more conservative successor (123–127), Guatemalan elites were not so patient. They encouraged Major Arana—the most conservative element of the junta that allowed for Arévalo's election—to attempt a coup, foiled by Arévalo but that led to three deaths, including Arana's own.[15]

Arévalo was succeeded in 1951 by Colonel Jacobo Arbenz, the minister of defense who had defended democracy in the Ubico transition, and who, thanks to his public reticence and prevailing prejudices of the day, won a wide spectrum of support. Organized labor was drawn to his support of democracy and became convinced of his progressive credentials, while members of the modernizing elite from his home town of Quezaltenango assumed he shared their sense that limited reforms would be economically beneficial and sought to "educate the prince" to their agenda (1991: 73). Likewise, a U.S. advisor's racism and ignorance of the man himself brought him to the conclusion that "… Arbenz is, in my opinion, essentially an opportunist who has strung along with the Arévalo bandwagon principally as a means of accumulating personal wealth and of giving ascendancy to his own political star. He has no admixtures of Indian blood, and is basically of an autocratic character" (73, 125).[16] Once in office, Arbenz in fact introduced a significant land reform and public works program. His agrarian reform plan, Decree 900, approved on 17 June 1952, involved the redistribution of all government-owned *fincas* and the expropriation of uncultivated land on large estates in exchange for 25-year government bonds at 3 percent interest (the same arrangement as the United States used in Formosa and Japan [Gleijeses 1991: 164; Schlesinger and Kinzer 1983: 54]).[17] The magnitude of the reform involved about 1.5 million acres from 107 national farms and 16.3 percent of the country's private arable land, which constituted only 3.9 percent of privately owned land outside of the UFCO's holdings (Schlesinger and Kinzer 1983: 55; Handy 1984: 132; Dunkerley 1988: 148). The number of beneficiaries has been assessed at "100,000 heads of families," or roughly 500,000 people based on the 1950 census (Gleijeses 1991: 156; Schlesinger and Kinzer 1983: 55; Handy 1984: 128).

The public works program was designed to create a national transportation infrastructure competitive with the U.S.-owned network through a large road system, a new Caribbean port, and a hydroelectric dam.[18] The plan largely followed the recommendations of a 1951 World Bank report on Guatemala (Gleijeses 1991: 165; Dunkerley 1988: 147). After the failure to balance the 1953–1954 budget, Arbenz sought to introduce the first income tax in Guatemalan history to assist in funding the reforms (Gleijeses 1991: 169; Schlesinger and Kinzer 1983: 54).[19] Arbenz was sympathetic to communism, joining the *Partido Guatemalteco de Trabajo* (PGT, Guatemalan Communist Party) in 1957, three years after his overthrow (Gleijeses 1991: 147). The Communist Party distinguished itself—even in U.S. circles (Lehman 1997: 212)—in its incorruptibility in executing land reforms (Schlesinger and Kinzer 1983: 58–63; Handy 1984: 131). Yet the reform program of the Arbenz administration was firmly capitalist in orientation: he and the PGT understood Guatemala to be at a semifeudal level of development, which required passing through a capitalist stage before socialism could be considered. As a leader of the PGT put it, "the PGT 'enthusiastically endorsed the thesis that Guatemala must first go through a capitalist stage. When we state this we were not trying to hoodwink anyone. We were convinced of it' " (Gleijeses 1991: 148). This meant that capitalist agriculture would be developed through small farmers; Arbenz stated clearly: "It is not our purpose to break up all the rural property of the country that could be judged large or fallow and distribute the land to those who work it. This will be done to *latifundia*, but we will not do it to agricultural economic entities of the capitalist type" (Dunkerley 1990: 226).

Despite their nationalist-capitalist orientation, the reforms did engender a certain transformation in the ensemble of social relations, particularly in the countryside. As anthropologist Richard Adams observed,

> An awaking of profound import did take place for many...but it was not what usually has come under the rubric of "ideological." It could better be called a "sociological awakening," for it amounted to a realization that certain of the previously accepted roles and statuses within the social system were no longer bounded by the same rules, and that new channels were suddenly opened for the expression of and satisfaction of needs. (in Gleijeses 1991: 161)

The oligarchy likewise perceived a change. Dunkerley (1988) observes: "[W]hatever its fundamental objectives, [the reform program] was perceived by the oligarchy as an unprecedented challenge to its economic base and a major assault upon the entire political culture erected upon hacienda" (148). The Arbenz reforms in fact were limited in their direct impact; however, they did potentially undermine the conditions of labor availability under disarticulation.

The backlash to Arbenz came from two quarters, the United States, influenced by the UFCO, and the Guatemalan elites, who benefited from the ambivalence of the military and the urban middle classes to the reform program.[20] Both of these sectors objected to the principles of the reform program and the social changes accompanying it: domestic elites saw a communist scare in the transformation of social relations while the United States saw one in Guatemala's increasing independence from its foreign policies in the region.

Landowners, both Guatemalan and foreign, routinely underreported the value of their holdings on tax statements, causing a reaction to the amount of compensation offered in the land redistribution. The UFCO objected vehemently to the principle of reappropriation— arguing that it required fallow land to rotate production to avoid disease—and to the amount offered, which it claimed was on the order of 25 times too little.[21] The UFCO also felt discriminated against by the 1947 Labor Code, with its limitations on rural unions to farms with more than 500 employees.[22] Guatemalan elites were also "exasperated" by the code and "began to brandish charges of communist infiltration with even greater gusto than did UFCO" (Gleijeses 1991: 99). Over the course of the reform era, the U.S. government similarly had grown to see "communism" everywhere in Guatemala. The UFCO certainly promoted this perception through an elaborate and well-financed public relations campaign that effectively involved leading U.S. newspapers in presenting its point of view (Schlesinger and Kinzer 1983: Chapter 6).[23]

Initially the United States engaged in a policy of harassment from a distance, denying military sales and economic assistance, both bilateral regional aid and a much needed World Bank loan.[24] When the Eisenhower administration came to power in the United States, the policy became much more interventionist, leading to a CIA-sponsored coup.[25] The operation, PBSUCCESS, involved isolating Guatemala diplomatically and convincing the military that U.S. intervention was imminent to abandon the Arbenz administration, while simultaneously maintaining "plausible deniability" about its intentions.[26] The campaign to isolate Guatemala diplomatically in particular involved a resolution in the Organization of American States that declared the internal control of an American state by a communist movement an actionable threat to the security of the whole region (Gleijeses 1991: Chapter 12; Schlesinger and Kinzer 1983: 142–145). Such diplomatic tactics, as well as measures within Guatemala such as the appointment of a brash, militant new ambassador, were designed to convince key players, most importantly the military, that U.S. intervention was imminent.[27] On 16 June 1954 Carlos Castillo Armas, formerly a colonel in the Guatemalan army, began his U.S.-sponsored coup against Arbenz. On 27 June, after a U.S.-assisted bombing campaign and a strategic misinformation campaign about the level of support for the coup leaders, Arbenz resigned.[28]

The Arbenz program was not a challenge to capitalism, as his enemies charged. It was a challenge to certain features of disarticulation. The land reform he proposed was limited to UFCO and state holdings; however, the transition to such small-scale holdings had the potential to undermine the basis of labor availability in the economy, and challenge the basic principles of modernization theory. The conservative backlash to his policies was wider than "mere" U.S. intervention, although Arbenz's strong reputation within the military would undoubtedly have maintained his presidency longer had the United States not gotten involved. The withdrawal of support from the military and the lack of strong support from the urban middle classes allowed for conservative elements to reassert their control.

This would require a stronger hand than before the reform era, which had raised expectations in the rural population: precisely the conditions to which emergent counterinsurgent state would address itself with U.S. support.

The Counterinsurgent State

Guatemala emerged from the Arana coup with a new "counterinsurgent-modernizing" raison d'etat, constructed to a significant degree with U.S. intervention. In this new order, the military was reoriented toward counterinsurgent warfare. New economic policies and foreign investment moved the economy away from its traditional focus into new areas of investment, constructing a new economic rationality among some sectors of the economic elite, and associated with new business associations in the process.

The counterinsurgent state targets all those who resist the logic of disarticulated modernization. In Guatemala, this comprised many elements: certainly the organized guerilla movements that emerged at different moments and in different regions (several of which involved military officers disaffected by the corruption and logic of the military in the counterinsurgent state), though also other forms of popular organizing, such as the cooperative movement. Ultimately, the counterinsurgent state targeted the indigenous population as a whole: counterinsurgency embodies the contradiction of protecting a disarticulated economy that relies on the subjective division between traditional and modern, while at the same time securitizing the traditional "Other" to such a degree that it generates an impulse toward its elimination. The military face of the modernizing counterinsurgent state can be genocidal, though this impulse can take other forms, such as religious/cultural conversion, as occurred under the evangelical movement in Guatemala.

The modernizing counterinsurgent state generates social effects through its policies. In Guatemala the convergence of two trends transformed the nature of popular organizing against the state from calls for socioeconomic justice to calls for racial equality and human rights. Most conspicuously, the racialized nature of the counterinsurgent state's repression and human rights abuses focused attention on those questions; however, growing class divisions and a greater capitalist sensibility within the indigenous population also shifted the emphasis in popular organizing, as would the changing bases of international support (discussed further in chapter 4).

The Guatemalan ensemble of social relations was reconstructed in the postreform era with significant involvement of the United States in the military and the economy. The modern Guatemalan military owes a significant debt to U.S. funding after the coup. Although the military was quite strong under the Ubico regime, there was a significant contribution by the United States after 1954, through the direct transfer of weaponry, training in the leadership of armed forces, and police assistance (Holden 1993: 288). The United States trained numerous Guatemalan military personnel both in the United States and at the U.S. Army School of the Americas then in Panama; in 1962 it established a secret base for counterinsurgency training in the department of Izabal, directed by members of U.S. Special Forces (Sharckman 1974: 197). Howard Sharckman (1974) argues this reconstruction of the Guatemalan military—including transforming its materiel, from tanks, artillery, bombers to less expensive light weapons, mobile communications, and helicopters—served as a model for other U.S. counterinsurgent military assistance projects.

Police training provided by USAID also focused on anticommunist ideology and counterinsurgency strategies, and "professionalizing" the police force. Over 30,000 Guatemalan police personnel received such training by 1970, which included programs on the "Threat to Latin America," the "Changing Society," and the "Implementation of Modern Scientific Aid" (199).[29] Although Guatemala at times distanced itself from the United States (notably during the Carter administration, because of its onerous emphasis on human rights), this was only after the United States had established it as one of the best trained and equipped militaries in the region. Furthermore, at this point it was able to purchase military supplies from Israel and the Argentine dictatorship.[30]

As the military developed institutionally, it also grew to become a significant economic actor. Initially the economic ambitions of the military were contained to the opportunistic, personal accumulation of senior officers (Dunkerley 1988: 462). For example, in the 1970s a sparsely populated area called the Northern Transversal Strip, marked for "colonization" as a development mechanism, was ultimately so appropriated by military elites that it became known as the "Land of the Generals." Later, however, this accumulation became more institutionalized, as per the military itself. The military established a bank and invested in such diverse activities as real estate construction, insurance, and manufacturing; likewise it often controlled semiautonomous state enterprises (462). As Regis Debray (1978) explains, with the creation of an Army Bank "military hegemony grows in time and in space with foreign investment... " (352).

The U.S. development strategy for postreform Guatemala was implemented through the World Bank, USAID, and the private U.S. consulting firm Klein and Saks (K&S).[31] These postintervention economic policies emphasized state support for private enterprise rather than state regulation. Prominent features of the World Bank/USAID/ K&S plan included dismantling restrictions on foreign investment and attracting U.S. investors to Guatemala ("a campaign in which K&S played a crucial role"), private sector concessions and subsidies, an emphasis on export agriculture and the financing of infrastructure through World Bank and U.S. funds (Jonas 1974: 79). Such financing insulated elites from taxation, a perennial problem in Guatemala, which has among the lowest taxes in Latin America and a highly regressive tax system.

The expansion of the "modernizing" business elite lies in the postintervention era and foreign participation in the economy. From the 1950s to the 1970s, U.S. investment in Guatemala increased significantly: 128.8 percent in the period 1959–1969, bringing it to US$888 million in 1969 (Tobis 1974: 132). The composition of this investment favored manufacturing over agriculture—so that it grew to account for 36.3 percent of U.S. direct investment (US$ 46.6 million) by 1970—and commercial capital, as illustrated in graph 3.1 (Tobis 1974: 133). Many firms were classified as "new industries" after acquisition, exempting them from corporate tax for five years and granting them duty-free imports (133).

The changes in U.S. investment in Guatemala were accompanied by a change in the composition of economic elites. Thus the *Comité*

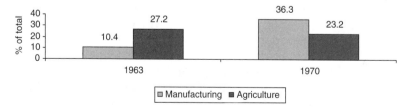

Graph 3.1   Composition of U.S. Foreign Direct Investment

Source: David, Tobis "The US Investment Bubble in Guatemala." In *Guatemala*, edited by Susanne Jonas and David Tobis, 132–142. Berkeley, CA: North American Congress on Latin America, 1974.

Coodinador de Asociaciones Agricolas, Comericiales, Industriales y Financieras (CACIF, The Coordinating Committee of Agricultural, Commercial, Industrial, and Financial Associations, 1957), *Asociación Nacional de Café* (ANACAFE, The National Coffee Association, 1960) and other postintervention business associations became increasingly powerful vis-à-vis their preintervention predecessors. CACIF and the American Chamber of Commerce increased in authority with the expansion of U.S. capital in Guatemala in the 1960s, both in traditional agricultural sectors and in manufacturing and commercial sectors (Dunkerley 1988: 463). CACIF began as a forum "to allow all of private enterprise to cooperate when necessary" and has since its inception promoted internationally oriented economic interests (Adams 1970: 340–341). "The general position of CACIF was conservative, however, and it did not hesitate to ridicule organizations that reflected a pre-1954 nationalism" (340). The composition of business associations is particularly significant because, as Dunkerley notes, "the bourgeoisie did not greatly depend upon direct representation through political parties.... [Policymaking] fell largely to the corporate associations of capital..." (Dunkerley 1988: 462–463).

The first guerilla movement in Guatemala emerged in 1962, led by disaffected army officers.[32] The CIA's use of a Guatemalan military base without proper army consultation provoked a nationalist coup attempt in November 1960. In 1961 those unsuccessful rebel leaders returned to join the PGT, which had committed itself to a strategy of guerrilla warfare. The *Fuerzas Armadas Rebeldes* (FAR, Armed Rebel Forces), as this effort would be later known, focused on the Eastern areas of Izabal province and the town of Zacapa. This movement suffered from two strategic problems. First, the military and political arms of the effort were kept separate: the guerrilla leadership was excluded from political decision making, which "engendered acute problems of coordination" (454). Second, the FAR and its related forces pursued a strategy of direct military confrontation without any organizational efforts among the population, which was later identified even by the FAR itself as "the overly adventurous and voluntarist features of a rigid *foquismo*" (after Ché Guevara's and Régis Debray's *foco* theory [452]).[33] (Figure 3.2 shows the insurgent regions of Guatemala.)

After the destruction of the FAR through the assassination of its remaining leadership in 1972, the resistance entered a phase of more secret activities that involved multicultural alliances. A group of dissident FAR members reorganized in the predominantly indigenous

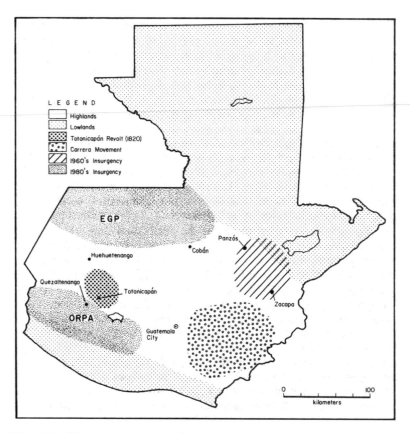

Figure 3.2   The Insurgent Regions of Guatemala over Time

Source: Courtesy of the Teresa Lonzano Long Institute of Latin American Studies, University of Texas at Austin.

region of El Quiché under the banner of the *Ejercito Guerrillero de los Pobres* (EGP, Guerrilla Army of the Poor). The EGP rejected *foco* theory and spent years cultivating a support base before it engaged in armed combat, initially in 1975 but more frequently from 1978 onward (455–456). The *Organización Revolucionaria del Pueblo en Armas* (ORPA, Organization of the People in Arms) similarly pursued a strategy of "gestation," having been established in 1971 but only emerging publicly in 1979 (Brockett 1988: 112). The ORPA, like the EGP, shared an emphasis on organizing in indigenous areas (the Western Highlands). Though smaller, ORPA attracted a broader base of support than the EGP, including middle-class intellectuals, and the FAR, whose program was less populist (Dunkerley 1988: 483). During this period the

Comité de Unidad Campesina (CUC, Committee of Peasant Unity), an indigenous-led but multicultural/multiracial peasant union emerged, also pursuing a strategy of secret organizing, going public only in 1978. This period was one of relatively less overt conflict between the state and popular forces; however, the 1976 earthquake would reopen this uneasy tension.

During this initial postcoup period, another form of popular organizing emerged in the form of *Acción Católica*, a religious developmentalist movement with the goal of creating small-scale farmer-entrepreneurs. This strategy emphasized transforming subsistence agriculture toward income generating cash crops (Arias 1990: 235). However, as Arturo Arias (1990) notes, "despite their reformist character, the growth of the cooperatives brought about serious conflicts with the local powers, thus accelerating the radicalization of *Acción Católica*'s members and their mentors" (233). The state tolerated the cooperative movement to the extent it could remain "apolitical." USAID supported cooperatives in its rural development program for the 1960s, but alienated participants through its attempt to be "nonpolitical," many of whom saw USAID as working to destroy the existing movement (Brockett 1988: 110). Participants became divided into those who feared being labeled communist—some members of *Acción Católica* and priests who argued that they "did not want to get involved in politics"—and those who felt disappointed with the failure to realize a political alternative and became radicalized through the experience (Arias 1990: 234).

The extensive organizational infrastructure of the cooperative movement allowed it to respond to the 1976 earthquake that devastated Guatemala, thus giving it the potential to control a great deal of the international aid that poured into the country. The cooperative movement interfaced with the international community and to an extent publicized the plight of indigenous Guatemalans, increasing the perception that it represented a threat to the state. In response, the army monopolized much of the aid, reinforcing social control while using the resources for the pursuit of individual profit (243). This situation was codified into law by the 1978 New Cooperative Law, which essentially put the cooperative movement under military control (Sollis 1995: 529). Counterinsurgency activities immediately after the earthquake targeted cooperative members, 200 of whom "disappeared" in the department of El Quiché in the year and a half following the earthquake (Brockett 1988: 111).

A number of public actions by progressive forces in the years leading up to the most brutal counterinsurgency campaign were met by reactionary responses that fuelled support for the guerrilla. By 1977 there was widespread support for union rights; a miners' march that year drew a crowd of 100,000 supporters in the capital (Dunkerley 1988: 471).[34] The next year, the CUC went public and organized thousands of Indians to march under its banner at the May Day demonstrations. Greg Grandin observes, "Not since 1839, when Rafael Carerra's peasant army occupied Guatemala City had this many Mayans gathered together *as Indians* in a show of oppositional force in the ladino capital" (Grandin 1997: 18, emphasis in original). In 1979, ORPA would make its efforts public as well.

The nature of the responses to these activities shows how the political involvement of the indigenous population provoked alarm. "Given the deep-seated mistrust between Mayans and ladinos, [its multiethnic character] perhaps was the CUC's most radical and threatening aspect" (Grandin 1997: 17). Thus later in May 1978, the army called indigenous peasants to the town of Panzós, ostensibly for a meeting to resolve conflicts over access to traditional lands that had been usurped for cattle farming, only to fire on the defenseless crowd it immediately buried in a mass grave.[35] In 1980, the leader of the CUC (Vincente Menchú, Rigoberta's father) and 39 peasants who took their case for protection from arbitrary repression to the Spanish embassy were burned alive in an army attack (which took place against the wishes of the Spanish ambassador).[36] These two events remain watersheds in the national consciousness and provoked greater sympathy for the guerrilla in the indigenous population.

Counterinsurgency operates with the rhetoric of development, but aims to remove the rural population from a context of potential guerrilla recruitment. In Guatemala two main strategies of control were employed: the destruction of villages (over 400 by the end of the campaign), with the relocation of the population into "model villages," and the forced recruitment of men into paramilitary civil patrols for rural surveillance. While outwardly their creation was defended through the discourse of development (and indeed with food to distribute from international relief efforts) model villages in fact impoverished peasants and subjected them to specific resocialization processes (Handy 1984: 262; Brockett 1988: 119).[37] "Even the military officer in charge of the National Reconstruction Committee... admitted that there were about 250,000 peasants, 'among them children who are forced to eat dirt'" (Handy 1984: 261). The further destruction of indigenous culture was explicitly promoted through techniques such as discouraging the use of Mayan languages among children, the assassination of Indian elders, and making different indigenous groups live together specifically to erode ethnic identities (Handy 1984: 260; Brockett 1988: 118).

Patrullas de Autodefensa Civil (PACs, Civilian Self-Defense Patrols) were created ostensibly to guard communities from the guerrilla. They included at their height 900,000 people, nearly 80 percent of the male population in rural indigenous areas (Human Rights Office of the Archdiocese of Guatemala 1999: 119). Although communities participated in PACs under threat of elimination, indoctrination was also used to promote participation. In the words of the Guatemalan army, "Civic education is part of psychological action; it begins by providing thorough information about the security forces' chances of success in the counter-subversion struggle" (Human Rights Office of the Archdiocese of Guatemala 1999: 121). As James Dunkerley notes, "the primary purpose of the patrols was less military than to ensure individual registration, control of movement, and dissemination of propaganda. The ambitious long-term objective was a coercive state-based "incorporation" of the *campesino* and particularly the Indian into the "nation" (Dunkerley 1988: 496–497).

Yet, despite the roots of its possibilities in racial anxiety and its genocidal activities on the one hand, the counterinsurgency project at the same time opens the possibility of social control through cultural and identity appropriation. Jennifer Schirmer (1998) describes the military's construction of the "sanctioned Maya" that is a model of the indigenous "constructed and continually reconstructed through the military's optic, deprived of memory, and mute to the recent 'subversive' past" (115). She argues,

> Such re-creational and guardian discourse should also alert us to the military's view of the indigenous community as a child needing to be disciplined, "ladinoized," entrepreneurized—that is, "forged" to fit the "new" Guatemalan state...Part of this forging, it is believed, is accomplished by appropriating Mayan symbols to "rescue the Indians" mentality until they feel part of the nation. (114)

Identity becomes part of the terrain for control, the economic dimension of which is manifest in the need to control the population in a specific modernization process.

The number of evangelical Protestants in Guatemala increased from 3 to 25 percent of the population in the period 1960–1990, giving it the most Protestants of any Latin American country (Rose and Brouwer 1990: 43).[38] In the words of the Project for Historical Memory:

> The army encouraged these sects as a way of controlling the population. The sects broadcast their own version of the violence and blamed the victims. They advocated structural changes in the religious life of the communities based on separation into small groups, messages legitimizing the army's power, and individual salvation. Their ceremonies involved mass emotional catharsis. Violence thus became the motivating force behind these evangelical sects, which installed themselves throughout much of the country. (Human Rights Office of the Archdiocese of Guatemala 1999: 47)[39]

Ríos Montt, who governed in the second half of the counterinsurgency (1981–1983) was indeed a member of a California-based evangelical church, the Church of the Word (*El Verbo*, in Guatemala). The rhetoric of the church—vehemently anticommunist—informed the counterinsurgency campaign, which became known as his "holy war against communism in the highlands" (Rose and Brouwer 1990: 47). It is interesting to observe that while the army justified its punishment of the people with the claim that the guerrillas had deceived them, "[t]he punishment is sometimes referred to by the displaced as 'the judgement' (*el jucio*), a reference to the Bible which legitimizes the punishment as an act of paternal authority" (Stepputat 1999: 71–72). Elites accepted evangelical churches because of their promulgation of "individual salvation rather than group solidarity and disciplined work under sanctioned authority" (Rose and Brouwer 1990: 44).

Much of the impetus, materials, organization, and funding for evangelical churches in Guatemala have come from the United States and are "perceived by many Guatemalans as being an innovative, modern product from North America" (44). Evangelical schools, which provide free, private education, have been particularly successful in Guatemala, where public education reaches only 60 percent of students (50–52).[40] Susan D. Rose and Steve Brouwer describe the educational materials associated with these churches: they strongly support free enterprise and condemn communism as the work of Satan, characterize the fight against communism as a religious one, promote private property (and suggest that Mayans' failure to embrace private property—their poor "stewardship" of the land—is why they have been dispossessed), and argue that poverty is the result of laziness and lack of discipline.[41] Unlike *Acción Católica*, for example, a developmentalist political agenda does not accompany the proselytizing of evangelical churches: they explicitly oppose public health care clinics and peasants' cooperatives (52).

The counterinsurgent moment "ethnicized" popular politics, in putting ethnic identity at the center of the conflict. The Maya in Guatemala involve 23 distinct linguistic groups where political consciousness historically was local rather than "pan-Mayan"; popular organizing needed to overcome these linguistic divisions (figures such as Rigoberta Menchú have commented on the paradox of relying on the colonial language to defend indigenous culture because of the difficulties of organizing in any other way). The focus on ethnicity opened up the debate as to what the nature of the "(pan-)Mayan" identity involved, and whether discrimination should be considered predominantly in terms of race or class. Grandin (1997) observes, "A closer examination of the language of the popular and revolutionary movement reveals a cultural struggle being waged not simply in the contested zone separating ladinos and Indians but within the ideological boundaries that mark the essence of what it means to be Mayan" (12–13). Arias (1990) also describes the challenges of this move:

> Ethnic identity has been transformed in the search for political force. Now, identity was a tangible, verbalized, phenomenon, around which the articulation of political practices was sought. But the symbolic practices, the worldview, and the unconscious codes had been discarded without the formation of new ones to substitute for them. Thus, in concrete practice, just as identity was being talked about more openly, it was experiencing its deepest crisis. (251)

The popular and influential peasant union, the CUC, was not an ethnically based organization: though predominantly indigenous, it engaged both Indians and ladinos in a class-based critique of Guatemalan politics. However, other, "Mayan nationalist" groups would seek to define ethnicity in terms that excluded class and preserved the Indian bourgeoisie (252–253). As the conflict progressed, the nature of organizing moved away from calls for material changes to questions of human and civil rights (Yashar 1997: 253). Moreover, external support proved more amenable to "Indian rights" than "peasant rights" or armed resistance. Grandin (2000) suggests, "as the repression mounted and the rebels lost ground, class-based Mayanism has increasingly sought legitimation by presenting the struggle in cultural terms, supported by increasing international attention to indigenous rights" (25). The new generation of "postcounterinsurgency community leadership...notably avoids directly addressing social problems such as land shortage or endemic poverty" (25).

Less obvious than these transformations in popular organizing are counterinsurgency's subjective effects. Counterinsurgency destroys what it constructs as the enemy, but it is also productive of a new social order: partly through the elimination of challenges and partly through resocialization through violence. The Recovery of Historical Memory Project (REMHI) of the Archdiocese of Guatemala's Human Rights Office is considered the most comprehensive survey of human rights abuses during the war. According to the REMHI interviews, counterinsurgency was characterized by constant tension in the rural population, generalized, indiscriminate violence against civilians, public displays of horror and blatant impunity for government perpetrators (Human Rights Office of the Archdiocese of Guatemala 1999: 9–10). Significantly, violence itself had explicit cultural overtones, including the way corpses were left to be found by indigenous communities, the targeting of children as victims, and the destruction of traditional crops (Human Rights Office of the Archdiocese of Guatemala 1999: 19, Chapter 2, 41).

The social and psychological effects of this indiscriminate climate of terror led to the disruption of community life and to an atomization of community forms. The societal effects involved restricted communication among people, withdrawal from community organizations, social isolation, and community distrust (Human Rights Office of the Archdiocese of Guatemala 1999: 10–11). This social disruption is reinforced on an individual level by feelings of humiliation, powerlessness, and difficulty in distinguishing the boundaries between the real and imagined (11–12). There are physical effects as well, which range from paralysis to acute panic attacks, and ailments such as immunological dysfunction and pain (11–12). There is some suggestion that suicide—a social issue that rarely affects indigenous cultures—increased dramatically as a result of the counterinsurgency campaign (15–16).[42]

Counterinsurgency's implicit justification for controlling the rural population is its presumed lack of rationality about the development project. A particular source of anxiety is the collective form where it is impossible to distinguish the naive peasant from the contaminated rebel. This anxiety is amplified by the indigenous, understood to be ontologically—racially—different and historically hostile. The counterinsurgency project deliberately aims to disrupt rural life, to disembed it from existing social networks, and to reconstruct society in a particular political-economic ideal. Its outward regulatory form is very conspicuous and violent. However, in the use of terror and other counterinsurgency techniques, an inward regulatory function is created. The new social form silences both community organizations and individual self-expression. Technologies of cultivating mistrust within a community are accompanied by technologies of cultivating shame within individuals, who internalize community atomization.

The nature of counterinsurgency as socially and subjectively productive must be considered in understanding the ensemble of social relations preceding the peace process. Counterinsurgency serves to disembed traditional cultures and to atomize them. The anxiety of culture, race, and modernity is resolved through the destruction and subsequent reconstruction of the "other." The "sanctioned Maya" reflects the selective use of cultural symbols in a dehistoricized reconstruction of identity in the service of the dominant groups' vision of the nation-state.

Neoliberalism and the Counterinsurgent State

The economic foundation of the counterinsurgent state came under pressure with the move toward neoliberalism. This transformation provoked a "passive revolution" among economic elites: the reassertion of civilian rule against the military, in a move that established the primacy of CACIF vis-à-vis economic policy and, nonetheless, preserved certain counterinsurgency structures in the constitution. At the same time, certain new sectors of the economy that have since been deemed "clusters" of growth, also challenged the logic of disarticulation.

The return to civilian government in Guatemala began in the late 1970s and 1980s. Military mismanagement and corruption in the 1970s had alienated junior officers and much of the organized private sector (McCleary 1999: 41). The Guatemalan economy deteriorated rapidly in the late 1970s and early 1980s: the foreign debt (previously the second lowest in Latin America) tripled, financed by short-term, high-interest loans: the payments by the mid-1980s amounted to 40 percent of the total value of exports (Moreno 1994: 45). By 1982, the tensions had become particularly pronounced: internationally, Guatemala had become a pariah, junior officers felt the military leadership was out of touch with the realities of the counterinsurgency that had been escalated in 1981, and economic elites were being asked to pay for the intensified military campaign while officers themselves profited through graft (McCleary 1999: 45–47).

These tensions led to two coups in the early 1980s: General José Efraín Ríos Montt in 1982 and General Oscar Humberto Mejía Víctores in 1983. Ríos Montt was initially viewed as someone who would resubordinate the military to economic elites, although he soon overstepped his remit with an independent (and evangelical) sense of modernization that alienated the private sector (Trudeau 1993: 60–63; McCleary 1999: 55).[43] Ríos Montt further alienated himself from economic elites in his declaration that he would serve additional time in office (to compensate for the electoral fraud perpetrated by his predecessor) and in his fiscal policy that marginalized CACIF (McCleary 1999: 52–55). He lacked a strong base in the military, relying on a young junta for his support (55). Thus, the military viewed the coup to replace him as a corrective to continue the basic principles of counterinsurgent "reform": "The message was right, but the messenger [Ríos Montt] was wrong" (55–56, quoting Francisco Beltranena).[44]

Under Mejía Víctores, Ríos Montt's plans for a National Constituent Assembly tasked with drafting a new constitution were realized in July 1984 elections. The new constitution, drafted a year later, included greater scope for political organizing, although it followed on an amnesty (covering the years 1982–1986) that significantly insulated the armed forces (Dunkerley and Sieder 1996: 83). The provisions of the new constitution facilitated the formation of political parties, recognized the multiethnic nature of the Guatemalan State, and created new offices such as those of the Human Rights Ombudsman and the Constitutional Court (Azpuru 1999: 102). However, it also legalized the institutions of counterinsurgency such as civil patrols (PACs), model villages, and the coordinating councils that subordinated development projects to military command (Dunkerley and Sieder 1996: 83). Jennifer Schirmer (1998) argues that military officers were aware of the "ingenuity" of "immersing counterinsurgency structures within the 1985 constitution written by the National Constituent Assembly" (77). As Robert H. Trudeau (1993) observes, "Each of these changes reduced the need for open military repression, while at the same time providing the appearance of new levels of popular participation and democracy" (66).

The less frequently noted "national discussion" of the Mejía Víctores regime took place between economic elites—CACIF—and the military.[45] As the early 1980s saw the tensions in the contradictions of military rule bring elite pressures for reform, CACIF reorganized to enhance its capacity to affect government policy: this restructuring was led by "a younger generation of entrepreneurs" who valued neoliberalism (McCleary 1999: 57). Restructuring initially alienated traditional agricultural elites, but they returned to CACIF in 1985 in the context of National Commerce Commission negotiations between CACIF and the government on the implementation of a September 1983 IMF credit agreement (60–61).[46] CACIF was able to pressure the resignation of both the minister of finance and the minister of economy of the Mejía Víctores government, in part through organizing a work stoppage that involved government officials (61). Ultimately, this confrontation between the government and CACIF was resolved through a "National Dialogue" (that also included some labor representation) in late April 1985, which consolidated CACIF's policy-making prowess:

> CACIF successfully had asserted its control over fiscal and economic policy. It had become the crisis negotiator par excellence and would remain the main defence instrument for the private sector. No administration henceforth could enact into law a bill relating to the economic and fiscal aspects of the country without negotiating beforehand with CACIF. (62)

The elections of 1986, although "procedurally correct," remained a contest of the right/center-right and were notable for their absence of discussion of both military accountability—corruption or human rights abuses—and socioeconomic reform (Trudeau 1993: 69–71). According to Trudeau, both the army and CACIF "made clear that they would not tolerate reform proposals after the inauguration" (71). Vinicio Cerezo, a Christian Democrat, won, having cultivated the support of CACIF with commitments to its economic agenda, promises not to introduce land reform, and concern for policies that might provoke capital flight (Dunkerley 1988: 501; 1990: 249).

CACIF's understanding of neoliberal development has been influenced through a long-standing conduit of intellectual and moral leadership, the business and management school, INCAE, begun by George Cabot Lodge (1999), then at the Harvard Business School, in conjunction with Walter Rostow in the context of John F. Kennedy's

Alliance for Progress.[47] Michael Porter's (1990) theory of *The Competitive Advantage of Nations* was circulated to CACIF through INCAE.[48] As noted in chapter 2, Porter's aim is to "move beyond comparative advantage to the competitive advantage of a nation," by promoting the construction of "clusters" of productivity and competitiveness (85). In *The Competitive Advantage of Nations*, the role of government is to promote the construction of "clusters" of related industries to improve international competitiveness including the provision of infrastructure and services ("transportation, communications, information, education, the legal and judicial system, taxation, capital markets and so forth") for the benefit of private industry (1996, 105). Government should reinforce the development of clusters through research assistance, investment-friendly policies and the protection of intellectual property (115). The *Competitive Advantage of Nations* views the state as a technocratic aide for private capital: "There will always be disagreements on social policy, but everyone should agree on competitiveness and the value of productivity growth. The biggest sign of economic health is often how small the differences are between the opposition and the ruling party on economic issues" (115).

There are four sectors of the economy with which CACIF's members are particularly associated, and which have risen in importance since the 1960s: banking, nontraditional agriculture, *maquila* production, and tourism.

After it had risen in importance throughout the postreform era, Guatemala liberalized and significantly expanded its financial sector at the end of the 1980s. This liberalization program involved several strategies designed to increase competitiveness and to strengthen the solvency of the sector, to modernize the financial system, and to improve "entry-exit" conditions in the financial services market (IMF 1995: 42–43). (The modernization efforts were supported by the Inter-American Development Bank [43]). The number of private banks nearly doubled in the period 1986–1994, increasing from 15 to 27 (110). The financial services sector is not limited to banks per se: it includes a number of large financial groups, which include both financial and nonfinancial enterprises, usually with offshore operations. Many also operate *fianciadoras*, which function in many ways as unregulated banks: they can provide financial services other than checking accounts and foreign trade transactions and are not subject to reserve requirements (1998: 26). The total number of banking and financial institutions rose from 25 in 1989 to 53 in 1997 (1998: 26).

Nontraditional agricultural products grew at a rate of about 15 percent a year in the period 1992–1997, as shown in graph 3.2 (30). The growth of this sector is attributed to two phenomena; the improvement of technology and cultivation methods, as well as the development of "niche" markets, such as supplying the United States with fresh berries in its off-season (30). Also understood as a "nontraditional" export by the IMF, the *maquila* sector began in Guatemala in 1978 with the *Zona Libre de Industria y Comercio* (ZOLIC, Industrial Free Trade Zone; Pérez Sáinz 1996: 165). According to the private sector organization for nontraditional exporters, the number of *maquila* enterprises rose from 41 in 1986 to 400 in 1992, going from a workforce of 5,000 to about 70,000 in the same period (166–168).[49] IMF data also shows a dramatic increase in the value of the sector: 21 percent per annum, 1991–1996, shown in graph 3.3 (IMF 1998: 30).

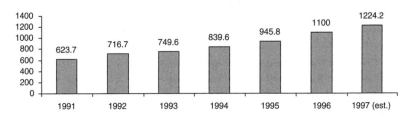

Graph 3.2 Nontraditional Agricultural Exports in Millions of US$

Source: IMF, "Guatemala: Recent Economic Developments." Washington, DC: International Monetary Fund, 1998.

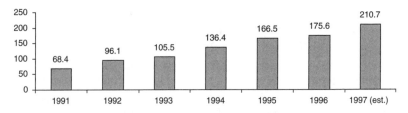

Graph 3.3 Guatemalan Maquila Exports in Millions of US$

Source: IMF, "Guatemala: Recent Economic Developments." Washington, DC: International Monetary Fund, 1998.

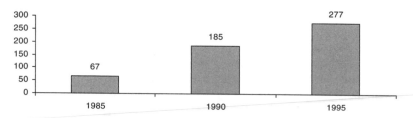

Graph 3.4   Guatemalan Tourism Earnings in Millions of US$

Source: Forrest D. Colburn and Fernando F. Sánchez, *Empresarios Centroamericanos Y Apertura Económica*. San José, Costa Rica: Educa, 2000.

Tourism exceeds *maquila* production in earnings and more than quadrupled in the period 1985–1995, as illustrated in graph 3.4.

Banking, nontraditional agricultural exports, *maquila*, and tourism all imply a different raison d'etat than that of the modernizing counterinsurgent state. A liberalized financial sector demands transparent government involvement in providing legal infrastructure for international capital, which cannot be guaranteed under military rule. Nontraditional agricultural products require a "disembedded" and flexible labor force, to a greater extent than the arrangement under "traditional" plantation agriculture; they also require new forms of marketing research for the identification and development of niche markets. The *maquila* sector similarly requires more flexible labor relations than those of the disarticulated order, and a particularly regulatory environment that includes tax and customs exemptions and favorable exchange rates (Pérez Sáinz 1996: 164). Indeed, the more recent development of the *maquila* sector consciously built on the weakness of the ZOLIC experience: the lack of infrastructure and labor, and the state's own managerial incapacity to deal with such projects (165). The *maquila* sector also presumes modernization. In Guatemala, as elsewhere, the sector is demographically specific, relying overwhelmingly on young, single women: women comprise 78 percent of the workforce and their average age is 21 years old (169–170). There is little job security in such positions, which offer very short contracts: in Guatemala the norm is 12 months (174). Juan Pablo Pérez Sáinz maintains that the *maquiladora* sector in Guatemala consciously located itself 50 kilometers away from the capital, to distance itself from organized labor and to position itself in a more docile, rural, indigenous workforce (173). Finally tourism requires the end of explicit political violence and the development of the state as a marketable destination. Colburn and Sánchez (2000) describe their interviews with business leaders in the region: "In Guatemala, they speak of the necessity of utilizing in a more aggressive manner not only their natural riches but their historical patrimony, such as the city of Antigua Guatemala and the Mayan ruins" (79, translation mine).

Conclusion: The Ensemble of Social Relations in Guatemala before the Peace Process

The ensemble of social relations in Guatemala comprises different subjectivities constructed through the mode of production and rearticulated as production changes: it reflects the extremely dense relationship between the material and the subjective, which is established across the "inside/outside" state boundary. The roots of the Guatemalan conflict lie in the thwarted attempt to challenge disarticulated production and the backlash that this engendered, a backlash that was to a certain extent organic to dominant elements in the ensemble of social relations though precipitated by and supported with U.S. power. This backlash cannot be understood in terms of the "pure" logic of capitalist accumulation, but a particular form of capitalism mediated through the "intellectual and moral leadership" of modernization theory and its understanding of difference. Modernizing counterinsurgency in Guatemala generated a number of paradoxes. It established the foundations for new sectors of the economy for which disarticulated production—the preservation of which is the very foundation of counterinsurgency—would be a hindrance. At the same time, in its attempt to securitize/eliminate modernization's "remainder" in violent excess, it produced new social conditions amenable to neoliberal principles of development.

One of the persistent themes across this story is the recurring question of how "liberal" modernization deals with the "other." In other words, how does "actually existing liberalism" address the subject of "the great transformation," as Karl Polanyi (1957) described the process of "disembedding" European culture in the transition to the liberal, market-based order? Under disarticulation, "traditional" society is strategically protected for the sake of production, though it is also denigrated, to justify exploitative labor practices. Modernizing counterinsurgency's paradoxes—its creation of new "neoliberal" forms of production under its remit of protecting disarticulation, and its disembedding of the traditional society through violence—produce less of a "great" transformation than a partial, confused transformation. These conditions and the ethico-political principles of neoliberal political theory are important to understand in considering the nature of the peace process, to which the next chapter turns.

4

The Peace Process

As chapter 3 illustrated, the ensemble of social relations entering the Guatemalan peace process can be characterized by a disarticulated mode of production reiterated and partially transformed by the modernizing, counterinsurgent state and its own further move toward neoliberalism. In this story, society is largely divided between "popular" forces—the groups constructed as "enemies" of the counterinsurgent state: the guerrilla, peasants involved in the cooperative movement, the indigenous—and economic and military elites, though these broad groups included diverse interests and perspectives. For example, the "popular" sector incorporated converts to evangelical Christianity, who share a neoliberal modernizing ethos with elements of the business classes; similarly, traditional agricultural elites were divided from "modernizing" economic elites on many issues.

The dominant story of the Guatemala peace process is that the peace process was inaugurated by a stalemate between two military forces—the guerrilla and the army—that could not conclusively win militarily and that the peace accords reflect a compromise of the two warring perspectives (Robinson 2000: 97). However, as will be outlined in further detail below, the peace process is better understood as a (second) passive revolution of certain elites, assisted by the international community, both through official channels and civil society.

The Guatemalan peace process should be understood in international and historical context. It followed a regional peace process that established certain parameters for the negotiations—particular understandings of democracy and human rights—while shifting foreign assistance in this period led to an "end of the revolutionary option" for resistance groups and contributed to a depoliticization of other civil society groups. The role that these regional efforts played in constructing "common sense" limits for the possibilities of the Guatemalan negotiations is a significant, if often overlooked, dimension of the peace process.

The negotiations themselves occurred in several stages, which may be characterized in terms of Gramscian political theory. The first phase was one of intellectual and moral leadership around the parameters of the negotiations, the end of the revolutionary option and agreement on the use of electoral politics. In the second phase, marked by a destabilizing coup, civil society was used as a site of elite-led consensus making. A third phase of UN conciliation institutionalized this mechanism of consulting civil society in terms that obscured the material bases of power among different groups. Indeed, this phase of the negotiations can be understood as one of *trasformismo*, where popular organizations were disciplined to participate as part of the "political center," and where CACIF's significant political influence was extended and validated. Finally, a number of issues were deferred until after the 1995 elections, where "propeace" forces won only a small victory in the unreformed electoral system, and thus this last phase of the negotiations was privileged elites under the threat of a return to violence.

The Guatemalan negotiations engaged in a practice of redefining and postponing discussion of the "essential" issues of disarticulation—the economic and the military—with consequences for the conceptualization of rights and the possibilities for the negotiations. Robinson (1996b) has described the deferral of certain kinds of popular claims in authoritarian-"democratic" transitions. He notes that in the dominant readings of such transitions, the requirement for orderly transitions leads to trade-offs between popular demands and the promise of participation in the consolidated, posttransition "democracy."[1] Trade-offs are not—as they are cast—temporary, transitional concessions; rather, they become structural features of the posttransition order (65). Robinson identifies the "equity" trade-off, the deferral of social justice and economic claims, and the military concession trade-off, the "preservation of existing military structures and promises not to prosecute militaries for human rights violations committed during dictatorships" (64). In Guatemala, analogous deferrals during the peace negotiations not only affected the quality of political participation but also constructed a definition of human and indigenous rights devoid of a socioeconomic dimension. The power of dominant interests was maintained through the preservation of state coercion and through the subjective effects of the persistence of impunity.

Regional Peace Processes

The Guatemalan national peace process follows on two regional peace processes, Contadora and Esquípulas, which established the international community in the region within parameters dictated by efforts to secure the progressive Sandinista government in Nicaragua.

Contadora

The first efforts at regional peace-building in Central America occurred through the Contadora Process in 1983, an initiative of Mexico, Venezuela, Colombia, and Panama to prevent the United States from getting directly militarily involved in the Sandinista revolution in Nicaragua (Bagley 1986: 2–3).[2] A primary element of the Contadora initiative's attempt to mitigate U.S. militarism involved redefining the conflicts as the result of internal considerations—poverty, injustice, repression—in contrast to the Reagan administration's claims of Soviet-Cuban subversion (Bagley 1986: 3; Moreno 1994: 56; Aguilar Zinser 1988: 101).[3] Nonetheless, during negotiations over the course of three years,[4] the Contadora process emerged with a rather paradoxical emphasis on conflicts *among* states in the region, not those *within* them, a construction that could appeal to both poles: the left Sandinstas in Nicaragua, who wished to eliminate Honduran and potentially Costa Rican support for the contras as well as the right-wing Salvadoran government under threat from the revolutionary *Frente Farabundo Martí de Liberación Nacional* (FMLN, Farabundo Martí National Liberation Front; Aguilar Zinser 1988: 103, 08).[5]

The United States participated in the Contadora process despite significant evidence that it would not accept the basic premise of recognizing the Nicaraguan revolution in exchange for its "containment" (Bagley 1986: 22).[6] Its objections were repeatedly framed in terms of questions of democracy and verification. The United States responded to the first declaration of the process, the Cancún Communiqué, with the objection that "only by ensuring free and open participation in the democratic process can the people of Central America achieve reconciliation within their societies" (Moreno 1994: 59, quoting the Congressional Record, 15 May 1984: S5758). The Reagan administration reacted similarly to the accord on procedural norms with the statement that, in addition to the reduction of military forces and the end of ties to Cuba and support for the FMLN in El Salvador, the United States wanted Nicaragua to "permit democratic pluralism to flourish at home" (Bagley 1986: 8, quoting then secretary of state George Schultz). Likewise, the Revised Act was met with the accusation that Nicaragua had rejected the key elements of that text relating to internal democratization (8). (The Sandinistas' unexpected acceptance of the Revised Act put the Reagan administration on the defensive.) "Democratization" became integrated into the Contadora texts and would represent a significant norm in future regional initiatives.[7]

The European Community (EC) initiated an annual conference with the Central American governments, the San José dialogue, in 1984 to provide a forum to discuss economic assistance and support for the Contadora process (Whitehead 1996: 233; Biekart 1999: 176). Initially, official European assistance often supported the Sandinista revolution (Biekart 1999: 175–176).[8] European governments, in contrast to the United States, understood the origins of the conflicts in terms of economic and social causes; however, after the early 1980s "open European support for the Sandinista government became less clear-cut and shifted towards more 'neutral' statements calling for the establishment of democratic principles and strict observance of human rights" (176).

A similar expansion and transformation can be observed in private European aid. Kees Biekart (1999) identifies four stages of European private aid activities in Central America: the arrival of such agencies in the early 1980s, their activities under counterinsurgency, their policy transitions around the 1987 Esquípulas II agreement and their interventions after 1989 (182). He argues there are several reasons for their significant growth, from a dozen prior to 1980 to over a hundred organizations by the late 1980s: support for the Sandinistas from progressive circles, the alternative they provided European governments to challenge discretely the Reagan administration, the larger trend in which European private aid agencies became increasingly significant in the international aid sector (182–184).[9] Initially, private aid largely involved emergency assistance (206). However, the democratic transitions in the region "generated confusion about the new 'political agenda' of private aid agencies and fuelled concern that the 'era of solidarity aid' had ended" (208). This development resulted in a new form of European private aid: "Instead of popular education and institutional support for strengthening organizations in civil society, support shifted to management and training methods to strengthen the capacity of organizations in order to increase their likelihood of economic sustainability" (208). OECD figures for European and U.S. bilateral assistance to the region over the period 1980–2000 are shown in graphs 4.1 and 4.2,[10] followed by multilateral aid figures for comparison in graphs 4.3 and 4.4.

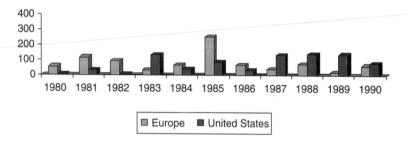

Graph 4.1   Bilateral Aid 1980–1990 in US$ Millions

Source: OECD, Aid Activity Database of the Dac. In www.oecd.org/dac/stats. (accessed 6 August 2003).

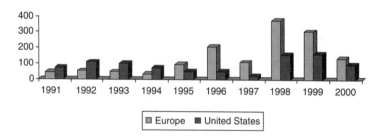

Graph 4.2   Bilateral Aid 1991–2000 in US$ Millions

Source: OECD, Aid Activity Database of the Dac. In www.oecd.org/dac/stats. (accessed 6 August 2003).

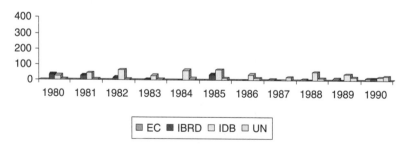

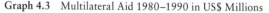

Graph 4.3   Multilateral Aid 1980–1990 in US$ Millions

Source: OECD, Aid Activity Database of the Dac. In www.oecd.org/dac/stats. (accessed 6 August 2003).

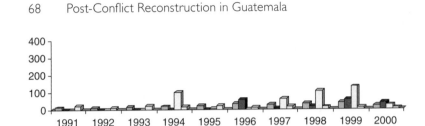

Graph 4.4   Multilateral Aid 1991–2000 in US$ Millions

Source: OECD, Aid Activity Database of the Dac. In www.oecd.org/dac/stats. (accessed 6 August 2003).

External actors and local elites have actively participated in constructing civil society in a particular image. Peter Sollis (1995) argues that in Guatemala the government was directly involved in NGO creation, particularly to promote microenterprise programs. "Mindful of the creative force represented by grass roots, political elites have devised a two-part strategy. While encouraging the arrival of US pentecostal church agencies, they have also organized their own NGOs" (534). As Sollis notes, "The scale of NGO funding questions the stereotype of NGOs as small players in Central America's unfolding drama. Hard data on funding is hard to gather because of the large number of funding sources, but estimates put the annual level of funding at over $200 million annually at the end of the 1980s" (527). Jenny Pearce (1998) notes that donor preferences have marginalized the more "political" and less "technocratic" NGOs, or subjected them to "capacity-building" programs (612). She argues:

> Most donors prefer the NGO as their model of a civil society organization, and many are engaged in turning organizations once seen as social empowerers into technical service deliverers and advocacy organizations on behalf of the poor. Words such as "empowerment" and "participation" are still used, but their meanings have become more anodyne and less political. (613)

And she reminds us that "associationalism" did exist prior to the 1980s, but was much less dependent on outside funding (613).

Although it failed to produce a peace plan for the region, the Contadora process established important understandings that would inform the parameters of future discussions: the weight given to defining the causes of conflict in "local" terms; the transformation of external support to favor a less "political" civil society, and a particular understanding of "democratization" qua electoral democracy. The process also set the stage for the Esquípulas agreements, which would play a more direct role in shaping the Guatemalan peace process.

Esquípulas

The Esquípulas meetings, initiated in 1986, are associated with the elections of Vinicio Cerezo in Guatemala and of Oscar Arias in Costa Rica. Cerezo called the first meeting, Esquípulas I, in late May 1986 to continue Guatemala's policy of "active neutrality" in the regional peace efforts as a way to reduce Guatemala's international isolation (Godoy 1987). (Indeed, at his inauguration in January 1986, Cerezo had the Central American heads of state in attendance endorse the Caraballeda declaration, essentially a reiteration of the Contadora process" 1984 Revised Draft treaty (Bagley 1986: 15; Moreno 1994: 69).) Esquípulas I did not create a clear plan for the end of conflict, but it did reiterate the principle of regional democracy—understood as Western-style liberal democracy—as a solution to conflict, and pressured Nicaragua to transform itself toward that ideal (Moreno 1994: 75).

Oscar Arias took up the regional peace process and invested it with active leadership and personal diplomacy, particularly vis-à-vis Western Europe and the (then) European Community (Andersen 1992: 444).[11] Indeed, the Arias effort understood that European support for the Sandinistas was waning and "capitalized on these attitudinal shifts, securing official support from both individual governments and the EC prior to the 1987 Esquípulas meeting" (451–452). Widespread support for the initiative divided both the Reagan and Thatcher governments between conservative hard-liners and more centrist Arias supporters ("Arias's Central American Peace Plan Gains European Support" 1987; Steele 1987).

Esquípulas II, the Arias peace plan, was signed on 7 August 1987. It called for the end of outside support to insurgencies, internal democratization and elections, and national reconciliation (Moreno 1994: 191).[12] In its emphasis on controlling insurgencies, the plan privileged the governments in office (requesting that "the irregular forces and insurgent groups operating in Central America...refrain from receiving such aid in order to demonstrate a genuine spirit of Latin Americanism" [195]). It also specifically thanked the EC and asked "the international community to respect and assist our efforts. We have our own approaches to peace and development but we need help in making them a reality. We ask for an international response which will guarantee development so that peace we are seeking can be a lasting one" (191–192). The construction of a regional peace process around the legality of the elected governments of the region, which was largely supported by European governments, also meant an end to private "solidarity" assistance: Esquípulas was perceived as the "end to the revolutionary option" by private European aid agencies (Biekart 1999: 209).

Laurence Whitehead (1996) argues that the primary difference between Contadora and Esquípulas involved the latter's stress on the "necessity for internally democratic processes" (245). According to interviews with the Costa Rican Foreign Minister, Arias "assured the Reagan administration that, unlike Contadora, his peace plan would result in the restructuring of the Nicaraguan policy" (Moreno 1994: 86–87). Such "democratization" was code for ensuring the peace process would not legitimize the Nicaraguan regime (87). Thus the Arias peace process "brought an imposing array of international pressures to bear on the Sandinistas, forcing them to democratize [sic]. The Sandinistas were confronted not only with the contras and the United States' economic embargo, but also with a more skeptical Western Europe and an increasingly reluctant Soviet Union" (134).

The Esquípulas program also amplified the involvement of multilateral agencies in the region. As Robert Andersen (1992) observes, "The Arias Peace Plan developed outside of the context of either the United Nations or the Organization of American States but, in contrast to Contadora, incorporated and heightened the profile of both organizations (particularly the United Nations) in the implementation of the accords" (444). The Esquípulas II agreement created a role for the UN as a monitoring force, the UN Observer Group in Central America (ONUCA, Observadores de las Naciones Unidas en Centroamerica). In principle, peace processes would occur simultaneously within the five countries of the Isthmus; however, the UN's "management of the armed conflicts," as Stephen Baranyi puts it, occurred sequentially: Nicaragua (1989–1990), El Salvador (1990–1994), and Guatemala (1994–1996) for the peace process itself, with an extended presence for the implementation of the agreements until 2004 (Baranyi 1996: 248). (The Salvadoran case particularly would serve as an example for the negotiators of the Guatemalan agreement, especially regarding the necessity of coordination between the UN and the IFIs [the IMF and the World Bank; Burgerman 2000; Whitfield 1999].)

European and U.S. involvement in Central America converged through the regional peace processes. Biekart (1999) suggests the mutual terrain of what were commonly understood to be divergent perspectives when he observes "The United States and the majority of European governments had different views about *how to rebuild the 'political centre'* that was destroyed by authoritarian regimes in the late 1970s, and about *how to strengthen civil society*" (173, emphasis added). Though their analyses of the causes of the region's conflicts differed ("local" versus "external"), Northern governments were unified in seeking to establish a political center and rebuild civil society. Whitehead (1996) captures the bounded nature of the United States-European Union differences in observing that not only was U.S. opinion deeply divided ("with many Democrats closer to Brussels than to the White House in their definitions of the issues"), but that "successful European policy could hardly be rated a moral affront to the United States" (234).[13] Whitehead emphasizes the *compatibility* of Western interests, characterizing the situation in terms of a "carrot and stick" approach, where "through a process of tacit co-operation the EC acquired the function of offering the carrots leaving the USA free to concentrate on administering the sticks" (235).

The regional peace processes created a particular landscape for international involvement in the region based on particular norms. Democratization was understood as narrow electoral, democracy and in terms that would allow for the "legitimate" reconstruction of the Nicaraguan polity. The simultaneous delegitimization of insurgency affected the possibilities for "solidarity" assistance and the revolutionary option. Civil society became the site for reconstructing the "political centre," and as the conflicts were increasingly secured, this assistance became increasingly technical in nature. The relative success of the Arias peace plan in consolidating international support for a "local" reading of regional conflicts—the "social bases of conflict"—in the face of the Reagan administration's policies nonetheless establishes quite narrow parameters for such issues. The norms that emerge out of the regional peace processes are constructed so as to allow for the continuation of elite rule, under the rubric of negotiated peace.

The Guatemalan Peace Process

The scale of the peace process in Guatemala is significant, involving on the order of 17 agreements over 8 years.[14] The initial phase of the negotiations involved several stages. In the agenda setting phase of the negotiations, the problematic of establishing a common terrain for negotiations involved the international sponsorship of discussions between the URNG and various social sectors that established the electoral system as a central legitimating feature of the process. A governmental crisis allowed private sector elites to lead a "consensus-building" process that would underscore its dominant position in civil society. UN conciliation in the peace process would further construct a legitimating role for civil society within significant limitations; in this process rights became understood as exclusively political and the "essential" issues of the economy and the military were deferred until after the 1995 elections, a moment of "democratic" participation that would in fact destabilize the peace process.

Agenda Setting

When speaking about the motivations to participate in the peace process, propeace members of CACIF cite issues such as the need for security for tourism, capital (financial regulations and the rule of law), and sufficient stability for long-term economic planning (Briz 2001; Pivaral 2001; Gonzalez 2001). The antipeace process perspective, by contrast, expressed itself through the sense that the military option of defeating the "illegal/lawless" insurgency still existed or that congress—not the "narrow, elitist" peace negotiations—was the appropriate venue for discussing political change (Gonzalez 2001; Briz 2001). The URNG describes its involvement in the peace process in terms of a gradual process of beginning to explore the possibility of a political solution, understood as the ability to establish the social bases of war as the foundation for negotiations (Noriega 2001; Asturias 2001).

The first phase of the peace process involved an agenda-setting process. Esquípulas II called for the formation of a *Comisión Nacional de Reconciliación* (CNR, National Reconciliation Commission), which sponsored a national dialogue that brought peace explicitly onto the national agenda. The URNG and the CNR signed the Oslo Accord, subtitled the "Basic Accord for the Search for Peace through Political Means" (30 March 1990) that promoted the idea of discussions between the URNG and various sectors of society. The URNG subsequently (June-October 1990) held meetings with political parties, CACIF, religious representatives, labor and popular organizations, and representatives of small business, cooperatives, and academe. These internationally hosted meetings resulted in a number of texts regarding goals for the process.

The meeting with the political parties resulted in the *Acuerdo de El Escorial,* signed by many political parties, the URNG, and the CNR. It contained five points promoting the Oslo Accord and institutional reform to advance democracy in Guatemala, including reform of the judicial system, respect for the rule of law and a cease-fire during the electoral process ('Acuerdo de El Escorial'). Thus the agenda of privileging electoral politics was established with the commitment of a cease-fire, but with no specifics on the reform of the electoral system to ensure participation. Indeed, electoral reform would be discussed only at the end of the peace process, after the 1995 presidential elections. The meeting between CACIF and the URNG failed to produce a joint document, although both sides did nonetheless issue declarations to express their good will toward the process.[15] CACIF noted in the first point of its declaration the importance of "the eradication of violence, as [the] necessary element for Guatemala to achieve sustainable and stable economic and social development" underscoring the economic purpose of the peace process ("Comunicado del CACIF en Ottawa").

Jorge Serrano Elías was elected in 1991, and continued the peace process, albeit initially only reiterating the Oslo Accord through a renegotiated "Agreement on the Procedure for the Search for Peace by Political Means" (Mexico, 26 April 1991). In the peace platform put forward by the URNG in May 1992, a particular understanding of development emerges: one of national development based upon education, health, nutrition, housing, support for small and medium producers and businesses, and the reform of land tenure, foreign trade, foreign investments, and taxation (URNG 1992b). (The negotiations would privilege and reconstruct the URNG's social development agenda in a particular way, while marginalizing its economic and fiscal agenda, as discussed below.) As the negotiations progressed, the URNG would become increasingly convinced that rural development rather than land reform was necessary to solve the problems in the countryside (Noriega 2001). Significantly, the URNG called for civil society representation with observer status in the negotiations (URNG 1992b).

The first phase of the peace process provided intellectual and moral leadership establishing certain elements of the peace process, particularly the question of the use of the unreformed electoral system to promote democracy and the need for economic development as part of the peace accords. It also established the URNG's support for the involvement of civil society, albeit a role limited and defined by the negotiating parties.

Crisis and "Consensus Inc."

The second phase of the peace process involves the crisis of the Serrano government that ended in an unsuccessful attempt to recover power through a self-coup (*auto-golpe* or *Serranazo*). Negotiations had stalled; the period leading to the *Serranazo* was marked by a period of social unrest and military exchanges. The government's coalition began to break down in early 1993, which led to the *auto-golpe* in May 1993 (Palencia Prado 1996).[16] The *auto-golpe* failed and brought the Human Rights Ombudsman to the presidency through a new mechanism, the *Instancia Nacional de Consenso* (INC, National Consensus Body).

The *Instancia* emerged from the *Foro Multisectoral*—CACIF's renamed Strategic Committee—that then invited broader participation, from the alternative/popular *Foro Multisectoral Social* (McCleary 1999: 110, 27). The "popular," "democratic" response to the *auto-golpe* was in fact strongly dominated by CACIF (192). The discourse of elite-led theories regarding the *Instancia* is that it was characterized by "compromise and negotiation" and that it "represented the political will of Guatemalan society" (192). In fact, popular organizations felt they had little alternative but to follow the private sector's lead. One union leader noted that "for the unions and popular movement there was no other choice but to participate in the [INC], despite the risk this represents. We had to take advantage of the spaces opening up...because to the contrary, only political and business sectors would have resolved the problem" (Central America Report 1993b). This sense may have been exacerbated by the failure of the URNG to take a stand on the crisis, due in part to its still tentative participation in the peace process at this stage (Noriega 2001; Azpuru 1999).

The international community strongly condemned the *Serranazo*, which assisted domestic actors in coalescing around a rejection of such *auto-golpe* tactics, yet also thus implicitly endorsed the resolution of the crisis in terms of the organization of "civil society" by economic elites (Jonas 2001; Central America Report 1993a).

UN Conciliation and the Civil Society Assembly

The bulk of the agreements were signed 1994–1996 in under UN conciliation. The resolution of the *Serranazo* led to the Ramiro de Leon Carpio assuming the presidency in June 1993. Despite having been Human Rights Ombudsman, de Leon Carpio's initial treatment of the peace process had a destabilizing effect in its introduction of a set of new rules for the negotiations. International pressure on the government led to the signing of a procedural accord bridging this impasse (Aguilera et al. 1996).

The 1994 Framework Accord (Mexico, 10 January) did three noteworthy things. First, it institutionalized the role of the international community in the peace process: UN involvement was intensified from observer status to that of moderator, and the Groups of Friend states (involving the United States, Spain, Mexico, Norway, Colombia, and Venezuela) was officially formed, tasked with providing "security and firmness" to the commitments (Palencia Prado 1996: 20).[17] Second, the Framework Accord collapsed into one theme the "socio-economic aspects" and "agrarian situation" (Baranyi 1995: 6). This is the first step in a narrow conceptualization of the agrarian situation, which would be further reified in the Socio-Economic Accord. Finally, the Framework Accord established a formal role for the *Asamblea de Sociedad Civil* (ASC, Civil Society Assembly).

The ASC emerged from the National Reconciliation Commission of the first phase of the negotiations, and was headed by Msgr. Quezada Turuño, the former president of that commission and ex-conciliator of the peace process. The Framework Accord gave the ASC the right to "advise" (in a nonbinding way) the formal negotiating process and the right to either accept or reject the accords; it became a parallel organization to the formal peace process.

The role given to the ASC is significant in several respects. The ASC was put into the position of informing the national discussion from the margin: needing to create its own consensus first, and then bring its positions to the table. In at least two areas, significant compromises took place in the ASC before reaching the formal negotiating table regarding indigenous autonomy and land (Sieder 1997: 68; Palma Murga 1997). Furthermore, CACIF, with its independent resources, did not participate in the ASC.[18] It had different access to the negotiations, lobbying the peace commission (COPAZ, Comisión Presidencial de la Paz), the Group of Friends, the UN moderation and even the URNG directly, rather than presenting its proposals directly to the negotiations as the ASC did (Krznaric 1999: 12).[19] Nonetheless, several ASC proposed texts (e.g., regarding the Armed Forces Accord) were adopted by the URNG and became the basis for negotiations with this support. The URNG held the view that the ASC played a big role in the negotiations and had excellent results as a reference point for popular claims (Asturias 2001).

The status of the ASC as a more publicly accountable body made it more vulnerable to pressure from international organizations. Roman Krznaric (1999) notes:

> After the withdrawal of Quezada Toruño from the presidency of the ASC and during much of the rest of 1995, the information flow from the [UN] moderation to ASC was limited, which undermined the Asamblea's lobbying efforts. At other times the UN moderation attempted to limit ASC lobbying efforts more directly. After the Xamán massacre of returned refugees on 5 October 1995, for example, the UN asked the Asamblea to "not make too much noise" about the massacre as this would damage the peace process. (12)

Thus, the ASC not only provided a forum for expressing opinions but also for containing that participation. Krznaric remarks that "Actors within the Asamblea and outside observers agree that it would have been possible to have had a greater impact on the negotiations. More of its proposals could have been accepted in the accords, particularly on the Socioeconomic theme. Efforts to make the negotiations more transparent also largely failed" (10).

The ASC is often described as an arena that built the political capacity of popular organizations. Susanne Jonas (2000b), for example, argues that the ASC gave groups that rejected electoral politics new political experiences that provided a basis for their participation in the 1995 elections (13). But the disciplining function of this new expertise is also clear: as Gabriel Aguilera suggests (unselfconsciously), "the ASC became another arena of permanent negotiation in which participants perfected their understanding of tolerance and mutual concessions, taking into account that they reflected heterogeneity in their political criteria and in the social interests that they reflected" (Aguilera et al. 1996: 23–23). The expectation is that organizations will converge into the "apolitical center," an area defined by powerful actors' sense of what is realistic and maintains stability. Thus the very claims of the ASC providing experience to popular organizations so that they might reincorporate into electoral politics expresses the logic of *trasformismo*.

The ASC was ultimately unsustainable. Three themes affected its longevity: the leadership vacuum left by the resignation of Mnsr. Quezada Turuño, the relatively specific mandate accorded to it by the Framework Accord, and the participation of some of the ASC in the 1995 elections as candidates for the *Frente Democratico de Nueva Guatemala* (FDNG, New Guatemala Democratic Front; Palencia Prado 1996; Krznaric 1999: 9–12). The ASC was not an "organic" political body, not because there was no pressure for social participation, but because it artificially aggregated too many positions.[20] The departure of FDNG candidates and the failure to replace them exacerbated tensions between "radical" and "centrist" positions, provoking the departure of the Atlixco (academic/small business) sector and ultimately the creation of another body (the Democratic Civic Forum for Peace, Foro Cívico Democrático por la Paz, FOCIDEP; Krznaric 1999: 10). The difficulty that the Atlixco sector perceived in relating to the popular movement illuminates the role this sector played as "organic intellectuals," supporting the status quo.[21]

Four agreements were signed before the 1995 elections: accords on human rights, the resettlement of refugees, "Historical Clarification" (i.e., the principle of establishing a truth commission), and indigenous rights. All four of these accords exclude or defer land and economic issues until the negotiations for the Socio-Economic Accord. The two accords on rights, which are considered quite successful, thus construct a mutually reinforcing understanding of rights as devoid of a socioeconomic dimension. Generally the guerrilla supported the order in which the issues were to be negotiated, based on the URNG's longstanding principle that substantive issues should precede operational issues (i.e., demobilization; Noriega 2001). Yet this deferral of key economic issues in particular to the elections had the effect of removing them from more popular pressures due to the tenuous outcome of the poll (discussed further below). The appeal to elections as part of the peace process in itself must be problematized: although little appears in the literature about objections to the elections—suggesting they were widely understood to be part of the "democratic" process—when asked whether electoral politics work for the left, the guerrilla and popular / Maya organizations suggest that they do not: either due to lack of resources and experience (Asturias 2001; Macahio 2001), or due to structural racism and exclusion (Raymundo 2001; Tiney 2001).[22]

"The Comprehensive Agreement on Human Rights" was agreed in March 1994. This accord's scope only applied to the immediate situation and established the UN verification mission (MINUGUA). Violations worsened in the period between the accord's signature and MINUGUA's arrival in November (Jonas 2000a: 45). Nonetheless, MINUGUA was successful in lifting the pronounced ambience of fear that existed before its arrival (Palencia Prado 1996: 34; Louise 1997: 57). It particularly functioned as a dissuasive presence against further human rights abuses, which indeed worsened after its final mandate expired in December 2004. MINUGUA undoubtedly played an important role in opening political spaces and reducing fear in Guatemala. However, the boundaries of its presence must also be considered. MINUGUA had an explicit institution-building mandate, which reflects the evolving notion of UN peacekeeping that emerged from Boutros Boutros-Ghali's *Agenda for Development,* with two main components: capacity building in juridical institutions and educational dissemination of human rights information (raising awareness of human rights). MINUGUA explicitly focused on civil and political rights as "priority rights" for verification, to the exclusion of economic and social rights (Baranyi 1995: 6). In 1995, Stephen Baranyi (1995) argued that this distinction "could undermine future demands for the respect of economic and social rights," which did indeed come to pass by the 1996 Socio-Economic Accord (6).[23]

In June 1994 the "Agreement on the Resettlement of Population Groups Uprooted by Armed Conflict" (Oslo, 17 June) and the "Agreement for the Establishment of the Commission to Clarify Past Human Rights Violations and Acts of Violence that have Caused the Guatemalan Population to Suffer" (23 June) were signed. The former involves the creation of a "comprehensive reintegration plan" to promote the safe return or resettlement of displaced people and refugees.[24] Though it recognized land and land tenure as elements of this process, it deferred the substantive discussion of them until the Socio-Economic Accord.[25] Because the accord would not go into immediate effect, it was subject to criticism by representatives of refugee committees (Jonas 2000a: 74).

The accord on Historical Clarification is considered the weakest of Guatemalan peace accords (Wilson 1997: 19). It created a commission for Historical Clarification limited in scope (only abuses "linked to the armed conflict"), time (six months, extendable to one year), legal prowess (no powers of search, seizure, nor subpoena) and that could not identify individual perpetrators (20). Gabriel Aguilera (1996) argues that, given serious disagreements, this accord was signed "only thanks to a particularly intense intervention of international actors, especially one of the friend countries, that principally pressured the insurgents" (18). The accord provoked public outrage and represented a loss of credibility for the URNG, which affected its ability to negotiate subsequent issues (Wilson 1997: 24; Aguilera et al. 1996: 18). This document was considered weak not only vis-à-vis the initial text proposed by the ASC, but also vis-à-vis the Salvadoran agreement for a truth commission (Baranyi 1995: 9).

With the November 1995 election in mind, the UN pressured the parties to conclude negotiations of substantive themes by August 1995 (Aguilera et al. 1996: 246). The Indigenous Rights Accord was signed in late March 1995. In many respects a far reaching accord, it recognizes the Guatemalan nation as "multi-ethnic, multicultural and multilingual," and "respect the identity and political, economic, social, and cultural rights of the Maya, Garifuna and Xinca peoples" ("Agreement on the Identity and Rights of Indigenous Peoples" 1995: para. 3–4). As noted in the introduction, Christopher Chase-Dunn (2000) calls the accord "a conceptual breakthrough that many other countries should emulate" (109). This achievement of the acknowledgment of indigenous rights—for example, to bilingual education, freedom from discrimination, the protection of indigenous names and sacred sites, and so on—given the history of the Guatemalan ensemble of social relations is very significant.[26]

In fact, it has been argued that the strength of the text of the Indigenous Rights Accord and the political mobilization of the indigenous community around the accords are two primary foundations for claims of "empowerment" during the peace process. Rachel Sieder (1997) argues that

> more than any other factor...it was probably the independence and self-confidence of Mayan actors in the peace process which confirmed the transformation in indigenous identity politics. During discussions of the [indigenous accord], it became evident that non-indigenous intermediaries were no longer necessary...(68)

Nonetheless, there are several drawbacks to how the accord was agreed. Notably, as per the structure of the negotiations generally, indigenous representatives were not able to sit at the negotiating table (68). Furthermore, there was significant compromise on the issue of Mayan autonomy within the ASC—that is, between Maya and non-Maya groups—before proposals reached the actual negotiation table (68). Kay Warren (1998) reports, "Mayanists hold that the accord process was seriously compromised by secrecy, limited Maya input, and disregard of indigenous norms of consultation with communities and elders. Of great concern is the fact that the final document dealt only obliquely with collective rights" (56).[27] Finally, two key issues were deferred to subsequent accords: the issue of Mayan lands and demilitarization in Mayan communities (Sieder 1997: 69–70; Aguilera et al. 1996: 247).

The text of the Indigenous Rights Accord engaged in two further "deferral" tactics. Key elements—centrally the redefinition of Guatemala as a "national unity, multiethnic, multicultural, and multilingual," the recognition of all existing languages, and the protection of spiritual practices ("Agreement on the Identity and Rights of Indigenous Peoples" 1995: IV A, IIIA2a, IIIC3)—would also be contingent on constitutional reform (dealt with in one of the final operational accords, as below). The agreement also relies on the establishment of joint commissions to explore education reform, "reform and participation" in national life and land rights. These commissions would be composed of equal numbers of government representatives and representatives of indigenous organization. Crucially, they were established to operate by consensus. In fact, the consensus requirement led to long delays in the resolution of the themes that the joint commissions were established to deal with and the indigenous organizations that participated in the commissions lost credibility among the popular sectors (Raymundo 2001; Tiney 2001; Macahio 2001).

The Guatemalan peace process before the 1995 elections was marked by the cultivation of consent through international support in agenda setting, through the resolution of the *auto-golpe*, and with mechanisms such as the ASC under UN mediation. UN conciliation was marked by an elaborate effort to involve civil society in the negotiations; however, one that did not overcome the pre-existing social power inequities in Guatemala; it functions precisely to preserve elite power and to cultivate the appearance of broad popular consent through "participation" in "openly contested" negotiations. While the UN's presence via MINUGUA clearly improved the conditions for popular organizing, which contributed to participation in formulating the Indigenous Rights Accord, the UN also undermined the URNG's position in the negotiations in its pressure for limited Historical Clarification. The categorical deferral of socioeconomic issues constructed a narrow understanding of rights as purely "political," devoid of socioeconomic content, while other deferral strategies—the electoral dimension of constitutional reform, consensus-driven joint commissions—would later compromise the implementation of the agreements.

Negotiating the "Essential"

The November 1995 elections would open up intraelite differences generated by internationalizing counterinsurgent modernization regarding the future of development in Guatemala. They resulted in a run-off between the CACIF-oriented *Partido de Anvanzada Nacional* (PAN, National Advancement Party) and the *Frente Republicano Guatemalteco* (FRG, Guatemalan Republican Front), which the PAN's Alvaro Arzú won by 2 percent. The FRG is the party of Efraín Ríos Montt; constitutionally barred from holding presidential office again, Montt was still seen to be the behind-the-scenes leader of the party. The PAN has a strong relationship with CACIF and fewer ties to the military; indeed Arzú, specifically sought independence from the military in the negotiations (Arnault 2001).

The FRG represented a right-wing, populist-military position that sought to continue Ríos Montt's counterinsurgent "development" program of *fusiles y frijoles* (guns and beans), evangelical renewal, and the promotion of nontraditional agrarian export-led growth. The FRG ran in the 1995 elections on a platform of economic liberalization and privatization as did the PAN, yet it sought to pursue a developmentalist project independent from CACIF (FRG 2001). The PAN, on the other hand, in its propeace platform, implied the resolution of counterinsurgency through the subordination of the military to civilian government with the support and "modernizing" economic agenda of CACIF, including sectors such as tourism, that required the end to military excess. Taken together the FRG-PAN showing illustrated above all an unreformed electoral system's preference for an elite-oriented solution to the contradictions of counterinsurgent modernization. Whatever the relative instability of the solutions represented by the FRG and the PAN, by this point popular forces had been "secured" by the peace process to a significant extent, through their incorporation into electoral politics and the governance project implied by an organized civil society.

To leftist analysts such as Edelberto Torres-Rivas (1997), the FRG/PAN contest reflected "the 'deideologification' of the electoral debate, the distaste for politics, that took place everywhere, which reduced itself to a poor [political] program, to a basic package of small material offerings and a millionaire's game of telegenic images" (25). Yet, two features of the election promoted a sense of contestation. One was the unprecedented call by the URNG for public participation. The second was the unexpected showing of the leftist coalition party *Frente Democrático Nueva Guatemala* (FDNG), which won 6 (of 80) seats. Jonas (2000a), for example, concludes "Until they actually occurred, such results had not been believed possible in Guatemala" (47). Clearly, however, the magnitude of this result was relatively insignificant vis-à-vis dominant interests. Electoral reform would be one of the last issues dealt with in the accords, as discussed below.

The narrow electoral victory of propeace forces would enhance the position of the PAN in the negotiations: "Armed with this specter [of the FRG], the PAN government was consistently able to gain a reluctant nod from the international community, even in the face of progress backwards [*sic*]" (176). It is in this context that the signing of the subsequent accords, dealing with socioeconomic issues, military reform, the reintegration of the guerrilla and electoral reform, should be considered.

Socio-Economic Accord

The Socio-Economic Accord was signed in May 1996. As with previous accords, notably the Indigenous Rights agreement, the ASC played a moderating role in bringing the text of a potential accord closer to dominant interests, which was then further compromised in the negotiations proper. The URNG saw the agreement in terms of the exigencies of external realities and the historical moment, but sought to emphasize the opportunities for future improvements that the accords afforded. International actors considered the accord a success in its ability to appeal to international donors (World Bank, IMF) and to powerful local actors, especially CACIF, which declared the accord a great achievement.

The ASC functioned as a forum for mitigating popular demands for land reform in its discussions of a potential Socio-Economic Accord, debating but ultimately not including in its proposals a redefinition of land ownership and use based on the "social function" of property (Palma Murga 1997: 76). Gustavo Palma Murga (1997) notes that

> The ASC proposals made tacit concessions to the neo-liberal preoccupations of the private sector. They recommended more "rational and

efficient use of the land" not only to increase production and meet historical grievances, but also to reflect the competitive "comparative advantage" of Guatemala in the new global economy. (76)

The negotiated texts of the accord received less enthusiastic reception from popular organizations, whose reactions varied from vocal opposition to resigned acceptance, concerned primarily with the possibilities for the accord to address land conflicts (78). Palma Murga argues that many popular organizations perceived that the guerrilla's concessions on land were related to concluding the negotiations quickly in order to further their own political ambitions in the post-conflict state (78). Ultimately the ASC did endorse the Socio-Economic Accord—after a two-month delay—in July 1996 (Jonas 2000a: 52).

The guerrilla had come to the conclusion that liberalism was an inevitable feature of the post-conflict state. Torres-Rivas (1997) notes that the URNG document, *Guatemala: Full Democracy, Revolutionary Goal at the End of the Millennium*, which articulates the position that the purpose of revolution can be democracy, also shows their decision to accept liberal democracy and self-regulating markets as the "scenario that must be lived with at the end of this century" (41).[28] A common response from *guerrilleros* regarding their compromises during the peace negotiations was that "the correlation of forces was such that..." such compromises were necessary (Noriega 2001; Asturias 2001). The official response of the URNG involved a cautiously optimistic emphasis on the positive: that the accord represented the first engagement in land reform in years (Palma Murga 1997: 78), and that the accord "is not a complete solution to all problems, but it opens avenues and establishes commitments oriented towards resolving them" (Monsanto 1996: 7). The URNG statement on the signing of the accord emphasized that the accord was not a blueprint for society, but a step towards peace and "the participation of all in its construction" (8).

The accord was widely understood, particularly in international organizations, to represent "an alternative to neoliberalism" in its support for government involvement in the economy (Jonas 2000a: 80–81). Thus,

for those with a more positive interpretation, especially the UN and other international officials, the glass was more than half full. From their perspective, the accord embodied a comprehensive approach that everyone could live with; it was acceptable not only to CACIF but also to the international financial institutions (IFIs) in Washington. (80–81)

CACIF's reaction was one of "enthusiasm," although it would resist elements of the accord in their implementation (2000a: 80).

In sum, many popular and leftists thus resigned themselves to the necessity of such an accord, and ultimately accepted its logic as the viable compromise position: a process of *trasformismo* made legitimate by the incorporation of the guerrilla into the post-conflict political order and the endorsement of civil society through the ASC, reflecting a trade-off logic of further participation. The agents of this process of *trasformismo* involved not just local modernizing elites, but international actors: foreign governments, the IFIs and the UN.

Military Reform and the Reintegration of the URNG

Robinson (1996b) argues that in authoritarian-"democratic" transitions, *controlled* demilitarization occurs because corrupt militaries obstruct capitalist modernization through their pursuit of economic privilege; they are necessary only to the extent that social control requires coercion (66). Controlled demilitarization involves the subordination of military authority to civilian elites, but not the elimination of coercive military potential (66). As social control can be effectively devolved through the promotion of democracy-cum-polyarchy and the reconstruction of civil society in an analogous vein, such demilitarization can occur, and is indeed advantageous to elites (66–69).

Within the peace process of a civil war, the notion of demilitarization involves more parties than just the state. Thus, in the Guatemalan peace process, there would be accords both on the Role of the Armed Forces in Society and on the demilitarization of the guerrilla. State forces to a large extent followed the logic of controlled demilitarization that Robinson outlines, yet by the time guerrilla forces are discussed, events that discredited the guerrilla would have opened the door for another the devolution of social control to an even more decentralized level: that of individual political subjectivity through impunity.

The controlled nature of demilitarization was in the first instance conducted through "self-purges" within the military before the negotiations proper, after which officers were not affected by the reductions called for in the accords (Schirmer 1998: 270–272; Molina Mejía 1999: 65). As a result of this preparation by the military, the ASC could construct a text that to a certain extent created the framework for the "Agreement on the Strengthening of Civilian Power and the Role of the Armed Forces in a Democratic Society."

The ASC, which had suffered significant organizational challenges by this point, put forward a rather reformist program.[29] As Torres-Rivas notes, the debate "took place as always with references to the unconstitutionality of different points...Nothing is said [in the accord] about substantive themes such as a new concept of national security, the significance of sovereignty in a global society, the utility of the military..." (Torres-Rivas 1997: 30, translation mine). He describes the negotiation as "a battle of percentages" in its narrow discussions around the precise levels of military reduction (30).

The Armed Forces Accord would be limited vis-à-vis the ASC proposal in a few important ways: while it redefined the role of the military as relating only to the external security of the country (narrowing its previous remit of both internal and external defense), it did so with the caveat that the president can call on the military for internal security in cases of emergency. The accord did not reduce the army to the degree sought by the ASC or achieved in El Salvador (it was reduced by 33 percent rather than 50 percent);[30] it also had very weak language and no verification measures for the demobilization of PACs. Certain counterinsurgency groups and their training facilities were not decommissioned, nor were some intelligence organs (Jonas 2000a: 85). Internal security was to be handled by a new National Police Force, which lacked details regarding membership criteria, another weakness vis-à-vis the Salvadoran example. Most of these elements of the Armed Forces Accord would be contingent on constitutional reforms (as with the Indigenous Rights Agreement). Although the reaction to the Armed Forces Accord was muted, those organizations that did issue statements were cautiously optimistic (Torres-Rivas 1997: 111).

The guerrilla made a significant tactical error during the 1996 negotiations: one faction of the URNG (ORPA) kidnapped an 86-year-old member of the oligarchy, Olga Novella, for ransom, and the government ultimately consented to exchange her for the perpetrator.[31] Kidnappings for ransom are not uncommon in Guatemala, but the timing and nature of this—apparently a fundraising exercise for ORPA and the future presidential campaign of its head, Rodrigo Asturias—seriously compromised the URNG's negotiating position (Noriega 2001). The head of the ORPA resigned from their negotiating team, and the international community stepped in to finalize the logistical accords that remained. (It is interesting but not surprising that this miscalculation by one sector of the guerrilla would [allegedly] involve the electoral process: it exposes the implications that increased material requirements for campaigning have for the Left.)

A series of final agreements were signed in December 1996, culminating in the "Accord for a Firm and Lasting Peace." These agreements were facilitated by the Friend Governments, which hosted a series of meetings in Europe involving both negotiators and civil society to sign the final operational accords, a tour to achieve closure in the face of the setback of the Novella affair. These operational accords treated establishing a cease-fire, constitutional reforms, and the demobilization of the URNG.

The Agreement on Constitutional Reform and the Electoral Regime called on the government to draft amendments to the constitution, as per the Indigenous Rights and Armed Forces agreements, and forward them to congress within 60 days of its entry into force ("Agreement on Constitutional Reforms and the Electoral Regime" 1996). Such amendments would require a two-thirds majority there and final approval in a national referendum. The accord also provided for the study of the reform of the electoral system, underscoring the authority of the *Tribunal Supremo Electoral*, established by the 1985 constitution.

The demobilization accord was very contentious because it reopened the sticky issue of amnesty. The agreement called for the creation of a special commission to involve the government, URNG, and international donor representatives, as well as a national law—a national reconciliation act—to be passed by the Guatemalan Congress (Jonas 2000a: 89). The law that emerged (Law for National Reconciliation, 1997) was ultimately very weak: it naturally needed to provide amnesty for "political crimes" to allow for the reincorporation of the URNG, but it understood "political crimes" to involve both directly taking up arms against the government as well as "related common crimes," "which cannot be shown to be motivated by personal goals" (in Jonas 2000a: 90). This provided wide scope to amnesty counterinsurgency forces. The FRG and CACIF supported the agreement, while human rights activists, religious authorities, members of the FDNG and a number of indigenous organizations objected to it (Torres-Rivas 1997: 133).

Impunity is mentioned as early as the 1994 Comprehensive Agreement on Human Rights, whose second section, "Commitment

Against Impunity," involves an agreement by the government not to sponsor legislation or other measures to prevent the prosecution of those responsible for human rights violations and to initiate legislation "so that enforced or involuntary disappearances and summary or extra-judicial executions may be characterized as crimes of particular gravity and punished as such" ("The Comprehensive Agreement on Human Rights" 1994: 2). Paragraph 3 stipulates that "No special law or exclusive jurisdiction may be invoked to uphold impunity in respect of human rights violations." However, in the (subsequent) agreement on the Role of the Armed Forces impunity is mentioned only once, in the context of the reform of the justice system, which "should be geared to preventing the judiciary from producing or covering up a system of impunity and corruption" ("Agreement on the Strengthening of Civilian Power and the Role of the Armed Forces in a Democratic Society" 1996: 9). Furthermore, though the agreement on the reintegration of the URNG's call for new legislation to address both "the right to know the truth" and "the right of redress" stipulated such an act should not neglect the necessity of combating impunity, the later sections on political crimes and related common crimes clearly provide wide scope for amnesty.

The legacy of the trauma of counterinsurgency is profound and has significant political effects. Impunity generates political subjective effects that are of concern here primarily in terms of their capacity to dissuade political engagement. Impunity is associated with depoliticization both because the psychodynamics associated with counterinsurgency's techniques of involving the population in its technologies of control and because of the "unreality" of making sense of the experienced world in a climate of denial.

The technologies of counterinsurgency involve actively incorporating the population in strategies of social control. This may be done in terms of forced resettlement and civil patrols, but it is also done through the exercise of spectacle. The use of spectacle occurs within the public-private obfuscation that characterizes counterinsurgency, for while it is intended to influence those immediately present, it is also denied by official sources. However, by forcing some to witness the atrocities of counterinsurgency, the perpetrators psychologically involve them in the violence, leading to a sense of shared responsibility. Frank Graziano writes of such spectacles in Argentina, "The public's collective body, united by and meaningful in relation to the body being brutalized, constituted the agency by which the macabre display was transformed into a ceremonial strengthening of the institutions in which they were now participating" (Zur 1995: 62). Counterinsurgency implicates the public in its own tyranny as the "audience-guarantor," forcing it to "[share] the State's power and truth because it [shared] in the spectacle" (62, quoting Graziano). Thus counterinsurgency carries out other forms of social denial in addition to its official denial. Moreover, the continued public denial of counterinsurgency both in terms of truth and accountability reiterates a depoliticized subjectivity.

The public denial of the trauma of counterinsurgency through impunity can lead to a sense of unreality that makes politics next to impossible. The absence of an acknowledgment of trauma "pervert the highest mental functions...the process of learning and knowing, and even that of imagining" such that "victims do not see truth and justice as feasible" (Rojas 1999: 20, 17). The symptoms of impunity are highly undemocratic: people report "impotence and frustration, that they did not any longer feel like a whole person with rights" (27). Dr. Paz Rojas (1999) writes of impunity in Chile: "The appearance of this new symptomatology, whose psycho-dynamism differed from that of crime, led us to think that, with time, impunity induces mechanisms of intrapsychic perturbation with consequences equal to or worse than torture" (25–26).

Raúl Molina Mejía (1999) describes the political/psychological manifestation of impunity as the technique "by which political options in a polity are restricted and controlled through the state's manipulation of fear" (58). He argues that not only does the continuation of coercion through silence preempt demands for social equality and justice generally, but in the case of Guatemala impunity affected the FDNG's support in the 1995 elections. He claims that although voters knew that individual ballots were secret, "the political inclination of each municipality would be immediately unveiled" (64). The legacy of counterinsurgency extends beyond its immediate manifestations, where the memory of violent repercussions extends into spheres such as voting behavior.

The agreements on military force and guerrilla demobilization reflect a controlled demilitarization. Traditional military apparatuses were subject only to limited reductions in a context where prior purges "counted" toward the peace process. In addition to these "objective" elements of coercion, the subjective element persists through military amnesties. The significant use of the ASC text engendered cautious but genuine consent in the case of the Armed Forces accord, while the accord on the guerrilla's demobilization could be used for less acceptable amnesties, justified under the exigencies of the crisis of Novella affair. The failure to adequately address the traumatic subjective effects of counterinsurgency's militarism through impunity leads to a depoliticization of the public. This occurs both at the more overt level of an awareness that individual rights may not secure the protection of the collectivity as well as the less visible psychological level, where the "unreality" of lived and constructed worlds cannot be reconciled.

Conclusion

International actors helped to establish key parameters of the Guatemalan peace process through their involvement in the Contadora and Esquípulas negotiations, by sponsoring informal talks among the guerrilla and other groups in society, in the negotiations themselves through the Group of Friend state and UN conciliation, and through their position as aid donors. This participation at times served to establish the "common sense" parameters of the negotiations; at others it explicitly disciplined different domestic groups. Overall, however, international actors served to assist in the preservation of elite outcomes (which proved to be the common denominator between what seemed at times to be antagonistic positions between the EU and United States). Thus the definition of democracy to come out of the regional peace processes—electoral democracy based on an unreformed constitution—was established as a "common sense" understanding of the Guatemalan peace process: unchallenged, though it predictably worked against progressive interests. These regional peace processes are also associated with the "end of the revolutionary option" and the transformation of support for popular-sector actors from solidarity to technical aid (and the transition from class-based to cultural and "rights"-based groups, as discussed in chapter 3). This made the direct involvement of the *Asamblea de la Sociedad Civil* in the negotiations a much safer prospect for elite groups, though at times the ASC would be directly disciplined by UN mediation, which can be understood through the Gramscian conception of *trasformismo*: co-optation that can occur at the "molecular" (individual) and group level. Ultimately, the deferral of the "essential" to the least democratic moment of the negotiations and the maintenance of the coercive apparatus of the state suggests that this should be understood in Gramscian terms as a passive revolution of elites. As noted in chapter 3, the democratization process can also be understood in such terms. However, the peace process differs in its significant involvement of the international community in promoting such negotiations and in implicitly assisting such an outcome.

Few observers of the peace process have objected to the negotiations themselves; many have argued that the accords produced, or at least provided, a blueprint for addressing the social bases of conflict, even if implementation has been flawed. As will be discussed in the next chapter, such claims about the text of the Socio-Economic Accord are problematic; furthermore, implementation, while extremely partial, nonetheless followed a neoliberal hierarchy of interests.

5

The Post-Conflict State

Perhaps the strongest claim made about the Guatemalan peace process is that the peace accords addressed the social bases of conflict. Even those who criticize the implementation of the accords often support the principle that the accords sought to balance macroeconomic stability with social spending, and as such represent "blueprints" with the potential to address the social bases of conflict in the post-conflict state. However, if the Socio-Economic Accord is read through a Gramscian lens as elaborated in chapter 2, the project of constructing neoliberal subjectivity through the social spending offered in the agreements becomes clear. (This does, in a sense, address the social bases of conflict, though in terms that aid rather than mitigate the transition to neoliberalism.) The implementation of the accords has indeed been problematic, though to a certain extent, the failures of the implementation reflect the logical extension of the peace process' elitist orientation; furthermore, as discussed below, the implementation of the accords reflects the priorities of neoliberal world order. In fact, through mechanisms such as the consultative group of international donors and "peace conditionality," international actors are directly implicated in the selective implementation of the accords. Thus, this discussion concludes with a reconsideration of the role of peace processes in the neoliberal world order.

(Re)articulating the Post-Conflict State: the Socio-Economic Accord

The "success" reading of the peace process understands the socioeconomic agreement as a significant compromise that accommodates both the neoliberal orientation of CACIF and the IFIs in its use of market mechanisms, for example, vis-à-vis the question of land, while addressing the guerrilla's agenda by strengthening the capacity for government in areas such as taxation and supporting social spending (Jonas 2000: 27). A critical perspective, however, seeks to examine the terms on which such a compromise is reached, particularly given the operation of power during the negotiations. The argument below is that the "compromise" perspective misses to a large extent how neoliberal considerations may be embedded in the elements of the accord that ostensibly reflect the URNG's agenda. An examination of the texts of the accords shows a strong neoliberal emphasis, both vis-à-vis the question of land, where such an orientation is commonly recognized, but also vis-à-vis fiscal and budgetary policy and spending and investment, where it is less so. Four areas will be considered in turn: land, fiscal and budgetary policy, growth, and social spending and investment.

The question of land is primarily addressed in the third section of the accord, the Agrarian Situation and Rural Development (1996) (see figure 5.1, "Outline of the Socio-Economic Accord"; the texts of the accord can be found in appendix 2). The accord begins with the statement that

> The transformation of the structure of land use and ownership must have as its objective the incorporation of the rural population into economic, social and political development so that the land constitutes, for those who work it, the basis of their economic stability, the foundation of their progressive social well-being and the guarantee of their freedom and dignity. (27)

Yet in the next paragraph this is collapsed into the commitment to "promote more efficient and more equitable farming" (28). By the fourth paragraph the logic has transformed into one of security property rights: "Solving the agrarian problem is a complex process covering many aspects of rural life, from modernization of production and cultivation methods to environmental protection, as well as security of property, adequate use of the land and of the labor force..." ("Agreement on the Social and Economic Aspects and Agrarian Situation" 1996: 30).

The primary mechanism with which the accord promotes the expansion of land ownership is through a National Trust Fund for Land, whereby the government buys land to "promote the establishment of a transparent land market" (34[a]). The government undertakes to

> Promote, through all means possible, the development of a dynamic land market that would enable tenant farmers who either do not have land or have insufficient land to acquire land through long-term transactions at commercial or favorable interest rates with little or no down payment. In particular, promote the issuance of mortgage-backed securities guaranteed by the State whose yield is attractive to private investors, especially financial institutions. (34[e])

Other measures to assist private land ownership include legal reforms to simplify awarding title and registering ownership and "an efficient,

---

I. Democratization and participatory development
   A. Participation and consensus building
   B. Participation of women in economic and social development
II. Social development
   A. Education and training
   B. Health
   C. Social security
   D. Housing
   E. Work
III. Agrarian situation and rural development
   A. Participation
   B. Access to land and productive resources
   C. Support structure
   D. Organization of the rural population for production
   E. Legal framework and juridical security
   F. Land register
   G. Labor protection
   H. Environmental protection
   I. Resources
IV. Modernization of government services and fiscal policy
   A. Modernization of government services
   B. Fiscal policy
V. Final Provisions

Figure 5.1   Outline of the Socio-Economic Accord

multiuser land registry system that is financially sustainable" (37[a], 38). Land would be acquired through the consolidation of uncultivated state land, the reappropriation of illegally settled lands, government purchases, including those supported by grants from foreign governments, international NGOs, and loans from IFIs (34[c]). There are also measures for the resolution of land disputes, a significant issue for areas where there have been displaced communities, and promises to promote legislation for a land tax from which small holdings would be exempt.

The accord functions to promote a national land *market* through the privatization of state land and through international assistance rather than pursuing genuine land reform. As Palma Murga (1997) describes it, "resolution of the agrarian problem is understood as a process of reallocating resources within a marginally reformed institutional context based on private ownership and the market" (78). Although the question of illegally occupied lands does reflect an issue of justice for many indigenous communities, it also reflects a way to discipline corrupt military officers who participated in such acquisitions, particularly in the 1970s: the areas noted in the accord—the *Franja Transversal del Norte* and the *Petén*—were those known as the "Land of the Generals."

Fiscal and budgetary policies are designed to strengthen the competitiveness of the country, which requires greater labor productivity and infrastructure. The accords call for an improvement in tax collection, a long-standing issue in Guatemala which had the lowest level of taxation in the Western Hemisphere for 1963–1983 (Dunkerley 1990: 231). In the accords, fiscal policy is defended through an appeal to productivity and competitiveness, the lack of government spending has led to low levels of education, health, and infrastructure, "which militate against increasing the productivity of labor and the competitiveness of the Guatemalan economy" ("Agreement on the Social and Economic Aspects and Agrarian Situation" 1996: 45). Taxation and spending are understood in terms of the "competitiveness of nations." The accords aim to increase the tax burden as a ratio of GDP by 50 percent from 1995 levels by 2000. Furthermore, the enforcement of more regressive taxation, i.e., value-added tax, comes before the enforcement of the obligations of large contributors (50[d, e, g]). Thus, the pursuit of taxation is cautious, and does not emphasize its redistributive potential. Taxation remains one of the most contentious issues in post–peace agreement politics (discussed further below).

The Socio-Economic Accord fundamentally prioritizes growth over everything else. The discourse of growth prefaces nearly every section of the agreements and growth precedes any mention of social development or justice every time either term appears in the accord. For example, the section "Social Development" argues that

> In the quest for growth, economic policy should be aimed at preventing processes of socio-economic exclusion, such as unemployment and impoverishment, and maximizing the benefits of economic growth for all Guatemalans. In seeking to ensure the well-being of all Guatemalans, social policy should foster economic development through its impact on production and efficiency. (14)

In this paragraph, the bottom line (literally) is that social policy should be designed to improve production and efficiency.

Regardless of whether growth in fact leads to development axiomatically, it will in the new Guatemalan State, for in fact social programs are designed to be contingent on a certain level of economic growth.[1]

> For its part, the Government undertakes to adopt economic policies designed to achieve steady growth in the gross domestic product of not less than 6 per cent per annum, which would enable it to implement a progressive social policy. (18)

Thus, the accords construct a situation where the country is invested in economic growth as a requirement for the social services promised in the agreements. A failure to produce the social services promised can thus be excused by pointing to slow growth.[2]

In this agreement, citizenship itself is defined as an economic good. The section "Democratization and Participatory Development" argues that functional, participatory democracy requires consensus building among "agents of socio-economic development" as well as citizen participation in "identifying, prioritizing and meeting their needs" (1). The assumption is that such participation is "essential in order to promote productivity and economic growth" (2–3).

The state must play the role of brokering this consensus—"essential in order to stimulate and stabilize economic and social growth"—"in order to be able to work effectively and efficiently to modernize the production sector, enhance competitiveness, promote economic growth and provide basic social services efficiently and universally" (2–3). A clear question that emerges is who will participate in this consensus. Point 4 acknowledges the right of indigenous and resettled peoples to "exercise their rights effectively and participate fully in decision making on the various matters affecting or involving them, *with full awareness of both their individual and collective obligations to society, which they will fulfill responsibly*" (4, emphasis added). The right to participate is limited to "matters affecting or involving them," while it is implied that indigenous peoples are located outside of society, an entity to which they nevertheless have established obligations. Not to acknowledge the individual and collective obligations is *irresponsible* and suggests a breach of the citizenship contract, presumably permitting the state to treat these groups and individuals differently.

There is an explicit subsection for the status of women. This, too, is an economic affair, as it begins by "recognizing women's undervalued contributions in all spheres of economic and social activity . . . the Parties agree that there is a need to strengthen women's participation in economic and social development on equal terms" (12). It is interesting to note where else women's rights are articulated: primarily in the Indigenous Rights Accord. Women are not mentioned in the Agreement on Constitutional Reforms and the Electoral Regime, nor in the Comprehensive Agreement on Human Rights, and only once in the Agreement on Resettlement of the Population Groups Uprooted by the Armed Conflict. Women's rights to protection are articulated in the indigenous agreement while their obligations as economic agents are articulated in the socioeconomic agreements, yet they do not explicitly appear much elsewhere in the accords. This reflects the construction of neoliberalism's need to manage the indigenous identity and socioeconomic subjectivity, more than a comprehensive "gendering" of the process.[3]

The accords go further than "merely" casting citizenship in terms of economic agency: they provide a blueprint for the construction of economic agents in their treatment of education and training, work, and the organization of the rural population for production.

Education is a highly economic good, "vital for economic modernization and international competitiveness" (21). Education and training should "contribute to the application of technical and scientific progress and, consequently, to the achievement of higher productivity, the creation of more jobs and increased income for the population and beneficial integration into the world economy" (21). The goal of education is thus to further the national economy and its globalized possibilities.

Work is defined in terms of the individual's development: it is "essential for the integral development of the individual, the well-being of the family and the social and economic development of Guatemala" (26). The role of labor is as "an essential element of social participation in socioeconomic development and *of economic efficiency*. In this respect, *the state's policy with regard to work is critical for a strategy of growth* with social justice" (26, emphasis added). The state is cast unambiguously as the guarantor of economic growth, and represents the manager who will mediate between growth and social justice. Organized labor's role is likewise expressed in terms of promoting economic efficiency. The accord's discourse on work involves the commodification of labor celebrated as beneficial for both the individual and the state, the latter of which controls the social dimensions of labor for the market.

The laborer in the neoliberal economy must possess a particular economic rationality. There is no mistaking that the accords aim to construct this rationality, as the subsection "organization of the rural population for production" evidences:

> Organizing the rural population is a decisive factor in transforming the inhabitants of the countryside into genuine protagonists of their own development...there is a need to promote a more efficient form of organization of small producers so that they can, in particular, take advantage of the support structure described in paragraph 35. (36)

As with the discourse on work, participating in the reorganized, productive rural economy is good for the individual, indeed liberating (one becomes a "genuine protagonist"). However, such participation requires becoming a microentrepreneur. The support structures in paragraph 35 involve the provision of infrastructure for the marketing of agricultural produce. The paragraph continues,

To this end, the Government undertakes to:

(a) Support micro-, small and medium-scale agricultural and *rural enterprises*...
(b) Tackle the problem of smallholdings through:
   (i) A firm and sustained policy of *support for smallholders so that they can become small-scale agricultural businessmen* through access to training, technology, credit and other inputs;
   (ii) Promoting, if the smallholders so desire, amalgamation of holdings in those cases where conversion into small businesses is not possible owing to the dispersal and size of the properties. (36, emphasis added)

Smallholdings are considered a problem that needs to be solved through conversion to microenterprise via training and technology. Farmers are to become businessmen, and if they are not able to due to the scale of their holdings, the government will assist them to consolidate into economies of scale.

As with land, the subsection on housing emphasizes privatization. There is a need "to give priority to the building of low-cost housing, through the appropriate financial arrangements, in order to enable as many Guatemalan families as possible to own their own homes" (25). The financing of new housing would occur with the proper incentives to investors and companies:

> Strengthen the securities market and make it more available as a source of funds to purchase housing, by...facilitating the selling of securities issued for housing operations, such as common and preferred stocks in construction companies, mortgage bonds and debentures, real estate participation certificates, supplemental letters, promissory notes and other documents related to rental with an option to buy. (25[f])

One of the striking things about this passage is the specificity of economic instruments to be employed in financing new housing, no doubt the "appropriate financial arrangements." There is no ambiguity about how the goal for low-income housing will be accomplished, the mechanisms involve strengthening the market, commodifying real estate, and providing more financing for construction companies. *Then* the government will provide subsidies to low-income families to purchase their houses (25[g]). Thus, housing is constructed to be governed by the market and lucrative to investors, despite the need for subsidies as well: it is a predominantly economic, rather than social, good. (Considering the contingency of social programs on the 6 percent increase in GDP, this approach seems even more precarious in terms of its ability to actually provide housing to the poor.)

Recalling CACIF's identification of tourism as a "cluster" of national competitiveness for economic development, the Socio-Economic Accord's treatment of culture in the rural sector reflects Porter's thesis as well. The preservation of culture is seen in economic terms as something for the state to *take advantage of.*

> These changes [promoting more efficient farming, etc.] will enable Guatemala to take full advantage of the capacities of its inhabitants and, in particular, the richness of the traditions and cultures of its indigenous peoples. It should also take advantage of the high potential

for agricultural, industrial, commercial and tourist development of those resources deriving from its wealth of natural resources. (29)

Clearly the implication is that the commercial and tourisitc development of natural resources might also apply to the traditions of indigenous peoples. In the neoliberal project, traditions represent a resource for the state to utilize. The state is the guarantor that "its" inhabitants are utilized as economic inputs. Indigenous peoples "in particular" are a rich commodity to be developed.

The Socio-Economic Accord relies on conventional neoliberal mechanisms—privatization and the market—for access/distributional issues around land and housing. More subtly and profoundly, perhaps, it aims to reconstruct the social as an expression of the market. It does this at the level of individual subjectivity through the creation of structures that inculcate market rationality in the conduct of nearly all areas of daily life. The citizen-entrepreneur embodies this ideal and becomes the subject of policymaking. Growth and efficiency appear as omnipresent goals. Social goods are consistently constructed in economic terms. Indeed, the rural population is explicitly reorganized for production, and the solution to land reform is the market, which "promises" growth out of the historical injustices acknowledged in the accords. This order homogenizes the diversity of economic relationships to the land into one governed by the rational actor and the market, with the sanctioned marginalization of groups that "irresponsibly" do not participate in full. Indeed, "the richness of the traditions and cultures" of indigenous peoples become commodities.

The Socio-Economic Accord exploits the need to address the social bases of conflict as an opportunity to reconstruct the integral state as a reflection of the market. The raison d'etat becomes neoliberal, while citizenship is constructed around the rationality and subjectivity of *homo economicus*. The Socio-Economic Accord has not been subject to criticism regarding the *nature* of its social spending, which raises interesting questions regarding the ethicopolitical purchase of neoliberalism's resolution to counterinsurgent modernization. Aesthetically, neoliberalism appears "democratic" to the extent that it embraces "(economic) rationality" as a social construct, unlike previous iterations of liberalism that could not reconcile the presumption of a "presocial" economic rationality with cultural difference. (Performatively and materially, as discussed in chapter 2, neoliberalism is in many senses *anti*democratic.) The accords generally have not been fully implemented; however, this pattern of implementation in many ways reinforces the neoliberal ethos of the texts.

Implementation of the Accords

Implementation of the accords has been uneven, though the patterns of implementation have been consistent with reasserting elite privilege in their emphasis on security, the guerrilla, and certain economic structures, while neglecting demilitarization of the state and the Indigenous Rights Accords. Most vivid is the failure of a referendum on constitutional reforms required to implement key elements of the peace agreements.

The operational accords, dealing with a definitive cease-fire, the demobilization of the guerrilla, and the return of refugees, were for the most part implemented very quickly (Salvesen 2002: 9). In principle, all of the accords were to be implemented by December 2000; however, this timetable was revised in December 1999 to extend until 2004; the rescheduled agenda included 119 outstanding commitments predominantly relating to the Socio-Economic Accord (66), the Armed Forces Accord (23), and the Indigenous Accord (18) (Salvesen 2002: 9). One of the most conspicuous obstacles to implementation is the electoral defeat of constitutional reforms necessary for the full implementation of the Indigenous Rights and Armed Forces Accords; taxation has also remained a persistent question, generating a new set of civil society negotiations around a *Pacto Fiscal* (fiscal pact).[4] Implementation had been at best partial from 1996, thus the impact of the 2000 elections that saw the defeat of the PAN by the FRG should not be overstated. Nonetheless, it was under the FRG that military funding began to exceed the limits stipulated by the peace agreements. (The URNG and by extension, the left umbrella party, the New Nation Alliance [ANN, *Alianza Nueva Nación*], suffered from the appearance of complicity with the PAN government and won nine seats [Buchanan 2000: 4].)

Perhaps the most fundamental failure of implementation involves the defeat of the constitutional reforms required by the Agreement on Constitutional Reforms and the Electoral Regime, and associated with key elements of the Armed Forces and Indigenous Rights Accords. The PAN embroiled the reforms in a complicated process that added numerous extraneous elements to the package and delayed their consideration, making them vulnerable to challenges from a well-organized and well-funded antireform campaign.[5] Throughout, the right challenged the validity of amending the constitution, taking its case to the Constitutional Court, which ruled on procedural grounds in February 1998 that the reforms were unconstitutional and sent them back to congress (Jonas 2000: 194). In the process of negotiation the number of measures grew from the 12 called for in the accords to 50 altogether.[6] The reforms were ultimately defeated, 56–44 percent, in a poll marked by very low voter turn out: 18.5 percent of registered voters (MINUGUA 2002b: 2). The negative result has been described in terms of a "punishment vote" against politicians for the lack of transparency in the development of the reforms in congress and a reflection of distrust of the political elite (Jonas 2000: 203; Salvesen 2002: 22). In addition, confusion about the complexity of the reforms may have affected the outcome: for example, new proposals added questions of municipal authority to demilitarization reforms such that the indigenous mayor of the second largest city in Guatemala opposed the measures, affecting the overall "No" vote there (Jonas 2000: 204).

By the time of the poll, both the PAN and the FRG officially supported the reforms, however, with dubious sincerity. The PAN, as noted, clearly had not taken an active leadership position on quickly achieving reforms, despite their congressional majority (with the argument that it needed to establish the legitimacy of the reforms with the FRG to ensure that it would not sabotage them during the referendum), nor did it actively promote the reforms closer to the referendum (95). The FRG decided to support the reforms in early April, "for opportunistic political reasons" (195). Jonas suggests that "many believed, in fact, that both were engaging in a kind of 'double discourse' with their formal 'Sí' masking indifference and internal divisions (PAN) or opposition (FRG)" (195). The left assumed that the reforms would pass and, preoccupied with the elections that year, did not mobilize for the cause (195). The "No" campaign involved scare mongering around ideas of "social chaos" and the "balkanisation" of Guatemalan into two countries (196–198). The defeat of the constitutional reforms would amount to the inability to implement central concerns of the Armed Forces and Indigenous Rights Accords.

The defeat of the constitutional reforms in 1999 included the defeat of an amendment to redefine the remit of the military to limit it exclusively to the external defense of the country. In June 2000, a decree further compromised this element of the peace process by formalizing the military's role in *internal* security (Salvesen 2002: 10). The central question of the creation of a new military doctrine had not been implemented by 2002 (10). There has been a failure to redeploy military detachments in areas of severe counterinsurgency activities, such as the Ixil triangle, and to reconstruct military education and training away from counterinsurgency doctrine and toward a meaningful appreciation of human rights.[7] While the military budget seemed to meet its target in 1997 and 1998 its proportion of GDP has been creeping beyond the 0.66 percent ceiling in the peace accords since 1999. The figure was 0.83 percent by 2000 and 0.94 percent by 2001 as the result of supplementary transfers to the Defense Ministry, which increased the congressionally approved allocation by 85 percent (MINUGUA 2002b: 19).

As with the redefinition of the role of the military, the redefinition of the Guatemalan nation as multiethnic, multicultural, and multilingual was defeated with the failure of the constitutional reforms. Very few measures of the accord have been implemented beyond those calling for the creation of commissions for further study (Salvesen 2002: 14–15). This has led MINUGUA to conclude in January 2002 that the Indigenous Rights accord has been the least implemented (MINUGUA 2002b: 6). The biggest success in the implementation of this accord is understood to be the creation of Joint Commissions of government and indigenous representatives (MINUGUA 2001: 30). Yet the Joint Commissions have not had substantive impact: their only accomplishments have been the drafting of further proposals, which has tarnished their credibility with indigenous organizations (Raymundo 2001).

In terms of the Socio-Economic Accord, social spending has only partially been implemented (Salvesen 2002: 16). The successes of implementation in the area of fiscal policy involve the creation of "information systems" for the surveillance of income and public spending. The tax administration (*Superintendencia de Administración Tributaria*, SAT, Tax Administration Authority) established an information sharing system to coordinate independent banks and the central bank in monitoring income (Salvesen 2002: 17). The SAT has also implemented the requirement for a Unified Tax Register to monitor compliance with tax obligations and a system of evaluation and control of public spending, the Integral System for Financial Administration (SIAF, Sistema integral para la administración financiera) has been established (Salvesen 2002: 17).

Most attention has been focused on the challenge of implementing the measures associated with the area of modernization and fiscal policy. The accords sought to increase taxation from 8 to 12 percent of GDP by 2000. By 1997 it was clear that the government was not going to meet the interim target of 10 percent by 1998, the commitment was rescheduled and (re)solved through a complex negotiation between civil society and the PAN government resulting in a new

Pacto Fiscal. The PAN government did attempt to create a more progressive property tax in late 1997; however, such measures were subject to a confused campaign of resistance. There were widespread protests against the tax (*Impuesto Unico Sobre Inmuebles*, IUSI, Consolidated Property Tax) in 1998, supported not only by the FRG but also by rural mayors who felt they would pay the political costs of higher taxes while the wealth would remain with the central government (Gamboa M. and Trentavizi 2001: 20; Jonas 2000: 171–172). In anticipation of the October 1998 meeting of the Consultative Group of international donors to the peace process, the government sought to reschedule its taxation targets. This led to a set of negotiations involving numerous civil society organizations, including CACIF, around the *Pacto Fiscal,* that lasted until May 2000 and rescheduled the 12 percent target until 2002, a deadline that was not met (Gamboa M. and Trentavizi 2001: 149; Salvesen 2002: 17; MINUGUA 2002b: 14). The primary tax measure that has been implemented involved raising the value-added tax from 10 to 12 percent.

The implementation of the Guatemalan peace accords has been only partial. The electoral defeat of the constitutional reforms compromised the possibility of full implementation at the outset. The Armed Forces Accord has not been fully implemented, in part due to the failure of the constitutional reforms that would have redefined its remit to external security, while the PNC has not replaced the military in internal security. Counterinsurgency doctrine remains part of both military theory and practice through the failure to reform military education materials and with its continued engagement in "social intelligence tasks." The Indigenous Rights Accord likewise suffered from the failure of the constitutional reforms and have been deemed the least implemented element of the substantive agenda. The Socio-Economic Accord has been partially implemented: notably vis-à-vis financial surveillance, while the international conditionality emphasizes the construction of a viable taxation regime, without regard to progressivity.

The pattern of implementation nonetheless reflects a hierarchy of neoliberal interests. In addition to securing the guerrilla, implementation has emphasized taxation and the surveillance of banking and public finance. These concerns reflect the logic of disciplinary neoliberalism as Stephen Gill describes it: the use of surveillance to affect conformity in fiscal policy under the IFIs and other elements of the G7 nexus and the (re)construction of taxation to extend it more broadly and regressively, privileging capital and increasing the burden on the lower classes (Gill 1995). The former expresses the need for elites to reproduce the neoliberal transnational bloc while the latter institutionalizes unequal economic hierarchies under the guise of an "activist tax state" that nevertheless relies upon increasingly regressive taxes (Gill 2003: 135–137).[8]

The ethicopolitical rationale for taxation appeals to the necessity of funding for the implementation of social services agreed to in the accords and indeed the sense that such an approach could in the process redistribute wealth and power in Guatemala (Jonas 2000: 169–170). However, as taxation is discussed in the *Pacto Fiscal* and as the basis for peace conditionality on one hand, the Integral System for Financial Administration for the "evaluation and control of public spending" is established on the other, ensuring state spending within the boundaries of the values implied by neoliberal restructuring, that is, the insulation of economic oversight from democratic decision making (Gill 2003: 132). The emergence of a problematic around the need to increase taxation to create sustainability in the domestic funding of the peace accords obscures the strategic nature of the selective implementation of taxation and financial surveillance mechanisms.

The Consultative Group and Peace Conditionality

At the end of the Guatemalan peace process a Consultative Group (CG) was created among key funders of the implementation of the accords, including the World Bank, the Inter-American Development Bank, other international organizations, and bilateral donors. The CG met in January 1997, just after the signing of the final accords, and pledged US$1.9 billion in aid for the process. Indeed, the actual contribution for the period 1996–1999 reached US$2.4 billion (Salvesen 2002: 29). By December 2001, the total value of external assistance amounted to US$3.2 billion, of which 78 percent came from multilateral agencies (Inter-American Development Bank 2002: 1). The IFIs and the EU provided 81 percent of the multilateral funding, that is, 63 percent of the external resources for financing the peace agreements (Inter-American Development Bank 2002: 2). The United States also represents a significant player, providing 45 percent of bilateral aid and about 10 percent of the overall amount. (For specific contributions, see table 5.1.) Jonas suggests that the IFIs were

Table 5.1   Outline of the Socio-Economic Accord

Agency or Country	Total Signed (Thousands of US$)
Bilateral	735,340.1
Germany	140,700.0
Spain	16,442.4
Canada	28,379.2
Denmark	7,076.2
Finland	8,438.9
Italy	12,918.4
Netherlands	14,224.4
Japan	73,954.5
Norway	37,622.0
United Kingdom	19,960.1
Sweden	29,771.3
Switzerland	13,331.6
United States	332,521.2
Multilateral	2,479,590.2
Central American Bank for Economic Integration	543,254.0
European Union	145,675.4
World Bank	329,295.3
Inter-American Development Bank	990,516.0
Organization of American States	11,257.0
UN Development Program	328,860.0
Other UN Agencies	130,732.50
Total	3,214,930.3

Source: Inter-American Development Bank, "Summary of Internationally Financed Projects: Document Presented to the Members of the Consultative Group of Guatemala." Washington, DC: Inter-American Development Bank, 2002.

inspired to give particular attention to Guatemala because of the perception that Guatemala had in recent years prudently managed its macroeconomic affairs so that the implementation of the peace accords could be an opportunity for poverty reduction without macroeconomic instability (Jonas 2000: 170).

The CG is seen as a strong example of "peace conditionality"—"the use of formal performance criteria and informal policy dialogue to encourage the implementation of peace accords and the consolidation of peace" (Boyce, 2002: 1025–1026)—particularly vis-à-vis taxation. Donors formally and explicitly stated the conditions of their assistance at the outset of the post-conflict reconstruction period, based primarily on the increase in fiscal revenues from 8 to 12 percent by 2000 (Salvesen 2002: 29). The conventional reading of this conditionality is that the aid pledged at the January 1997 CG meeting was to be a temporary measure to assist the peace process, which in principle would ultimately become domestically sustained through greater taxes and spending on social programs (Jonas 2000: 170). However, peace conditionality vis-à-vis Guatemala has not been contingent on a progressive understanding of taxes and, as noted above, one of the most tangible areas of increased taxes is in the regressive VAT. Jonas reports, "As one analyst put it, in the Guatemalan case, many IMF staff believed that distributional inequalities should be addressed through spending more than through progressive taxes" (128).

While the conceptual redefinition of the state vis-à-vis militarism and multiculturalism in the constitutional reforms is left to the uncertain fate of the electoral process, the fiscal reconstruction of the state vis-à-vis taxation and the creation of surveillance for the protection of international capital becomes an area of international pressure and peace conditionality.

Conclusion: Peace Processes in the Neoliberal Era

This book began with an argument for a critical theoretical reading of peace processes as a way of addressing the absence of political theory in examining post-conflict societies. It then provided a reading of Gramscian political theory to provide exegesis of how Gramsci's work might be applied to the particular problematic of peace processes in the post–Cold War world. It argued that both the structural and subjective dimensions of Gramsci's understanding of power are important in understanding politics, and in particular, that the lens of articulation provides a helpful way of conceptualizing the material and subjective differences between developing and industrialized countries in particular world orders. This lens is indeed extremely useful in analyzing the nature of counterinsurgent modernization, which not only cannot be reduced to either its subjective or material dimension and must be understood as an interplay between the two, but relies on the operation of politics—through intellectual and moral leadership and coercion—across social fields, domestic and international, as well. Gramscian analysis in its attention to both faces of power provides a holistic account of the ontology and contradictions

of conflict, which allows for an understanding of the subjective legacies of conflict as well as disrupts any static accounts of the "social
bases of war" that cannot account for changing material interests
over time. Such material interests are important for understanding
the operation of power in peace negotiations themselves; here
Gramsci's theorization of the possibilities for progressive social change
again offers helpful analytical tools: of particular significance for the
Guatemalan case are the ideas of the passive revolution and *trasformismo*. These concepts embrace the complex negotiation (in the fullest
sense of the term) between powerful and subaltern groups during
periods of social change and express the qualified contingency such
moments represent for meaningful transformation. Among the parameters for such transformation is the logic of world order and the pressure it exerts in establishing new raisons d'etat, which is particularly
evident in the Guatemalan case in the peace accords and their project
for the post-conflict state, as well as in the selective practices of implementation and peace conditionality.

A Gramscian reading of the Guatemalan peace process raises a
number of implications and questions for peace research. First it challenges liberal readings, such as the one offered by Paris, that critique
the failure to achieve a redistribution of wealth in Guatemala without
rigorously examining the nature of neoliberal development or the
peace negotiations themselves; the Guatemalan process appears to
have met his own recommendations of "institutionalization before liberalization," which involve waiting until conditions are ripe for elections, designing electoral systems that reward moderation, promoting
good civil society, and adopting conflict-inhibiting economic policies
(which include the "balance" ostensibly achieved in Guatemala) (Paris
2004: Chapter 10). Paris faults the implementation of the accords for
the failure to achieve the desired outcomes; however, if his criteria of
"institutionalization before liberalization" were largely met, how
should the failure to implement truly be understood? A Gramscian
analysis would suggest that what Paris attributes to the challenges of
liberalism in post-conflict settings reflects in fact much deeper problems of liberal political theory and in particular its antinomies vis-à-vis
non-Western societies. (A Gramscian reading, as should be clear, also
finds the criteria for "institutionalization before liberalization" and
other aspects of such an approach highly problematic.)

The apparent disconnect between the agreement of the accords
and their partial implementation can in large part be understood by
the neoliberal logic of such implementation. It suggests that of equal
importance to the blueprints for the post-conflict state was the

opportunity to reconstruct civil society through the peace process itself.

This process is more comprehensive than what Robinson describes in his study of authoritarian-democratic/polyarchic transitions, involving many more facets of the international community than merely the United States (as would be expected in the Gramscian analysis offered here). The Guatemalan case suggests that much as the prospect of "democracy" was co-opted through intellectual and moral leadership in Robinson's study, the idea of addressing the "social bases of war" served as a form of intellectual and moral leadership privileging neoliberalism as a solution to counterinsurgent modernization. (It also suggests the utility of further studies of consultative groups, which provide conspicuously little public information regarding their practices.)

Finally, a Gramscian reading of this case provides interesting insight into the nature of neoliberalism across an articulated world order. Neoliberalism's ethicopolitical appeal is that it understands identity and economic rationality as *constructed*: it resolves liberal modernization's anxiety about difference by universalizing the construction of neoliberal rationality and market discipline. It does not assume rationality to be associated with a presocial subject, thus it removes any ontological basis for understanding rationality and difference, "deracializing" liberalism's encounter with nonmarket forms of production. It allows for the kind of small-scale capitalist development that was understood as threatening to the disarticulated state (although it is unlikely to sustain support for it beyond constructing initial market conditions and rationalities), diffusing that source of conflict. However, in its construction of market logic as subjectivity, neoliberalism affects the same dislocation to nonmarket *cultures* as liberal modernization theories. It does not allow for nonmarket-based production and thus insists that culture be understood in thin terms, disembedded from social reproduction. As neoliberalism assumes identity to be socially constructed, while making an argument for market rationality as the only form of rationality, the basis for protecting culture becomes its commodification.

The Guatemalan case poses many challenges to the analyst: an extremely diverse society, a very long legacy of conflict and social injustice, and a complex relationship with external actors with the potential for significant influence on the small, developing state. Examining the Guatemalan peace process through the lens of Gramscian political theory requires an exegesis of Gramsci's work; such effort is neverthe-

less greatly rewarded by the richness of his theorizat power and the possibilities for progressive social cl vides insight into the historical construction of socia tural difference, and the operation of power across form boundaries. The Guatemalan case, in turn, provides a to examine the "actually existing" conditions of capita historically and in the "postcolonial" era, and how soc conflict are reproduced as production and world o Gramscian framework provides insight into the com ments—material, ideational, subjective—that lead to th or rearticulation of particular social conditions during pe formation and change. Though gaining understanding cesses, as Gramsci warned us, indeed leads to a certain pes the prospects for social justice, it is also a necessary pre truly emancipatory politics.

Political Chronology of Guatemala

This appendix was created by the author based on the following sources: Ralph Lee Woodward Jr., *Central America: A Nation Divided*, 3rd ed. (New York: Oxford University Press, 1999). Jeremy Armon, Rachel Sieder, and Richard Wilson, eds., *Negotiating Rights: The Guatemalan Peace Process*, 2nd ed. (London: Concilliation Resource, 1997).

1821	Guatemala declares independence from Spain.
1822	Central America annexes itself to Mexican Empire.
1823	Central America declares independence from Mexico and forms United Provinces of Central America.
1824	Central American states ratify republican constitutions.
1826	Central American governments sign Treaty of Friendship and Commerce with United States.
1826–1829	Bloody civil war in Guatemala between Liberals and Conservatives.
1829	Liberals emerge victorious in Guatemala.
1831–1838	Liberal Mariano Gálvez launches bold liberal and anticlerical policies.
1837–1840	Cholera epidemic in Central America.
1839	Conservative Rafael Carrera comes to power in War of the *Montaña*.
1839–1842	Liberal program dismantled.
1847	Guatemala declared a Republic.
1848	Carrera resigns in face of popular uprising.

1849	Carrera returns to power as armed forces chief. Mariano Paredes is officially President until 1851.
1854–1865	Carrera serves as Perpetual President of Guatemala.
1865	Carrera Dies.
1871	Conservative leader General Vicente Cerna overthrown by Liberal revolt.
1873	Liberal Justo Rufino Barrios becomes dictator of Guatemala.
1885	Barrios killed in El Salvador.
1898	President José M. Reyna assassinated.
1898–1920	Manuel Estrada Carbrera seizes power and establishes dictatorship.
1899	United Fruit Company formed.
1921	Guatemalan "Unionist" government overthrown by military.
1931–1944	Dictatorship of Jorge Ubico.
1944	Ubico resigns in face of protests.
1945	New Constitution ratified.
1945–1950	Juan José Arévalo leads reformist administration.
1949	Francisco J. Arana assassinated, and revolt of Guardia de Honor follows.
1950–1954	Jacobo Arbenz elected President of Guatemala.
1952	Agrarian reform law goes into effect. Guatemalan Labor Party (PGT) formed.
1954	Carlos Castillo Armas overthrows Arbenz with aid of US.
1957	Castillo Armas assassinated.
1958	Common market plan developed and treaty signed.
1958–1963	Conservative Migeul Ydígoras Fuentes elected President.
1960	Leftist revolt suppressed. Survivors form MR-13 guerilla movement.
1963	Military, led by Minister of Defense Enrique Peralta Azudia, ousts Ydígoras and pursues hard-line against leftists.
1975	Guerilla Army of the Poor (EGP) launches guerilla activity in northern Quiché Department.
1977	Guatemala rejects US military aid when Jimmy Carter links it to greater human rights observance.
1978	General Fernando Romeo Lucas García becomes President in fraudulent election. Escalates repressive

	policies. Rejuvenated Rebel Armed Forces (FAR) renew guerilla activities.
1981	US resumes arms sales to Guatemala.
1982	Guatemalan Military coup in March ousts General Lucas and installs a junta headed by General Efraín Ríos Montt. Ríos Montt assumes Presidency on June 9. Guatemalan National Revolutionary Unity (URNG) formed as umbrella group for rebel groups.
1983	Military coup in August ousts Ríos Montt and installs Defense Minister Oscar Humberto Mejías Victores.
1985	Military agrees to elections.
1986	Civilian rule reestablished with inauguration of Vinicio Cerezo. Oscar Arias elected President of Costa Rica.
1987	Esquipulas II Peace Agreement signed.
1988	URNG meets with National Reconciliation Commission established by Esquipulas II.
1990	Msgr. Rodolfo Quezada Toruño becomes official 'conciliator' of emerging Guatemala peace process, UN secretary general invited to observe. URNG meets with other sectors of society.
1991	Jorge Serrano Elías elected President. Mexico Accord signed.
1993	Serrano attempts 'auto-golpe'. *Instancia Nacional de Consenso* (National Consensus Body, INC) resolves crisis, installs Human Rights Ombudsman Ramiro de León Carpio as President.
1994	Civil Society Assembly (ASC) formed. Five peace accords signed.
1995	Indigenous Rights Accord signed. Alvaro Arzú of the PAN party wins December elections by a two percent margin.
1996	Eight peace agreements signed, including the final peace accord, 'The Agreement on a Firm and Lasting Peace', on 29 December.

Text of the Socio-Economic Accord

Agreement on Social and Economic Aspects and Agrarian Situation

THE SITUATION IN CENTRAL AMERICA: PROCEDURES FOR THE ESTABLISHMENT OF A FIRM AND LASTING PEACE AND PROGRESS IN FASHIONING A REGION OF PEACE, FREEDOM, DEMOCRACY AND DEVELOPMENT

Letter dated 24 May 1996 from the secretary general addressed to the President of the General Assembly

I have the honour to transmit herewith the text of the Agreement on Social and Economic Aspects and Agrarian Situation, concluded on 6 May 1996 between the Presidential Peace Commission of the Government of Guatemala and the General Command of the Unidad Revolucionaria Nacional Guatemalteca (URNG) (see annex). The signing ceremony took place at the Mexican Foreign Ministry in the presence of Mr. Angel Gurría, Foreign Minister, and, amongst others, senior officials of the countries that are members of the Group of Friends of the Guatemalan Peace Process (Colombia, Mexico, Norway, Spain, the United States of America and Venezuela), representatives of the Assembly of Civil Society and other Guatemalan personalities.

This Agreement, which is the fruit of intensive negotiations initiated a year ago, contains a comprehensive package of commitments on several issues critical to the building of a lasting peace and sustainable development in Guatemala. Based on a shared perception that conflict resolution is inseparable from significant change in social and economic policy, the parties have agreed on a broad array of measures to permit wider participation in decision-making at all levels; to increase and redirect government spending towards social development; to promote a more efficient and equitable agrarian structure; to modernize public administration; and to produce a sustained increase in public revenue. At the heart of the strategies outlined in the agreement is the concept, consistent with the thinking of the United Nations, that enhanced social participation in all aspects of development is key to both improved social justice and sustainable economic growth. The Agreement reflects an agenda of social and economic change widely supported in Guatemala. On 22 May 1996, the text of the Agreement was submitted to the Assembly of Civil Society for its endorsement.

With the signing of the Agreement on Social and Economic Aspects and Agrarian Situation, the peace process in Guatemala is gathering new momentum. The cessation of offensive military action declared by both parties in March has held. The suspension by the URNG of its practice of levying "war tax", with effect from 6 May, will broaden support for the peace process within Guatemala. Advances in the negotiations will, in turn, facilitate the difficult struggle against impunity to which the Government of President Arzú is committed. Better prospects for an early peace will also enhance the impact and effectiveness of the verifying and institution-building activities of the United Nations Mission for the Verification of Human Rights and of Compliance with the Commitments of the Comprehensive Agreement on Human Rights in Guatemala (MINUGUA). In a public statement dated 6 May 1996, I congratulated the parties on their achievements and encouraged them to build upon those positive developments as they considered the next item on the negotiating agenda, namely, "Strengthening civilian power and the role of the army in a democratic society". This process will begin on 7 and 8 June 1996 in Mexico City.

The Agreement will enter into force with the signing of the Agreement on a Firm and Lasting Peace, which is to be the culmination of negotiations held under United Nations auspices since January 1994. At the request of the parties, and subject to authorization by the appropriate United Nations organ, MINUGUA will then expand its activities to cover verification of all agreements reached. While the latter's comprehensiveness will make verification a particularly complex task, experience has shown that the presence of the Verification Mission is a key factor in the broad process of building peace and consolidating democracy in Guatemala. In due time I intend, therefore, to recommend that the mandate of MINUGUA be extended, as requested by the parties, and that the Mission be provided with the sound financial basis it needs to continue to make its critical contribution to the peace process.

Support by the United Nations system for implementation of the peace accords will be another key contribution to the consolidation of peace and democracy in Guatemala. The comprehensiveness of the accords, combined with the limited availability of external assistance and the expectations of Guatemalan people that peace will soon produce tangible benefits, will call for the redoubling of our efforts, in close collaboration with the Government of Guatemala, to coordinate the United Nations system's response to the demand for verification, good offices and technical assistance to help implement the accords. To ensure an integrated approach, I have called a meeting of relevant United Nations specialized agencies, bodies and programmes, under the chairmanship of the Under-Secretary-General for Political Affairs, to discuss how the United Nations system can best work together in this endeavour.

I would be grateful if you would bring the contents of the present letter to the attention of the members of the General Assembly.

(Signed) Boutros BOUTROS-GHALI

ANNEX

Agreement on Social and Economic Aspects and Agrarian Situation concluded on 6 May 1996 between the Presidential Peace Commission of the Government of Guatemala and the Unidad Revolucionaria Nacional Guatemalteca

Whereas:

A firm and lasting peace must be consolidated on the basis of social and economic development directed towards the common good, meeting the needs of the whole population,

This is necessary in order to overcome the poverty, extreme poverty, discrimination and social and political marginalization which have impeded and distorted the country's social, economic, cultural and political development and have represented a source of conflict and instability,

Socio-economic development requires social justice, as one of the building blocks of unity and national solidarity, together with sustainable economic growth as a condition for meeting the people's social needs,

Rural areas require an integral strategy that facilitates access by small farmers to land and other production resources, offers juridical security and promotes conflict resolution,

It is essential, both for the realization of the production potential of Guatemalan society and for the achievement of greater social justice, that all sectors of society participate effectively in finding a way to meet their needs, particularly in setting public policies that concern them,

The State should pursue democratization in order to expand those possibilities for participation and strengthen its role as a leader of national development, as a legislator, as a source of public investment and a provider of services and as a promoter of consensus -building and conflict resolution,

This Agreement seeks to create or strengthen mechanisms and conditions to guarantee the effective participation of the people and contains the priority objectives for Government action to lay the foundations of this participatory development,

The implementation of this Agreement should enable all the country's social and political forces to face together, in a cooperative and responsible way, the immediate tasks of combating poverty, discrimination and privilege, thus building a united, prosperous and just Guatemala that will afford a dignified way of life to its people as a whole,

The Government of Guatemala and the Unidad Revolucionaria Nacional Guatemalteca (hereinafter referred to as "the Parties") have agreed as follows:

I. DEMOCRATIZATION AND PARTICIPATORY DEVELOPMENT

A. Participation and consensus-building

1. In order to pursue a true, functional and participatory democracy, the process of social and economic development should be democratic

and participatory and include: (a) consensus-building and dialogue among agents of socio-economic development; (b) consensus-building between these agents and State bodies in the formulation and implementation of development strategies; and (c) effective citizen participation in identifying, prioritizing and meeting their needs.

2. Expanded social participation is a bulwark against corruption, privilege, distortions of development and the abuse of economic and political power to the detriment of society. Therefore, it is an instrument for the eradication of economic, social and political polarization in society.

3. In addition to representing a factor in democratization, citizen participation in economic and social development is essential in order to promote productivity and economic growth, achieve a more equitable distribution of wealth and train human resources. It ensures transparency in public policies and their orientation towards the common good rather than special interests, the effective protection of the interests of the most vulnerable groups, efficiency in providing services and, consequently, the integral development of the individual.

4. In this spirit, and in line with the agreements already concluded on the resettlement of the population groups uprooted by the armed conflict and on identity and rights of indigenous peoples, the Parties agree on the importance of establishing or strengthening mechanisms allowing the citizens and different social groups to exercise their rights effectively and participate fully in decision-making on the various matters affecting or involving them, with full awareness of both their individual and collective obligations to society, which they will fulfil responsibly.

5. Strengthening social participation means that greater opportunities in social and economic decision-making should be offered to organized groups. This assumes that all kinds of grass-roots organizations representing different interests will be recognized and encouraged. It requires, in particular, the guarantee of full and effective rights for rural and urban workers and small farmers to participate, as organized entities, in the process of building consensus with the business sector or at the national level. For this purpose, flexible laws and administrative regulations must be passed to grant legal personality or other forms of legal recognition to those organizations requesting it.

6. This also assumes a major effort to promote a culture of consensus and capacity-building in business, labour and other types of organizations in order to increase their ability to plan and negotiate and effectively to assume the rights and duties inherent in democratic participation.

Consensus-building

7. Building consensus at the national, departmental and communal levels and among rural and urban units of production is essential in order to stimulate and stabilize economic and social growth. State structures must be adapted to fulfil this role of building consensus and reconciling interests, in order to be able to work effectively and efficiently to modernize the production sector, enhance competitiveness, promote economic growth and provide basic social services efficiently and universally.

Participation at the local level

8. Bearing in mind that the people who live in a department or municipality, whether business owners, workers, members of cooperatives or community representatives, are the ones who can best define the measures that benefit or affect them, a package of instruments must be adopted for institutionalizing the decentralization of social and economic decision-making, involving a real transfer of government funds and of the authority to discuss and decide locally on the allocation of resources, how projects will be executed and the priorities and characteristics of government programmes or activities. In this way, government bodies will be able to base their actions on proposals arising from the reconciliation of interests among the various segments of society.

9. Through this Agreement, the Government commits itself to take a series of steps designed to increase the people's participation in the various aspects of public life, including social and rural development policies. This series of reforms must enable structures that generate social conflict to be replaced by new relationships that ensure the consolidation of peace, as an expression of harmonious life together, and the strengthening of democracy, as a dynamic and perfectible process from which advances can be achieved through the participation of various segments of society in shaping the country's political, social and economic choices.

10. In order to reinforce the people's ability to participate and, at the same time, the State's management capacity, the Government agrees to:

Communities

(a) Promote a reform of the Municipal Code so that deputy mayors are appointed by the municipal mayor, taking into account the recommendations of local residents in an open town council meeting;

Municipalities

(b) Foster social participation in the context of municipal autonomy, pursuing the process of decentralization to give more authority to municipal governments, and consequently, strengthening their technical, administrative and financial resources;

(c) Establish and implement as soon as possible, in cooperation with the National Association of Municipalities, a municipal training programme that will serve as a framework for national efforts and international cooperation in this field. The programme will stress the training of municipal staff who will specialize in executing the new duties that will be the responsibility of the municipality as a result of decentralization, with an emphasis on land use planning, a land register, urban planning, financial management, project management and training of local organizations so that they can participate effectively in meeting their own needs;

Departments

(d) Promote in the Congress a reform of the Act concerning the governance of the departments of the Republic, to the effect that the governor of the department would be appointed by the President of the Republic, taking into consideration the candidates nominated by the non-governmental representatives of the departmental development councils;

Regions

(e) Regionalize health care, education and cultural services for indigenous people and ensure the full participation of indigenous organizations in the design and implementation of this process;

System of urban and rural development councils

(f) Take the following steps, bearing in mind the fundamental role of urban and rural development councils in ensuring, promoting and guaranteeing the people's participation in the identification of local priorities, the definition of public projects and programmes and the integration of national policy into urban and rural development:

(i) Re-establish local development councils;

(ii) Promote a reform of the Urban and Rural Development Councils Act to broaden the range of sectors participating in departmental and regional development councils;

(iii) Provide adequate funding for the council system.

B. Participation of women in economic and social development

11. The active participation of women is essential for Guatemala's economic and social development, and the State has a duty to promote the elimination of all forms of discrimination against women.

12. Recognizing women's undervalued contributions in all spheres of economic and social activity, and particularly their efforts towards community improvement, the Parties agree that there is a need to strengthen women's participation in economic and social development on equal terms.

13. To this end, the Government undertakes to take the specific economic and social situation of women into account in its development strategies, plans and programmes, and to train civil servants in analysis and planning based on this approach. This undertaking includes the following:

(a) Recognizing the equal rights of women and men in the home, in the workplace, in the production sector and in social and political life, and ensuring that women have the same opportunities as men, particularly with regard to access to credit, land ownership and other productive and technological resources;

Education and training

(b) Ensuring that women have equal opportunities for education and training in the same conditions as men, and that any form of discrimination against women that may be found in school curricula is eliminated;

Housing

(c) Ensuring that women have equal access to housing of their own by eliminating the obstacles and impediments that affect women in relation to rental property, credit and construction;

Health

(d) Implementing nationwide comprehensive health programmes for women, which involves giving women access to appropriate information, prevention and health care services;

Labour

(e) Guaranteeing women's right to work, which requires:

(i) Using various means to encourage vocational training for women;

(ii) Revising labour legislation to guarantee equality of rights and opportunities between men and women;

(iii) In rural areas, recognizing women as agricultural workers to ensure that their work is valued and remunerated;

(iv) Enacting laws to protect the rights of women who work as household employees, especially in relation to fair wages, working hours, social security and respect for their dignity;

Organization and participation

(f) Guaranteeing women's right to organize and their participation, on the same terms as men, at the senior decision-making levels of local, regional and national institutions;

(g) Promoting women's participation in public administration, especially in the formulation, execution and supervision of government plans and policies;

Legislation

(h) Revising national legislation and regulations to eliminate all forms of discrimination against women in terms of economic, social, cultural and political participation, and to give effect to the government commitments deriving from the ratification of the Convention on the Elimination of All Forms of Discrimination against Women.

II. SOCIAL DEVELOPMENT

14. The State is responsible for promoting, guiding and regulating the country's socio-economic development so as to ensure economic efficiency, increased social services and social justice in an integrated manner and through the efforts of society as a whole. In the quest for growth, economic policy should be aimed at preventing processes of socio-economic exclusion, such as unemployment and impoverishment, and maximizing the benefits of economic growth for all Guatemalans. In seeking to ensure the well-being of all Guatemalans, social policy should foster economic development through its impact on production and efficiency.

15. Guatemala requires speedy economic growth in order to create jobs and enhance social development. The country's social development, in turn, is essential for its economic growth and for better integration into the world economy. In this regard, better living standards, health, education and training are the pillars of sustainable development in Guatemala.

State responsibilities

16. The State has inescapable obligations in the task of correcting social inequities and deficiencies, both by steering the course of development and by making public investments and providing universal social services. Likewise, the State has the specific obligations, imposed by constitutional mandate, of ensuring the effective enjoyment, without discrimination of any kind, of the right to work, health, education and housing, as well as other social rights. The historical social imbalances experienced in Guatemala must be corrected, and peace must be consolidated, through decisive policies which are implemented by both the State and society as a whole.

Productive investments

17. The country's socio-economic development cannot depend exclusively on public finances or on international cooperation. Rather, it requires an increase in productive investments that create adequately paid jobs. The Parties urge national and foreign entrepreneurs to invest in the country, considering that the signing and implementation of an agreement on a firm and lasting peace are essential components of the stability and transparency required for investment and economic expansion.

Gross domestic product

18. For its part, the Government undertakes to adopt economic policies designed to achieve steady growth in the gross domestic product of not less than 6 per cent per annum, which would enable it to implement a progressive social policy. At the same time, it undertakes to implement a social policy aimed at ensuring the well-being of all Guatemalans, with emphasis on health, nutrition, education and training, housing, environmental sanitation and access to productive employment and to decent pay.

The State's leadership role

19. To meet this objective and to enable the State to play its leadership role in social policy, the Government undertakes to:

(a) Apply and develop the regulatory framework to guarantee the exercise of social rights and provide social services through public entities and, where necessary, through semi-public or private entities, and supervise the adequate provision of such services;

(b) Promote and ensure the participation, in accordance with the regulatory framework, of all social and economic sectors that can cooperate in social development, particularly in providing full access to basic services;

(c) Ensure that the public sector provides services efficiently, considering that the State has a duty to give the population access to quality services.

20. In response to the population's urgent demands, the Government undertakes to:

(a) Increase social investment significantly, especially in the areas of health, education and employment;

(b) Restructure the budget so as to increase social expenditure;

(c) Give priority to the neediest sectors of society and the most disadvantaged areas of the country, without short-changing other sectors of society;

(d) Improve the administration of government resources and investments by decentralizing them and making them less concentrated and bureaucratic, reforming budget performance mechanisms by giving them autonomy in decision-making and financial management to guarantee their efficiency and transparency, and strengthening supervisory and auditing mechanisms.

A. Education and training

21. Education and training have a fundamental role in the country's economic, cultural, social and political development. They are central to the strategy of equity and national unity, and vital for economic modernization and international competitiveness. Reform of the educational system and of its administration is therefore necessary, as is the implementation of coherent and forceful State policies in the field of education, in order to achieve the following objectives:

(a) To affirm and disseminate the moral and cultural values and the concepts and behaviour patterns which are the foundations of democratic coexistence, including respect for human rights, for the cultural diversity of Guatemala, for the productive work of its people and the protection of the environment and for the values and mechanisms of power-sharing and social and political consensus-building which constitute the basis of a culture of peace;

(b) To avoid the perpetuation of poverty and of social, ethnic, sexual and geographical forms of discrimination, particularly those which arise from the divide between urban and rural society;

(c) To contribute to the application of technical and scientific progress and, consequently, to the achievement of higher productivity, the creation of more jobs and increased income for the population, and beneficial integration into the world economy.

22. In response to the country's needs in the field of education, the Government undertakes to:

Spending on education

(a) Implement significant increases in the resources allocated to education. By the year 2000, the Government proposes to step up public spending on education as a proportion of gross domestic product by at least 50 per cent over its 1995 level. These targets will be revised upwards in the light of future developments in State finances;

Adjustment of educational curricula

(b) Adjust educational curricula in accordance with the objectives set out in paragraph 21. These adjustments will take into account the conclusions of the Education Reform Commission established by the Agreement on Identity and Rights of Indigenous Peoples;

Coverage

(c) Expand, as a matter of urgency, the coverage of education services at all levels, and in particular the provision of bilingual education in rural communities, by means of:

(i) The integration of children of school age into the educational system, ensuring that they complete the pre-primary and primary levels and the first level of secondary school; in particular, by the year 2000, the Government undertakes to provide access, for all those between ages 7 and 12, to at least three years of schooling;

(ii) Literacy programmes in as many languages as is technically feasible, with the participation of suitably qualified indigenous organizations; the Government undertakes to raise the literacy rate to 70 per cent by the year 2000; and

(iii) Education, training and technical courses for adults;

Occupational training

(d) Develop, with appropriate and efficient methodology, training programmes in communities and enterprises for the retraining and technical updating of workers, with emphasis on the inhabitants of isolated areas and rural communities, with support from those sectors which are able to collaborate in this undertaking;

Training for participation

(e) Provide training to enable social organizations at the municipal, regional and national levels to take part in socio-economic development, including the fields of public administration, fiscal responsibility and consensus-building;

Civic education programme

(f) Design and implement a national civic education programme for democracy and peace, promoting the protection of human rights, the renewal of political culture and the peaceful resolution of conflicts. The mass media will be invited to participate in this programme;

Community-school interaction and community participation

(g) In order to encourage the enrolment of children in the educational system and to lower the school drop-out rate, the Government undertakes to encourage effective community and parental participation in the various aspects of the education and training services (curricula, appointment of teachers, school calendar, etc.);

Financial support

(h) Develop scholarship and student grant programmes, economic support and other incentives, to enable needy students to continue their education;

Training of school administrators

(i) Develop continuing education programmes for teachers and school administrators;

Advisory commission

(j) For the purpose of designing and implementing the educational reform to be carried out by the Ministry of Education, an advisory commission attached to the Ministry will be set up, consisting of participants in the educational process, including representatives of the Education Reform Commission set up pursuant to the Agreement on Identity and Rights of Indigenous Peoples;

Higher education and research

(k) State-run higher education, the management, organization and development of which is the sole responsibility of the Guatemalan University of San Carlos, is a key factor in achieving economic growth, social equity, the dissemination of culture and a greater pool of technological know-how. The Government of the Republic undertakes to provide to the University of San Carlos, in a timely manner, the funding which is its prerogative under a constitutional mandate. With all due respect to the autonomy of the University, the parties urge the authorities of that distinguished institution to give favourable consideration to all initiatives which increase its contribution to the country's development and help to consolidate peace. The Government undertakes to heed such contributions and initiatives and to respond appropriately. Particular importance is attached to the development of the University's regional centres and of its internship programmes, especially in the poorest sectors. The Parties also urge the business sector to devote increased efforts to applied technological research and to human resources development, forging closer exchange links with the University of San Carlos;

Educational outreach workers

(l) Pursuant to the Agreement on Resettlement of the Population Groups Uprooted by the Armed Conflict and the Agreement on Identity and Rights of Indigenous Peoples, community educational outreach workers shall be incorporated into the national education system, and due regard shall be given to suitable curricula for indigenous communities and uprooted population groups.

B. Health

23. The Parties agree on the need to promote a reform of the national health sector. This reform should be aimed at ensuring effective exercise of the fundamental right to health, without any discrimination whatsoever, and the effective performance by the State, which would be provided with the necessary resources, of its obligation with regard to health and social welfare. Some of the main points of this reform are as follows:

Concept

(a) It would be based on an integrated concept of health (including prevention, promotion, recovery and rehabilitation) and on humanitarian and community-based practice emphasizing the spirit of service, and it would be applied at all levels of the country's public health sector;

National coordinated health system

(b) One of the responsibilities of the Ministry of Health is to formulate policies to provide the entire Guatemalan population with integrated health services. Under the coordination of the Ministry of Health, the health system would combine the work of public agencies (including the Guatemalan Social Security Institute) and private and non-governmental organizations involved in this sector to implement actions designed to enable the whole Guatemalan population to have access to integrated health services;

Low-income population

(c) The system would create the conditions for ensuring that the low-income population has effective access to quality health services. The Government undertakes to increase the resources it allocates to health.

By the year 2000, the Government proposes to step up public spending on health as a proportion of gross domestic product by at least 50 per cent over its 1995 level. This target will be revised upwards in the light of future developments in State finances;

Priority care

(d) The system would give priority to efforts to fight malnutrition and to promote environmental sanitation, preventive health care and primary health care, especially maternal and child care. The Government undertakes to allocate at least 50 per cent of public health expenditure to preventive care and undertakes to cut the 1995 infant and maternal mortality rate in half by the year 2000. In addition, the Government undertakes to maintain the certification of eradication of poliomyelitis, and to eradicate measles by the year 2000;

Medicine, equipment and inputs

(e) The Ministry of Public Health and Social Welfare will revise current rules and practices with regard to the manufacture and marketing of drugs, equipment and inputs and will promote measures to ensure that these are in sufficient supply and that they are affordable and of high quality. In the case of popular basic or generic drugs, ways of purchasing them will be studied and applied in order to ensure transparency in their marketing, quality and pricing to ensure that services are provided efficiently;

Indigenous and traditional medicine

(f) The system would enhance the importance of indigenous and traditional medicine, promoting its study and renewing its concepts, methods and practices;

Social participation

(g) The system would encourage active participation of municipalities, communities and social organizations (including groups of women, indigenous people, trade unions and civic and humanitarian associations) in the planning, execution and monitoring of the administration of health services and programmes, through local health systems and urban and rural development councils;

Administrative decentralization and
enhancement of local autonomy

(h) The decentralized organization of the various levels of health care should ensure that health programmes and services are offered at the community, regional and national levels, which are the basis of the national coordinated health system.

C. Social security

24. Social security is a mechanism for expressing human solidarity and promoting the common good, laying the foundations for stability, economic development, national unity and peace. Under the Political Constitution of the Republic, the Guatemalan Social Security Institute, an autonomous body, administers the social security system. The Parties consider that appropriate measures should be taken to expand its coverage and increase its benefits and the quality and efficiency of its services. To that end, the following should be taken into account:

(a) The administration of the Guatemalan Social Security Institute should be completely autonomous, in accordance with the constitutional principle of coordination with health agencies under the national coordinated health system;

(b) Under the International Labour Organization convention ratified by Guatemala, social security should include programmes for medical care and benefits in the areas of sickness, maternity, disability, old age, survival, job-related accidents and illnesses, employment and family welfare;

(c) The application of the principles of efficiency, universality, unity and compulsoriness to the operation of the Guatemalan Social Security Institute should be reinforced and guaranteed;

(d) The financial soundness of the Institute should be strengthened through a system of tripartite control of contributions;

(e) New ways of managing the Institute with the participation of its constituent sectors should be promoted;

(f) The Institute should be effectively incorporated into the coordinated health system;

(g) Conditions should be created that will facilitate the universal coverage of all workers by the social security system.

D. Housing

25. It has been recognized that there is a need to institute a policy, in accordance with the constitutional mandate, to give priority to the building of low-cost housing, through appropriate financial arrangements, in order to enable as many Guatemalan families as possible to own their own homes. To this end, the Government undertakes to:

Planning

(a) Closely monitor land management policies, especially urban planning and environmental protection policies, to enable the poor to have access to housing and related services in hygienic and environmentally sustainable conditions;

Standards

(b) Update health and safety regulations applicable to the construction industry and monitor compliance with them; coordinate with municipalities to ensure that construction and supervision standards are homogeneous, clear and simple, in an effort to provide high-quality, safe housing;

Housing stock

(c) Promote a policy to increase the stock of housing in Guatemala, in an effort to enable more people from low-income sectors to rent or own their own homes;

(d) Increase the supply of housing-related services, housing options and high-quality, low-cost building materials; in this context, apply anti-trust regulations to the production and marketing of building materials and housing-related services in accordance with article 130 of the Constitution;

Finance and credit

(e) Implement monetary policies designed to reduce the cost of credit significantly;

(f) Strengthen the securities market and make it more available as a source of funds to purchase housing, by offering first and second mortgages and facilitating the selling of securities issued for housing operations, such as common and preferred stocks in construction companies, mortgage bonds and debentures, real estate participation certificates, supplemental letters, promissory notes and other documents related to rental with an option to buy;

(g) Design a direct subsidy mechanism and apply it to the demand for low-cost housing, to benefit the most needy sectors. To this end, strengthen the Guatemalan Housing Fund to improve its capacity to grant funds to assist those living in poverty and extreme poverty;

Participation

(h) Stimulate the establishment and strengthening of participatory arrangements, such as cooperatives and self-managed and family businesses, to ensure that the beneficiaries are able to participate in the planning and construction of housing and related services;

Regularization of the land situation

(i) Promote the legalization, access to and registry of land, not only in the vicinity of Guatemala City but also for urban development in the province capitals and municipalities, together with the implementation of building projects in villages and on farms, especially rural housing;

National commitment

(j) In view of the size and urgency of the housing problem, national efforts should be mobilized to solve it. The Government undertakes to allocate to the housing promotion policy no less than 1.5 per cent of the tax revenue budget, beginning in 1997, giving priority to the subsidy for low-cost housing options.

E. Work

26. Work is essential for the integral development of the individual, the well-being of the family and the social and economic development of Guatemala. Labour relations are an essential element of social participation in socio-economic development and of economic efficiency. In this respect, the State's policy with regard to work is critical for a strategy of growth with social justice. In order to carry out this policy, the Government undertakes to:

Economic policy

(a) Through an economic policy designed to increase the use of the labour force, create conditions for the attainment of rising and sustained levels of employment, while sharply reducing structural underemployment and making possible a progressive increase in real wages;

(b) Encourage measures in coordination with the various social sectors to increase investment and productivity within the framework of an overall strategy of growth with social stability and equity;

Protective labour legislation

(c) Promote, in the course of 1996, legal and regulatory changes to enforce the labour laws and severely penalize violations, including violations in respect of the minimum wage, non-payment, withholding and delays in wages, occupational hygiene and safety and the work environment;

(d) Decentralize and expand labour inspection services, strengthening the capacity to monitor compliance with the labour norms of domestic law and those derived from the international labour agreements ratified by Guatemala, paying particular attention to monitoring compliance with the labour rights of women, migrant and temporary agricultural workers, household workers, minors, the elderly, the disabled and other workers who are in a more vulnerable and unprotected situation;

Occupational training

(e) Establish a permanent, modern vocational instruction and training programme to ensure training at all levels and a corresponding increase in productivity through a draft law regulating vocational training at the national level;

(f) Promote coverage by the national vocational instruction and training programmes of at least 200,000 workers by the year 2000, with an emphasis on those who are joining the workforce and those who need special training to adapt to new conditions in the labour market;

Ministry of Labour

(g) Strengthen and modernize the Ministry of Labour and Social Welfare, ensuring its leading role in Government policies related to the labour sector and its effective deployment in the promotion of employment and in labour cooperation. To that end, it undertakes to:

Participation, coordination and negotiations

(i) Promote the restructuring of labour relations in enterprises by encouraging labour management cooperation and coordination with a view to the development of the enterprise for the common good, including possible profit-sharing arrangements;

(ii) Facilitate the procedures for the recognition of the legal personality of labour organizations;

(iii) In the case of agricultural workers who are still hired through contractors, propose reforms for the speedy and flexible legal recognition of forms of association for the negotiation of such hiring; and

(iv) Promote a culture of negotiation and, in particular, train persons to settle disputes and coordinate action for the benefit of the parties involved.

III. AGRARIAN SITUATION AND RURAL DEVELOPMENT

27. It is essential and unavoidable to solve the problems of agrarian reform and rural development in order to address the situation of the majority population, which live in rural areas and is most affected by poverty, extreme poverty, injustice and the weakness of State institutions. The transformation of the structure of land use and ownership must have as its objective the incorporation of the rural population into economic, social and political development so that the land constitutes, for those who work it, the basis of their economic stability, the foundation of their progressive social well-being and the guarantee of their freedom and dignity.

28. Land is central to the problems of rural development. From the conquest to the present, historic events, often tragic, have left deep traces in ethnic, social and economic relations concerning property and land use. These have led to a situation of concentration of resources which contrasts with the poverty of the majority and hinders the development of Guatemala as a whole. It is essential to redress and overcome this legacy and promote more efficient and more equitable farming, strengthening the potential of all those involved, not only in terms of productive capacity but also in enhancing the cultures and value systems which coexist and intermingle in the rural areas of Guatemala.

29. These changes will enable Guatemala to take full advantage of the capacities of its inhabitants and, in particular, the richness of the traditions and cultures of its indigenous peoples. It should also take advantage of the high potential for agricultural, industrial, commercial and tourist development of those resources deriving from its wealth of natural resources.

30. Solving the agrarian problem is a complex process covering many aspects of rural life, from modernization of production and cultivation methods to environmental protection, as well as security of property, adequate use of the land and of the labour force, labour protection and a more equitable distribution of resources and the benefits of development. This is also a social process whose success depends not only on the State, but also on a combination of efforts on the part of the organized sectors of society, in the awareness that the common good requires breaking with the patterns and prejudices of the past and seeking new and democratic forms of coexistence.

31. The State has a fundamental and vital role in this process. As the guide for national development, as a legislator, as a source of public investment and provider of services and as a promoter of social cooperation and conflict resolution, it is essential for the State to increase and refocus its efforts and its resources towards the rural areas, and to promote agrarian modernization, in a sustained manner, in the direction of greater justice and greater efficiency.

32. The agreements already signed on human rights, on the resettlement of populations uprooted by armed confrontation and on the identity and rights of indigenous peoples contain commitments which constitute essential elements of a global strategy for rural development. It is in line with these provisions that the Government undertakes, through this Agreement, to promote an integral strategy covering the multiple elements which make up agrarian structure, including land ownership and the use of natural resources; credit systems and mechanisms; manufacturing and marketing; agrarian legislation and legal security; labour relations; technical assistance and training; the sustainability of natural resources and the organization of the rural population. This strategy includes the aspects described below.

A. Participation

33. The capacity of all actors involved in the agricultural sector must be mobilized to make proposals and to take action, including indigenous peoples' organizations, producers' associations, business associations, rural workers' trade unions, rural and women's organizations or universities and research centres in Guatemala. To that end, in addition to the provisions of other chapters of this Agreement, the Government undertakes to:

(a) Strengthen the capacity of rural organizations such as associative rural enterprises, cooperatives, small farmers' associations, mixed enterprises and self-managed and family businesses to participate fully in decisions on all matters concerning them and to establish or strengthen State institutions, especially those of the State agricultural sector, involved in rural development so that they can promote such participation, particularly the full participation of women in the decision-making process. That will strengthen the effectiveness of State action and ensure that it responds to the needs of rural areas. In particular, participation in development councils will be promoted as a framework for the joint formulation of development and land use plans;

(b) Strengthen and expand the participation of tenant farmers' organizations, rural women, indigenous organizations, cooperatives, producers' trade unions and non-governmental organizations in the National Agricultural Development Council as the main mechanism for consultation, coordination and social participation in the decision-making process for rural development, and in particular for the implementation of this chapter.

B. Access to land and productive resources

34. Promote the access of tenant farmers to land ownership and the sustainable use of land resources. To that end, the Government will take the following actions:

Access to land ownership: land trust fund

(a) Establish a land trust fund within a broad-based banking institution to provide credit and to promote savings, preferably among micro-, small and medium-sized enterprises. The land trust fund will have prime responsibility for the acquisition of land through Government funding, will promote the establishment of a transparent land market and will facilitate the updating of land development plans. The fund will give priority to the allocation of land to rural men and women who are organized for that purpose, taking into account economic and environmental sustainability requirements;

(b) In order to ensure that the neediest sectors benefit from its services, the fund will set up a special advisory and management unit to serve rural communities and organizations;

(c) Initially, the fund will limit its activities to the following types of land:

(i) Uncultivated State land and State-owned farms;
(ii) Illegally settled public land, especially in Petén and the Franja Transversal del Norte, which the Government has pledged to recover through legal action;

(iii) Land acquired with the resources allocated by the Government to the National Land Fund and the National Peace Fund for that purpose;

(iv) Land purchased with grants from friendly Governments and international non-governmental organizations;

(v) Land purchased with loans secured from international financing agencies;

(vi) Undeveloped land expropriated under article 40 of the Constitution;

(vii) Land acquired from the proceeds of the sale of excess land, as determined by comparing the actual dimensions of private property with the dimensions recorded at the land register department, which has become the property of the State;

(viii) Land which the State may purchase pursuant to Decree No. 1551, article 40, on agricultural development areas;

(ix) Land which the State may purchase for any purpose; and

(x) Miscellaneous grants;

(d) The Government will promote and enact legislation to regulate all the activities of the land trust fund. Such legislation will establish, inter alia, the fund's aims, functions and financing and acquisition mechanisms, and the allocation, origin and destination of land. In 1999, the extent to which the allocation targets have been met will be assessed and, if need be, the functioning of the land allocation programme will be adjusted;

Access to land ownership: funding mechanisms

(e) Promote, through all means possible, the development of a dynamic land market that would enable tenant farmers who either do not have land or have insufficient land to acquire land through long-term transactions at commercial or favourable interest rates with little or no down payment. In particular, promote the issuance of mortgage-backed securities guaranteed by the State whose yield is attractive to private investors, especially financial institutions;

Access to the use of natural resources

(f) By 1999, allocate to small and medium-sized farmers' groups legally incorporated as natural resources management ventures, 100,000 hectares within multi-use areas for sustainable forest management, the management of protected areas, eco-tourism, conservation of water sources and other activities compatible with the sustainable potential use of the natural resources of such areas;

(g) Promote and support the participation of the private sector and grass-roots community organizations in projects for the management and conservation of renewable natural resources through incentives, targeted direct subsidies or funding mechanisms on soft terms, in view of the non-monetary benefits that the national community derives from such projects. Given the benefit that the international community receives from the sustainable management and conservation of the country's forest and biogenetic resources, the Government will actively promote international cooperation in this venture;

Access to other productive projects

(h) Develop sustainable productive projects especially geared towards boosting productivity and the processing of agricultural, forestry and fishery products in the poorest areas of the country. In particular, for the period 1997–2000, guarantee the implementation, in the poorest areas, of a Government agricultural sector investment programme in the amount of 200 million quetzales in the agriculture, forestry and fisheries sectors;

(i) Promote a renewable natural resources management programme which fosters sustainable forestry and agro-forestry production, as well as handicrafts and small- and medium-scale industry projects that give added value to forest products;

(j) Promote productive ventures related, inter alia, to agro-processing industries, marketing, services, handicrafts and tourism with a view to creating jobs and securing fair incomes for all;

(k) Promote an eco-tourism programme with the broad participation of communities which have received appropriate training.

C. Support structure

35. Prerequisites for a more efficient and just agricultural structure include not only more equitable access to productive resources but also a support structure that will enhance farmers' access to information, technology, training, credit and marketing facilities. Over and above its commitment to social investment as set forth in the chapter on social development, including in particular investment in

health, education, housing and employment, the Government also
undertakes to:

Basic infrastructure

(a) Engage in judicious public investment and foster a climate condu-
cive to private investment with a view to upgrading the infrastructure
available for sustainable production and marketing, especially in
areas of poverty and extreme poverty;

(b) Develop a rural development investment programme with emphasis on basic infrastructure (highways, rural roads, electricity,
telecommunications, water and environmental sanitation) and productive projects, for a total amount of 300 million quetzales annually
during the period 1997–1999;

Credit and financial services

(c) Activate the land fund not later than 1997, while simultaneously
promoting conditions that will enable small and medium-scale farmers to have access to credit, individually or in groups, on a financially
sustainable basis. In particular, with the support of the private sector
and non-governmental development organizations, the Government
proposes to strengthen local savings and credit agencies, including
associations, cooperatives and the like, with a view to enhancing their
function as sources of credit providing small and medium-scale farmers with financial services efficiently and in accordance with local
needs and conditions;

Training and technical assistance

(d) Strengthen, decentralize and broaden the coverage of training programmes, especially programmes designed to enhance rural people's
managerial skills at various levels. The private sector and
non-governmental organizations will be enlisted in the implementation
of this action;

(e) Develop technical assistance and job training programmes that
will upgrade the skills, versatility and productivity of the labour force
in rural areas;

Information

(f) Develop an information collection, compilation and distribution
system for the agriculture, forestry, food processing and fisheries

sectors, one that will provide small producers with reliable information on which to base their decisions relating to seeds, inputs, crops, costs and marketing;

Marketing

(g) Develop a system of storage centres and duty-free zones with a view to facilitating the processing and marketing of agricultural products and fostering rural employment.

D. Organization of the rural population for production

36. Organizing the rural population is a decisive factor in transforming the inhabitants of the countryside into genuine protagonists of their own development. In view of the vital role of small and medium-scale enterprises in combating poverty, creating rural jobs and promoting more efficient land use, there is a need to promote a more efficient form of organization of small producers so that they can, in particular, take advantage of the support structure described in paragraph 35. To this end, the Government undertakes to:

(a) Support micro-, small and medium-scale agricultural and rural enterprises by strengthening the various ways of organizing them, such as associative rural enterprises, cooperatives, small farmers' associations, mixed enterprises and self-managed and family businesses;

(b) Tackle the problem of smallholdings through:

(i) A firm and sustained policy of support for smallholders so that they can become small-scale agricultural businessmen through access to training, technology, credit and other inputs;

(ii) Promoting, if the smallholders so desire, amalgamation of holdings in those cases where conversion into small businesses is not possible owing to the dispersal and size of the properties.

E. Legal framework and juridical security

37. Guatemala is in need of reform of the juridical framework of agriculture and institutional development in the rural sector so that an end can be put to the lack of protection and dispossession from which small farmers, and in particular indigenous peoples, have suffered, so as to permit full integration of the rural population into the national economy and regulate land use in an efficient and environmentally sustainable manner in accordance with development needs. To this

end, and taking into account in all cases the provisions of the Agreement on Identity and Rights of Indigenous Peoples, the Government undertakes to:

Legal reform

(a) Promote a legal reform which will establish a juridical framework governing land ownership that is secure, simple and accessible to the entire population. This reform will need to simplify the procedures for awarding title and registering ownership and other real estate rights, as well as to simplify administrative and judicial formalities and procedures;

(b) Promote the establishment of an agrarian and environmental jurisdiction within the judiciary through the enactment of the relevant legislation by the Congress;

(c) Promote the revision and adjustment of the legislation on undeveloped land so that it conforms to the provisions of the Constitution, and regulate, inter alia through incentives and penalties, the underutilization of land and its use in ways incompatible with sustainable natural resource utilization and preservation of the environment;

(d) Protect common and municipal land, in particular by limiting to the strict minimum the cases in which it can be transferred or handed over in whatever form to private individuals;

(e) With respect to community-owned land, to regulate participation by communities in order to ensure that it is they who take the decisions relating to their land;

Prompt settlement of land conflicts

(f) To establish and apply flexible judicial or non-judicial procedures for the settlement of disputes relating to land and other natural resources (in particular, direct settlement and conciliation), taking into account the provisions of the Agreement on Resettlement of the Population Groups Uprooted by the Armed Conflict and the Agreement on Identity and Rights of Indigenous People. In addition, to establish procedures that will make it possible:

(i) To define formulas for compensation in the case of land disputes and claims in which farmers, small farmers and communities in a situation of extreme poverty have been or may be dispossessed for reasons not attributable to them;

(ii) To reinstate or compensate, as appropriate, the State, municipalities, communities or individuals when their land has been usurped or has been allocated in an irregular or unjustified manner involving abuse of authority;

(g) Regulate the award of title to the lands of indigenous communities and beneficiaries of the Guatemalan Institute for Agrarian Reform who are in lawful possession of the land assigned to them;

Institutional mechanisms

(h) By 1997, to have started the operations of a Presidential office for legal assistance and conflict resolution in relation to land, with nationwide coverage and the task of providing advice and legal assistance to small farmers and agricultural workers with a view to the full exercise of their rights, and in particular of:

(i) Advising and providing legal assistance to small farmers and agricultural workers and/or their organizations upon request;

(ii) Intervening in land disputes at the request of a party with a view to arriving at a just and expeditious solution;

(iii) In the case of judicial disputes, providing advice and legal assistance free of charge to small farmers and/or their organizations when they so request;

(iv) Receiving complaints of abuses committed against communities, rural organizations and individual small farmers and bringing them to the attention of the Office of the Counsel for Human Rights and/or of any other national or international verification mechanism.

G. Land register

38. On the basis of the provisions of paragraph 37, the Government undertakes to promote legislative changes that would make it possible to establish an efficient decentralized multi-user land registry system that is financially sustainable, subject to compulsory updating and easy to update. Likewise, the Government undertakes to initiate, by January 1997 at the latest, the process of land surveying and systematizing the land register information, starting with priority zones, in particular with a view to the implementation of paragraph 34 on access to land and other production resources.

H. Labour protection

39. The Government undertakes to promote better participation of rural workers in the benefits of agriculture and a reorientation of labour relations in rural areas. It will place particular emphasis on applying to rural workers the labour policy outlined in the relevant section of the present agreement. An energetic labour protection policy, combined with a vocational training policy, is in line with the requirements of social justice. It is also needed in order to attack rural poverty and promote an agrarian reform aimed at more efficient use of natural and human resources. Accordingly, the Government undertakes to:

(a) Ensure that the labour legislation is effectively applied in rural areas;

(b) Pay urgent attention to the abuses to which rural migrant workers, young tenant farmers and day labourers are subjected in the context of hiring through middlemen, sharecropping, payment in kind and the use of weights and measures. The Government undertakes to adopt administrative and/or penal sanctions against offenders;

(c) Promote reform of the procedures for recognition of the legal personality of small farmers' organizations with a view to simplifying such recognition and making it more flexible through the application of the 1975 International Labour Organization Convention 141 on organization of rural workers.

I. Environmental protection

40. Guatemala's natural wealth is a valuable asset of the country and mankind, in addition to being an essential part of the cultural and spiritual heritage of the indigenous peoples. The irrational exploitation of Guatemala's biogenetic and forest resource diversity endangers a human environment that facilitates sustainable development. Sustainable development is understood as being a process of change in the life of the human being through economic growth with social equity, involving production methods and consumption patterns that maintain the ecological balance. This process implies respecting ethnic and cultural diversity and guaranteeing the quality of life of future generations.

41. In this sense, and in line with the principles of the Central American Alliance for Sustainable Development, the Government reiterates the

following commitments:

(a) To adjust educational curricula and training and technical assistance programmes to the requirements of environmental sustainability;

(b) To give priority to environmental sanitation in its health policy;

(c) To link physical planning policies, particularly urban planning, with environmental protection;

(d) To promote sustainable natural resource management programmes that will create jobs.

J. Resources

42. In order to finance the measures mentioned above, and in view of the priority assigned to modernizing the agriculture sector and rural development, the Government undertakes to increase the State resources allocated to this area by, inter alia:

Land tax

(a) Promoting, by 1997, the legislation and mechanisms for the application, in consultation with municipalities, of a land tax in the rural areas from which it is easy for the municipalities to collect revenues. The tax, from which small properties will be exempt, will help to discourage ownership of undeveloped land and underutilization of land. Taken as a whole, these mechanisms ought not to encourage deforestation of land use for forestry;

Tax on undeveloped land

(b) Establishing a new tax schedule for the annual tax on undeveloped land which imposes significantly higher taxes on privately owned unutilized and/or underutilized land.

IV. MODERNIZATION OF GOVERNMENT SERVICES AND FISCAL POLICY

A. Modernization of government services

43. Government services should become an efficient tool of development policies. To this end, the Government undertakes to:

Decentralization and redistribution

(a) Deepen the decentralization and redistribution of the powers, responsibilities and resources concentrated in the central Government in order to modernize, render effective and streamline government services. Decentralization should ensure the transfer of decision-making power and sufficient resources to the appropriate levels (local, municipal, departmental and regional) so as to meet the needs of socio-economic development in an efficient way and promote close cooperation between government bodies and the population. This implies:

(i) Promoting an amendment to the Executive Authority Act and the Departmental Control and Administration Act and, in particular, to Decree No. 586 of 1956, which will make it possible to simplify, decentralize and redistribute government services;

(ii) Promoting the decentralization of support systems, including the purchasing and procurement system, the human resources system, the information-gathering and statistical system and the financial management system.

National auditing

(b) Reform, strengthen and modernize the Comptroller's Office.

Professionalization and advancement of public servants

44. The State should have a skilled labour force which can ensure the honest and efficient management of public funds. To this end, it is necessary to:

(a) Establish a career civil service;

(b) Adopt legal and administrative measures to ensure real compliance with the Integrity and Accountability Act;

(c) Promote criminal sanctions for acts of corruption and misappropriation of public funds.

B. Fiscal policy

45. Fiscal policy (revenue and expenditure) is the key tool enabling the State to comply with its constitutional commitments, particularly those relating to social development, which is essential to the quest for the common good. Fiscal policy is also essential to Guatemalan sustainable development, which has been impaired by low levels of education, health care and public security, a lack of infrastructure and other factors which militate against increasing the productivity of labour and the competitiveness of the Guatemalan economy.

Budgetary policy

46. Budgetary policy should respond to the need for socio-economic development in a stable context, which requires a public spending policy consistent with the following basic principles:

(a) Giving priority to social spending, the provision of public services and the basic infrastructure needed to support production and marketing;

(b) Giving priority to social investment in health care, education and housing; rural development; job creation; and compliance with the commitments entered into under the peace agreements. The budget should include sufficient resources for strengthening the organizations and institutions responsible for ensuring the rule of law and respect for human rights;

(c) Efficient budget performance, with an emphasis on decentralization, redistribution and auditing of budgetary resources.

Tax policy

47. Tax policy should be designed to enable the collection of the resources needed for the performance of the State's functions, including the funds required for the consolidation of peace, within the framework of a tax system consistent with the following basic principles:

(a) The system is fair, equitable and, on the whole, progressive, in keeping with the constitutional principle of ability to pay;

(b) The system is universal and compulsory;

(c) The system stimulates saving and investment.

48. The State should also ensure efficiency and transparency in tax collection and fiscal management so as to promote taxpayer confidence in government policy and eliminate tax evasion and fraud.

Tax collection target

49. Bearing in mind the need to increase State revenues in order to cope with the urgent tasks of economic growth, social development and building peace, the Government undertakes to ensure that by the year 2000, the tax burden, measured as a ratio of gross domestic product, increases by at least 50 per cent as compared with the 1995 tax burden.

Fiscal commitment

50. As a step towards a fair and equitable tax system, the Government undertakes to address the most serious issue relating to tax injustice and inequity, namely, evasion and fraud, especially on the part of those who should be the largest contributors. In order to eradicate privileges and abuses, eliminate tax evasion and fraud and implement a tax system which is, on the whole, progressive, the Government undertakes to:

Legislation

(a) Promote an amendment to the Tax Code establishing harsher penalties for tax evasion, avoidance and fraud, both for taxpayers and for tax administration officials;

(b) Promote an amendment to the tax laws designed to eliminate loopholes;

(c) Evaluate and regulate tax exemptions strictly so as to eliminate abuses;

Strengthening of tax administration

(d) Strengthen the existing auditing and collection mechanisms, such as cross-checking, tax identification numbers and tax credits for withholding of income tax and value-added tax;

(e) Simplify and automate tax administration procedures;

(f) Ensure the correct and prompt application or reimbursement of tax credit and punish severely those who do not return withheld value-added tax to the tax authorities;

(g) Create a special programme for large contributors in order to ensure that they comply fully with their tax obligations;

(h) Implement administrative structures specifically geared to the revenue collection and auditing programmes and to the application of the relevant tax laws;

(i) Strengthen the capacity of municipalities to exercise their authority to collect taxes;

Participation

(j) Ensure that the urban and rural development councils contribute to the definition and monitoring of tax policy within the framework of their mandate to formulate development policies;

Civic education

(k) Within academic curricula, continue to promote knowledge of, respect for and compliance with tax obligations as part of coexistence in a democratic society.

Enforcement of tax policy

51. The failure to fulfil tax obligations deprives the country of the resources needed in order to address the backlog of social needs affecting Guatemalan society. The Government undertakes to impose exemplary penalties on those who engage in various types of tax fraud, to modernize and strengthen tax administration and to give priority to spending on social needs.

V. FINAL PROVISIONS

1. This Agreement shall form part of the agreement on a firm and lasting peace and shall enter into force at the time of the signing of the latter agreement.

2. In order to ensure that this Agreement serves the interests of Guatemalans, the Government shall initiate immediately the programming and planning activities which will enable it to comply with the investment commitments contained herein.

3. In accordance with the Framework Agreement, the Secretary-General of the United Nations is requested to verify compliance with this Agreement.

4. This Agreement shall be disseminated as widely as possible; to this end, the cooperation of the mass media and of teaching and educational institutions is requested.

Mexico City, 6 May 1996

For the Government of the Republic of Guatemala
Gustavo PORRAS CASTEJÓN
Raquel ZELAYA ROSALES
Brigadier General Otto PÉREZ MOLINA
Richard AITKENHEAD CASTILLO

For the Unidad Revolucionaria Nacional Guatemalteca
General Command
Commander Pablo MONSANTO
Commander Rolando MORÁN
Commander Gaspar ILOM
Carlos GONZALES

For the United Nations
Marrack GOULDING
Under-Secretary-General
Jean ARNAULT

Notes

1 Introduction

1. Sir Marrack Goulding, "Preface," in *Of Centaurs and Doves: Guatemala's Peace Process*, ed. Susanne Jonas (Oxford: Westview Press, 2000), xiii.
2. More recently peace research has engaged with critical theory, largely focused on the work of Jürgen Habermas and its implications for power relations in speech acts, such as peace negotiations, and on Gadamer's hermeneutics. Oliver Ramsbotham, Tom Woodhouse, and Hugh Miall, *Contemporary Conflict Resolution*, 2nd ed. (Cambridge: Polity Press, 2005), Chapter 14.

2 Reading Gramscian Politics

1. The following relies heavily on Quintin Hoare and Geoffrey Nowell Smith's selections from and translations of the Prison Notebooks. Antonio Gramsci, *Selections from the Prison Notebooks of Antonio Gramsci*, ed. and trans. Quintin Hoare and Geoffrey Nowell Smith (London: Lawrence and Wishart, 1991). This translation, originally published in 1971 and reprinted six times, is a widely respected, and the most widely available, English-language collections of these works. E.J. Hobsbawm, "The Great Gramsci," *The New York Review of Books*, 4 April 1974, 39. Another English language translation of the Prison Notebooks, which aims to translate the *quaderni* in sequence, can be found in Antonio Gramsci, *Prison Notebooks, Volumes 1–3*, trans. Joseph A. Buttigieg (New York: Columbia University Press, 1991, 1996, 2007). Derek Bootham translated and edited further *quaderni*, focused less directly on political questions in Antonio Gramsci, *Further Selections from the Prison Notebooks of Antonio Gramsci*, ed. and trans. Derek Bootham (London: Lawrence and Wishart, 1995). Hoare has also edited and translated selections from Gramsci's political writings of 1910–1920 and 1921–1926: Antonio Gramsci, *Selections from the Political Writings 1910–1920*, ed. Quintin , trans. John Mathews (London: Lawrence and Wishart, 1977); Antonio Gramsci, *Selections from the Political Writings 1921–1926*, ed. and trans. Quintin Hoare (London: Lawrence and Wishart, 1978). A collection of Gramsci's cultural writings is found in

Antonio Gramsci, *Selections from Cultural Writings*, ed. David Forgacs and Geoffrey Nowell-Smith, trans. William Boelhower (London: Lawrence and Wishart, 1985) and Pedro Cavalcati and Paul Piccone, eds., *History, Philosophy and Culture in the Young Gramsci* (St. Louis: Telos Press, 1975). David Forgacs provides a collection of shorter excerpts of Gramsci's original works in *A Gramsci Reader: Selected Writings 1916–1935* (London: Lawrence and Wishart, 1988). The most comprehensive collection of commentaries on Gramsci's political theory can be found in Martin James' four-volume series: *Antonio Gramsci: Critical Assessments of Leading Political Philosophers* (London: Routledge, 2002). Joan Nordquist, ed., *Antonio Gramsci: A Bibliography, Social Theory: A Bibliographic Series* (Santa Cruz, CA: Reference Research Services, 1987), while a bit dated, includes works by and about Gramsci as well as references to reviews of such works. Giuseppe Fiori's biography is considered the definitive description of Gramsci's life available in English, Guiseppe Fiori, *Antonio Gramsci: Life of a Revolutionary*, trans. Tom Narin (New York: E.P. Dutton & Co., 1971). A simpler introduction to Gramsci's life and work is found in Anne Showstack Sassoon, ed., *Approaches to Gramsci* (London: Writers and Readers, 1982), while a brief introduction to his politics can be found in Roger Simon, *Gramsci's Political Thought* (London: Lawrence and Wishart, 1991). Walter L. Adamson, Carl Boggs, and Alastair Davidson all have written book-length treatments of Gramsci's life and politics: Walter L. Adamson, *Hegemony and Revolution: A Study of Antonio Gramsci's Political and Cultural Theory* (Berkeley: University of California Press, 1980); Carl Boggs, *The Two Revolutions: Antonio Gramsci and the Dilemmas of Western Marxism* (Boston: South End Press, 1984); Alastair Davidson, *Antonio Gramsci: Towards an Intellectual Biography* (London: Merlin Press, 1977); while Anne Showstack Sassoon, *Gramsci's Politics* (Minneapolis: University of Minnesota Press, 1987), focuses more exclusively on his politics. For discussions of the history and genealogy of hegemony with reference to Gramsci, see Ernesto Laclau and Chantal Mouffe, *Hegemony and Socialist Strategy: Towards a Radical Democratic Politics*, 2nd ed. (London: Verso, 2001); Peter Ghosh, "Gramscian Hegemony: An Absolutely Historicist Approach," *History of European Ideas* 27, no. 1 (2001): 1–43; Chantal Mouffe, ed., *Gramsci and Marxist Theory* (London: Routledge and Kegan Paul, 1979); Joseph A. Woolcock, "Politics, Ideology and Hegemony in Gramsci's Theory," *Social and Economic Studies* 34, no. 3 (1985): 199–210; Thomas R. Bates, "Gramsci and the Theory of Hegemony," *Journal of the History of Ideas* 36, no. 2 (1975): 351–366; Joseph Femia, "Hegemony and Consciousness in the Thought of Antonio Gramsci," *Political Studies* 23, no. 1 (1975): 75–93; James, *Antonio Gramsci*, vol. 2, part 8.

2. Marcus Green provided an interesting discussion of this in "Gramsci's Concept of Subaltern Social Groups," panel discussion at *Hegemony, Subalternity, and the Question of the Intellectuals,* York University, Toronto, October 20, 2006.

3. The ethicopolitical element in Gramsci's work is credited to the influence of Benedetto Croce. This is Forgacs' own translation of one of the Prison

Notebooks (Quaderno 10, I§12), and does not refer to a particular work by Croce; Croce did nonetheless write a volume specifically on ethics and politics: Benedetto Croce, *Etica E Politica* (Bari: Laterza, 1931); in English, Benedetto Croce, *Politics and Morals*, trans. Salvatore J. Castiglione (New York: Philosophical Library, 1945).

4. "Here again military organisation offers a model of complex gradations between subaltern officers, senior officers and general staff, not to mention the NCO's, whose importance is greater than is generally admitted. It is worth observing that all these parts feel a solidarity and indeed that it is the lower strata that display the most conspicuous esprit de corps, from which they derive a certain 'conceit' which is apt to lay them open to jokes and witticisms." Gramsci, *Selections from the Prison Notebooks of Antonio Gramsci*, 13, fn.

5. James Scott's critique of hegemony (which does not engage directly with Gramsci's texts) is in fact based on an argument akin to Gramsci's two consciousnesses. Much of what he attributes to "hegemony" in his critique would be understood as domination in the reading of Gramsci offered here. James C. Scott, *Weapons of the Weak: Everyday Forms of Peasant Resistance* (New Haven: Yale University Press, 1985).

6. Lukes indeed examines Gramsci in his discussion of the difficulties of working with a three-dimensional view of power. Steven Lukes, *Power: A Radical View* (London: Macmillan, 1974), 47–48.

7. Nonetheless, Lukes' schema is more useful for drawing out the key dimensions of how Gramsci's conception differs from the mainstream (i.e., in the realm of consciousness), than, for example, Paul Hirst's critique of IR, drawn from Hindess's later work, which does not get to questions of ideology and political subjectivity. Paul Hirst, "The Eighty Years' Crisis, 1919–1999—Power," *Review of International Studies* 24, no. 5 (1998): 134–135.

8. Hirst charges Robert Keohane with incoherence, and argues that Susan Strange, rather than ending in incoherence, ultimately adopts a conventional definition anyway. Hirst, "The Eighty Years' Crisis, 1919–1999—Power," 134 n6.

9. Robinson examines core-periphery relations exclusively through the lens of U.S. foreign policy, which acts as on behalf of "an emergent transnational elite" in a "power-over" frame. This emphasis on the United States as agent and power as domination has serious consequences for Robinson's empirical work, where he overstates the role, for example, of USAID-funded research institutes in Guatemala, which, rather than playing a determining role were subject to a complex process of appropriation and manipulation by local elites. William I. Robinson, "Neoliberalism, the Global Elite, and the Guatemalan Transition: A Critical Macrosocial Analysis," *Journal of Interamerican Studies and World Affairs* 42, no. 4 (2000): 89–107. (For a critique of the empirical limitations of *Promoting Polyarchy*, see William LeoGrande, "Deciding to Intervene: The Reagan Doctrine and American Foreign Policy; Promoting Polyarchy: Globalization, US Intervention, and Hegemony," *The Journal of Politics* 60, no. 1 [1998]: 306–310.) Given Robinson's project is to theorize global politics from the perspective of developing countries, it is ironic that his framework marginalizes the specific

experiences of (class hierarchies within) the South in constructing such an order.

10. Gramsci's perspective provides a radical interpretation of the term passive revolution, taken from Vincenzo Cuoco who used the phrase to describe the Neapolitan revolution of 1799 wherein an enlightened bourgeoisie introduced moderate reforms (without popular participation) to preempt genuine revolution. Forgacs, *A Gramsci Reader*, 413 n4. Cuoco's conception is echoed in the contemporary democratic transition literature of Guillermo A. O'Donnell, Philippe C. Schmitter, and Laurence Whitehead, eds., *Transitions from Authoritarian Rule: Prospects for Democracy* (Baltimore: Johns Hopkins University Press, 1986), critiqued by William I. Robinson, *Promoting Polyarchy: Globalization, US Intervention, and Hegemony*, vol. 48, *Cambridge Studies in International Relations* (Cambridge: Cambridge University Press, 1996).

11. For a thorough discussion of potentially conflicting elements within Gramsci's understanding of the state, see Perry Anderson, "The Antinomies of Antonio Gramsci," *New Left Review*, no. 100 (1976–1977): 5–78. Nevertheless, Peter Ghosh argues that Gramsci maintained "a relentless insistence that the only legitimate state is seamlessly bound to, and arises from, society. So what looks like Gramsci's confusion in the usage of terms, his 'failure' to find 'a single, wholly satisfactory conception of "civil society" or the State' is really a significant misunderstanding on the part of his classical 1970s commentators." He goes so far as to argue that Anderson's "problems and confusions are all self-inflicted." Ghosh, "Gramscian Hegemony" 5.

12. Here one might note the difference between this reading of Gramsci and that of Louis Althusser, who rejected the notion of an independent civil society altogether, arguing that "churches, parties, trade unions, families, schools, newspapers, cultural ventures" in fact all constitute "Ideological State Apparatuses," Louis Althusser, *Lenin and Philosophy, and Other Essays* (New York: Monthly Review Press, 1971) in Anderson, "The Antinomies of Antonio Gramsci," 35. Such a position destroys the subtlety of Gramsci's contribution to understanding the relationship between power and knowledge and arbitrarily reifies the state.

13. Razeto Miliaro and Misuraca argue that the root of this discrepancy lies in their two different readings of Hegel. Luis Razeto Migliaro and Pasquale Misuraca, "The Theory of Modern Bureaucracy," in *Approaches to Gramsci*, ed. Anne Showstack Sassoon (London: Writers and Readers, 1982), 77.

14. There is a debate as to whether historical blocs are necessarily hegemonic. There is nothing in what I have read of the *Prison Notebooks* in English (i.e., an incomplete record) that convinces me that it must be, though several commentators have come to that conclusion. Adamson seems to be in the minority in arguing "hegemonies always grow out of historical blocs but not all historical blocs are hegemonic." Adamson, *Hegemony and Revolution*, 177–178. Boothman argues that more than hegemony, Grasmci should be considered "the theorist of the historical bloc," which he reads as hegemonic though certainly not static. Gramsci, *Further Selections from the Prison Notebooks of Antonio Gramsci*, liii, xii. What is of significance for the discussion here is the heterogeneous nature of the historical bloc as a unifying

logic for the ensemble of social relations. Stephen Gill has compared the Gramscian historical bloc to Foucault's notion of a discursive formation, "a set of ideas and practices with particular conditions of existence which are more or less institutionalised, but which may be only partially understood by those that they encompass." Stephen Gill, "Globalisation, Market Civilisation, and Disciplinary Neoliberalism," *Millennium: Journal of International Studies* 23, no. 3 (1995): 403. The stronger analogue in Foucault's work may be the concept of a "dispositif" or apparatus: "the system of relations" that can be established between "a thoroughly heterogeneous ensemble consisting of discourses, institutions, architectural forms, regulatory decisions, laws, administrative measures, scientific statements, philosophical, moral and philanthropic propositions" Michel Foucault, "The Confession of the Flesh," in *Power/Knowledge: Selected Interviews and Other Writings 1972–1977*, ed. Colin Gordon (Brighton: Harvester Press, 1980), 194. Nonetheless, a central difference between the historical bloc and Foucault's concepts, as Gill notes, is that the historical bloc explicitly involves attention to the power of capital as a social relation. Gill, "Globalisation, Market Civilisation, and Disciplinary Neoliberalism," 404. On the compatibility between Gramsci and Foucault, see Barry Smart, *Foucault, Marxism and Critique* (London: Routledge and Kegan Paul, 1983); Anna Marie Smith, *Laclau and Mouffe: The Radical Democratic Imaginary* (London: Routledge, 1998); Michèle Barrett, *The Politics of Truth: From Marx to Foucault* (Stanford: Stanford University Press, 1991).

15. While sympathetic to the general observation that greater theorizing of development-related issues within a Gramscian frame is necessary, there are at least two significant problems with Robinson's critique. One is though he rejects what he describes as an emphasis on intraelite consensus among what he calls the "Italian School" of IPE, his work nonetheless remains focused on U.S. foreign policy: how the "new instruments of intervention [are] developed in the United States and then applied around the world," arguably committing the same error through a pronounced U.S. centrism. Robinson, *Promoting Polyarchy*, 30, 34. Furthermore, in many important respects his claims appear to reproduce rather than supersede the earlier Gramscian analyses that he critiques. This sense is reinforced by how little Robinson himself documents the "novelty" of his claims vis-à-vis previous work in Gramscian IPE, especially Cox and Augelli and Murphy, even as his argument in many cases seems to echo their arguments, particularly Cox's discussion of the internationalization of production and the state, which is uncited in, but very similar to, Robinson's discussion of globalization. Robinson, *Promoting Polyarchy*, 31–41.

16. To be clear, for Cox and Gramscian analysis generally, core and periphery are general heuristic devices and do not refer, for example, to strict categories as in world systems theory. Robert W. Cox, *Production, Power and World Order: Social Forces in the Making of History*, vol. 1, *Power and Production* (New York: Columbia University Press, 1987), 321.

17. For an excellent discussion of the role of social scientists in developing such "intellectual and moral leadership" to justify the United States' role in the

South in this period, see Irene L. Gendzier, *Managing Political Change: Social Scientists and the Third World* (Boulder, CO: Westview Press, 1985).

18. Indeed, the "rational peasant" school aspired to demonstrate that peasant societies could be studied through conventional economic models, while on the other side, "social modernisation" theorists aspired to show how the resistance of "traditional" sectors to adopt the inherently desirable "modern" culture was a sociopsychological issue. Tariq Banuri, "Development and the Politics of Knowledge: A Critical Interpretation of the Social Role of Modernization Theories in the Development of the Third World," in *Dominating Knowledge: Development, Culture and Resistance*, ed. Federique Apffel Marglin and Stephen A. Marglin (Oxford: Oxford University Press, 1990), 43–44.

19. "Whereas the fully proletarianized worker loses both control of the production process and ownership of the means of production, the semiproletarianized worker maintains these two forms of control. Because semiproletarians seek to protect this control, they compete fiercely on the labor market and accept wages below the price of subsistence." Alain de Janvry, *The Agrarian Question and Reformism in Latin America* (Baltimore: Johns Hopkins University Press, 1981), 84.

20. For a discussion of how neoliberalism became more acceptable as public policy from specific cases such as the fiscal crisis in New York City in the 1970s, see David Harvey, *A Brief History of Neoliberalism* (Oxford: Oxford University Press, 2005), Chapter 3.

21. Cox has described the process as "a collective effort of ideological revision undertaken through various unofficial agencies . . . then endorsed through more official consensus-making agencies like the OECD." Cox, *Production, Power and World Order*, vol. 1, 282. See also Stephen Gill, *American Hegemony and the Trilateral Commission* (Cambridge: Cambridge University Press, 1990).

22. It should be noted that the popularity of Gramsci among "Western Marxists" from the first availability of the Prison Notebooks in Europe involved precisely the alternative his work offered to the Stalinist trajectory "actually existing communism" had taken.

23. The term Washington Consensus was coined by John Williamson. Paul Krugman has observed: "By 'Washington' Williamson meant not only the U.S. government, but all those institutions and networks of opinion leaders centred in the world's de facto capital—the International Monetary Fund, World Bank, think tanks, politically sophisticated investment bankers, and worldly finance ministers, all those who meet each other in Washington and collectively define the conventional wisdom of the moment." Paul Krugman, "Dutch Tulips and Emerging Markets: Another Bubble Bursts," *Foreign Affairs* 74 (1995): 28.

24. As Harvey notes, "Neoliberals are particularly assiduous in seeking the privatization of assets. The absence of clear private property rights—as in many developing countries—is seen as one of the greatest of all institutional barriers to economic development and the improvement of human welfare.

Enclosure and the assignment of private property rights is considered the best way to protect against the so-called 'tragedy of the commons.'" Harvey, *A Brief History of Neoliberalism*, 65.

25. Thomas Lemke, "The Birth of Bio-Politics': Michel Foucault's Lecture at the Collège De France on Neo-liberal Governmentality," *Economy and Society* 30, no. 2 (2001): 190–207, represents a reconstruction from audio tape of Michel Foucault's exploration of neoliberal governmentality in his 1979 lectures at the Collège de France, which are not available in text form. Discussions of how governmentality relates to Foucault's other work can be found in Colin Gordon, "Introduction," in *Power: Essential Works of Foucault 1954–1984*, ed. James D. Faubion (New York: The New Press, 2000), xi–xli and Arpád Szakolczai, "From Governmentality to the Genealogy of Subjectivity: On Foucault's Path in the 1980s" (Florence: European University Institute, 1993).

26. "The economy embraces the entirety of human action to the extent that this is characterized by the allocation of scant resources for competing goals." Lemke, "The Birth of Bio-politics," 197.

27. Here the term neoliberal is used for consistency; Cox uses the term "hyper-liberal" for what is called neoliberal here; while "neoliberal" refers to Keynesianism in his schema.

28. The common use of discourses of social and human capital reflect this rationality. See, for example, the critiques of Ben Fine; inter alia Ben Fine, "The Developmental State Is Dead—Long Live Social Capital?" *Development and Change* 30 (1999): 1–19.

29. Gramsci made popular Romain Rolland's maxim "Pessimism of the intelligence, optimism of the will" in the pages of *Ordine Nuovo*. Gramsci, *Selections from the Prison Notebooks of Antonio Gramsci*, 175, fn75.

3 The Ensemble of Social Relations in Guatemala

1. A comprehensive description can be found in Julio Castellanos Cambranes, *Coffee and Peasants: The Origins of the Modern Plantation Economy in Guatemala, 1853–1897* (Stockholm: Institute of Latin American Studies, 1985), Chapter 1. Concineal was a natural dye made from the concineal insect, replaced by synthetic alternatives in European markets by the 1860s.

2. As in many Latin American countries, elite political debates in Central America at independence (1821) were polarized between liberals and conservatives. Liberals favored free-trade, the expansion of commercial agriculture, and sought to constrain the power of the Catholic church; conservatives sought "a return to the past," supporting the church and the "customs of colonial society" rather than the further commercialization of agriculture and increased trade, which invited greater foreign influence in Guatemala. Cambranes, *Coffee and Peasants*, 34.

3. The peasant revolt involved many contributing factors, among them the previous liberal regime's attempt to privatize and systematize land tenure,

which threatened indigenous communal property. Frederick Stirton Weaver, "Reform and (Counter)Revolution in Post-independence Guatemala: Liberalism, Conservatism and Postmodern Controversies," *Latin American Perspectives* 26, no. 105 (1999): 136.

4. Both conservatives and liberals supported various coercive labor practices against the indigenous. Under the colonial plantation system, indigineity was both an economic and an ethical question: forced labor was considered a moral necessity. Colin M. MacLachlan, *Spain's Empire in the New World: The Role of Ideas in Institutional and Social Change* (Berkeley: University of California Press, 1988), 48. The indigenous view of land and labor as a single unit was likewise considered problematic and force was philosophically and theologically defended as an acceptable measure to institutionalize the concept of private property. MacLachlan, *Spain's Empire in the New World*, 48.

5. The paragraph concludes by noting "Not surprisingly, the Indians protested these abuses: 'Under Liberal laws which guarantee our rights, we believe that no one may be forced to work against his will and that all coercion of this sort is illegal.' Such complaints met with little response." David McCreery, "'An Odious Feudalism': Mandamiento Labor and Commercial Agriculture in Guatemala, 1858–1920," *Latin American Perspectives* 13, no. 1 (1986): 108.

6. Smith reminds us that the signifiers that distinguish Indians from non-Indians today (religion, dress, political forms) "are not surviving pre-Hispanic forms but a fusion of native and Spanish traditions." Carol A. Smith, "Origins of the National Question in Guatemala: A Hypothesis," in *Guatemalan Indians and the State, 1540 to 1988*, ed. Carol A. Smith (Austin: University of Texas Press, 1990), 74.

7. For a pithy description of the banana sector as a vertical (and externally oriented) enclave, see Edelberto Torres-Rivas, *History and Society in Central America*, trans. Douglass Sullivan-González (Austin: University of Texas Press, 1993), 30–41. For a more detailed discussion of its expansion via control of transport, see Charles David Kepner, *The Banana Empire: A Case Study of Economic Imperialism* (New York: Russell and Russell, 1967); Paul J. Dosal, *Doing Business with the Dictators: A Political History of United Fruit in Guatemala 1899–1944* (Wilmington, DE: Scholarly Resources, 1993).

8. Ubico came to office when Guatemala had accrued a US$5 million debt, the interest on which threatened to consume nearly all government income. Jim Handy, *Gift of the Devil: A History of Guatemala* (Toronto: Between the Lines, 1984), 94. See also Kenneth J. Grieb, *Guatemalan Caudillo, the Regime of Jorge Ubico: Guatemala, 1931–1944* (Athens: Ohio University Press, 1979), Chapter 12; Paul J. Dosal, *Power in Transition: The Rise of Guatemala's Industrial Oligarchy, 1871–1994* (Westport, CT: Praeger, 1995), Chapter 4. "The formal advisory council foreshadows the origins of CACIF: To the industrialists, development policy should fall within the exclusive domain of the fuerzas vivas (a favorite self-description of the private sector in the 1980s), the planters, merchants, bankers, and industrialists who own productive enterprises and create jobs." Dosal, *Power in Transition*, 72.

9. See Cindy Forster, *The Time of Freedom: Campesino Workers in Guatemala's October Revolution* (Pittsburgh: University of Pittsburgh Press, 2001), 29–30, for a discussion of the "official myths" constructed to promote the idea that Ubico was popular among the peasantry, part of the "historical record" that has been adopted by many scholars.

10. "In the end, United Fruit was compelled to hire Ladinos alongside the descendants of West Indians, even though the company's 'scientific' racism led it to believe workers of African descent were best suited to banana production." Forster, *The Time of Freedom*, 16.

11. The officers were joined by civilian leaders as well. The transitional junta included Captain Jacobo Arbenz Guzmán, who would succeed Arévalo, Major Francisco Arana, who would lead a coup against Arévalo, and Jorge Toriello, a civilian.

12. As Dunkerley observed in 1988, the lack of scholarly treatment of this period given its later importance is somewhat surprising. James Dunkerley, *Power in the Isthmus: A Political History of Modern Central America* (London: Verso, 1988), 134. Since then a few volumes have been published: Forster, *The Time of Freedom*; Jim Handy, *Revolution in the Countryside: Rural Conflict and Agrarian Reform in Guatemala, 1944–1954* (Chapel Hill: University of North Carolina Press, 1994); Piero Gleijeses, *Shattered Hope: The Guatemalan Revolution and the United States, 1944–1954* (Princeton: Princeton University Press, 1991). Gleijeses provides the most thorough and well-documented political account, and is thus most relied upon here.

13. In an April 1945 speech, Arévalo claimed 'In Guatemala there is no agrarian problem . . . The problem is that the peasants have lost their desire to till the soil because of the attitudes and politics of the past. My government will motivate them, but without resorting to any measures that hurt other classes.' Gleijeses, *Shattered Hope*, 47.

14. See also Dunkerley, *Power in the Isthmus*, 40.

15. The plot and its demise are described in Gleijeses, *Shattered Hope*, Chapter 3. There had been other minor coup attempts against Arévalo as well; however, none save Arana's was seriously threatening.

16. See also Richard H. Immerman, *The CIA in Guatemala: The Foreign Policy of Intervention* (Austin: University of Texas Press, 1982), 106. Arbenz was in fact of middle-class origins, although quite fair given that his father was German; in 1939 he married a member of the Salvadoran upper class, María Vilanova, who is credited with introducing him to progressive politics and literature. The charge of personal self-interest is particularly illogical given that Arbenz was the only officer to resign in protest of the military's occupation of congress to strong arm it into selecting General Ponce during deliberations for Ubico's successor. Gleijeses, *Shattered Hope*, 139–140.

17. Government-owned *fincas* were lands appropriated from German farmers during World War II, which the Ubico administration took under U.S. pressure; see Dosal, *Power in Transition*, 79.

18. Schlesinger and Kinzer as well as Gleijeses emphasize that the strategy was to introduce competition rather than nationalization to improve Guatemalan

access to transport services. Stephen Schlesinger and Stephen Kinzer, *Bitter Fruit: The Untold Story of the American Coup in Guatemala* (New York: Anchor Books, 1983), 53; Gleijeses, *Shattered Hope*, 165.

19. For a discussion of taxation in the Arévalo period, see John H. Adler, *Public Finance and Economic Development in Guatemala* (Westport, CT: Greenwood Press, 1970).

20. For discussions of U.S. involvement in Guatemala: Walter LaFeber, *Inevitable Revolutions: The United States in Central America*, 2nd ed. (New York: W.W. Norton & Company, 1993); Schlesinger and Kinzer, *Bitter Fruit*; Dosal, *Doing Business with the Dictators*; Nick Cullather, *Secret History: The Cia's Classified Account of Its Operations in Guatemala, 1952–1954* (Stanford: Stanford University Press, 1999); Gleijeses, *Shattered Hope*.

21. Dunkerley suggests that 85 percent of the UFCO's land was fallow and that 653,197 of its 917,659 acres were subject to reappropriation, of which 15 percent were earmarked. Dunkerley, *Power in the Isthmus*, 149, James Dunkerley, "Guatemala since 1930," in *Cambridge History of Latin America*, ed. Leslie Bethell (Cambridge: Cambridge University Press, 1990), 227. Handy puts the figure at 250,000 of 350,000 manzanas. Handy, *Revolution in the Countryside*, 171. The company claimed on the order of 25 times the compensation offered by the government: Q15,854,849 versus the offered Q609,572. Handy, *Revolution in the Countryside*, 171–172; or, $15.8 million, at $75 per hectare versus the government figure of $627,527 at $2.99 per hectare, Dunkerley, "Guatemala since 1930," 227.

22. Handy argues that two other fincas fit in this category, while Gleijeses claims that four did. Handy, *Revolution in the Countryside*, 171; Gleijeses, *Shattered Hope*, 94.

23. Indeed anonymous reports from one of the UFCO's lobbyists that alleged Guatemala aspired to take over the Panama canal (a total fabrication, which would have been impossible for the limited range of the Guatemalan air force) became part of State Department and CIA reports. Schlesinger and Kinzer, *Bitter Fruit*, 107. The CIA was alleged to have distributed the UFCO's public relations reports to U.S. government officials as its own. Schlesinger and Kinzer, *Bitter Fruit*, 95.

24. "As Assistant Secretary Miller later explained to Congress, the World Bank 'sent a mission down there . . . to make some recommendations for loans. We asked [them]. . . . not to do that, that we . . . would exercise the veto power against such loans.'" Gleijeses, *Shattered Hope*, 128–129. Dunkerley similarly observes that the UFCO and the U.S. government "began to talk of the reform with the broad approval of the World Bank as 'persecuting' and 'victimizing' private enterprise." Dunkerley, *Power in the Isthmus*, 149.

25. Analyses of the Eisenhower administration decision making often note the prominent positions of John Foster Dulles, secretary of state, and his brother, Allan, head of the CIA, who had served as legal counsel to UFCO during the Ubico administration. Many of the concessions they negotiated for the company were undone by the 1952 Agrarian Reform. John Foster Dulles in particular was a forceful and visible member of the administration, dogmatically anticommunist. However, as Richard Immerman points out,

"Rather than supporting the standard portrait of Dulles leading by the strings a passive president and an overawed collection of advisers, the papers of the Eisenhower administration reveal a foreign policy resulting from a high degree of multiple advocacy, with the final decisions remaining firmly within the Oval Office." Immerman, *The CIA in Guatemala*, 14. Nonetheless, the Dulles brothers were particularly well-placed advocates for intervention, who allegedly even went so far as to manipulate the press (by discrediting a New York *Times* reporter to his editor) to affect the coverage of the coup. Schlesinger and Kinzer, *Bitter Fruit*, xiii.

26. Allan Dulles' assistant Richard Bissell stated: "The figleaf was designed to deny US involvement . . . yet the success of the operation hinged on convincing the Guatemalans that the US was indeed involved." Gleijeses, *Shattered Hope*, 247.

27. In fact, Ambassador John Peurifoy was the only U.S. diplomatic staff to know details of the operation, which was organized through the CIA. Gleijeses, *Shattered Hope* , 252. Immerman notes: "Without massive external assistance, including foreign troops, Castillo Armas could not possibly win an armed confrontation. Consequently, Allen Dulles and the other top CIA officials based their strategy on the assessment that both Arbenz and his military staff could be deceived into believing that Castillo Armas was at the head of a major insurrectionary force and that, if necessary, direct United States support waited in the wings. Perceiving such a challenge, the strategists predicted, the military would desert the revolution and Arbenz would resign. The actual scenario followed the CIA prognosis almost exactly." Immerman, *The CIA in Guatemala*, 162.

28. Details of the coup are related in Schlesinger and Kinzer, *Bitter Fruit*, Chapters 12 and 13; Immerman, *The CIA in Guatemala*, Chapter 7; Gleijeses, *Shattered Hope*, Chapter 14.

29. For the magnitude of such aid, see Robert H. Holden, "The Real Diplomacy of Violence: United States Military Power in Central America, 1950–1990," *The International History Review* 15, no. 2 (1993): 305. He notes: "it would seem that the United States gave the Guatemalan police forces during the 1960s nearly all of their handguns and nearly half their shoulder weapons. . . ." (305–306).

30. "At least until 1981 the Israeli connection represented a clear alternative to US military aid; thereafter it tended to become more of a surrogate although still providing the Guatemalan military with an appreciably wider margin of independence from Washington than was possessed by their regional counterparts. . . . Argentine expertise in urban counter-insurgency operations gained during the 'dirty war' in Buenos Aires resulted in the effective destruction of ORPA's (guerrilla group, discussed further below) network in the capital in 1981." Dunkerley, *Power in the Isthmus*, 490. "Given Israel's own dependence on US military hardware, and Washington's traditional interest in shutting out potential nonhemispheric military suppliers, it seems   likely that Israel stepped in only with the permission—perhaps even encouragement—of the United States." Holden, "The Real Diplomacy of Violence, 304.

31. Jonas claims that the World Bank was pressured to approve an US$18.2 million highway loan to Guatemala; the United States had rejected Arbenz' petition for the same loan. Here USAID is used for simplicity; during the early 1950s the agency was called the International Cooperation Agency. Susanne Jonas, "'Showcase' for Counterrevolution," in *Guatemala*, ed. Susanne Jonas and David Tobis (Berkeley, CA: North American Congress on Latin America, 1974), 77.

32. For a timeline of this period, see Dunkerley, *Power in the Isthmus*, 450–452. Régis Debray's reflections on the period can be found in his *Revolution on Trial: A Critique of Arms*, trans. Rosemary Sheed, vol. 2 (New York: Penguin Books, 1978). For discussions of the Maya in this period from an anthropological perspective, see, inter alia Beatriz Manz, *Refugees of a Hidden War* (Albany: State University of New York Press, 1988); Ricardo Falla, *Massacres in the Jungle: Ixcán, Guatemala, 1975–1982*, trans. Julia Howland (Boulder, CO: Westview Press, 1994); Robert M. Carmack, ed., *Harvest of Violence: The Maya Indians and the Guatemalan Crisis* (Norman: University of Oklahoma Press, 1988); Smith, *Guatemalan Indians and the State, 1540 to 1988*. The classic biography from an indigenous perspective is Rigoberta Menchú, *I, Rigoberta Menchú: An Indian Woman in Guatemala*, trans. Ann Wright (London: Verson, 1984). Discussions of the controversies it raised can be found in Arturo Arias, ed., *The Rigoberta Menchú Controversy* (Minneapolis: University of Minnesota Press, 2001).

33. *Foco* theory posits that under some conditions of extreme exploitation a revolutionary consciousness essentially already exists and thus a small group of guerrillas can initiate a revolution and the people will follow, without any need for extensive outreach or organization.

34. The success of this march and other instances of Indian-Ladino cooperation encouraged the CUC to be a multiethnic rather than Indigenous-based organization.

35. Dunkerley notes: "According to later military reports a major clash with 'subversives' took place, which explained neither the immediate burial of the dead in a single mass grave—alleged to be dug by tractors two days earlier—nor the fact that only one soldier was hurt, with a slight wound to the leg. Well before the church issued its detailed version of a premeditated mass execution the regime's clumsy rendition of events had been undermined by eye-witness accounts . . . . " Dunkerley, *Power in the Isthmus*, 477. See also Handy, *Gift of the Devil*, 245–246.

36. Handy notes that "Only the ambassador and one peasant survived. The peasant was later kidnapped from the hospital where he was recuperating from his injuries." Handy, *Gift of the Devil*, 247.

37. External actors accepted the developmentalist pretext for the model villages. USAID and the international NGO CARE established positions for joint military assistance/development programs. Howard Sharckman, "The Vietnamization of Guatemala: US Counterinsurgency Programs," in *Guatemala*, ed. Susanne Jonas and David Tobis (Berkeley, CA: North American Congress on Latin America, 1974), 194. Roads, for example, and other infrastructure that was ostensibly for development, had a strong

military purpose. Charles Brockett notes: "The Agency for International Development, which provides much of the financing, defends [roads] as meeting developmental objectives, but many observers in the region see other purposes: 'You'll see right away that there is always a military outpost at the end of all the roads in the Altiplano. The roads are for the security of the country.'" Charles D. Brockett, *Land, Power and Poverty: Agrarian Transformation and Political Conflict in Central America*, ed. Gilbert W. Merkx, *Thematic Studies in Latin America* (Boston: Unwin Hyman, 1988), 119.

38. For a study of religious divisions in Guatemala and their economic significance from an anthropological perspective, see Sheldon Annis, *God and Production in a Guatemalan Town* (Austin: University of Texas Press, 1987).

39. The RHEMI report is admittedly sponsored by the Catholic church, which has itself been divided between conservatives and liberation theologians throughout the war.

40. In fact, public education reaches 75 percent of students aged 7–14 in urban areas and 34 percent in rural areas.

41. In a comic but disturbing passage, they note that one pamphlet wrongly quotes Stalin as having advised people to "undermine the loyalty of citizens in general, and young people in particular, by making it easy for them to obtain drugs of all kinds, giving them alcohol, extolling their savagery, and strangling them with sexual literature." Susan D. Rose and Steve Brouwer, "The Export of Fundamentalist Americanism: US Evangelical Education in Guatemala," *Latin American Perspectives* 17, no. 4 (1990): 45.

42. The report notes that in Rabinal municipality, there had been only one suicide in the 10 years prior to the government campaign there, while during the repression there were 8 suicides in a 2-year period. The forensic anthropologists coordinating many of the investigations into the human rights abuses in Guatemala have published a volume on the massacres in that region: Equipo de Antropoloígia Forense de Guatemala, *Las Masacres En Rabinal*, 2nd ed. (Guatemala: EAFG, 1997).

43. Ríos Montt was Guatemala's first evangelical president. For a discussion of the relationship between his faith and his presidency, see David Stoll, *Is Latin America Turning Protestant? The Politics of Evangelical Growth* (Berkeley: University of California Press, 1990), Chapter 7. Rachel McCleary notes that "Ríos Montt preached on Sunday radio as part of his 'New Guatemala' propaganda campaign. He used the opportunity to preach moral values, but he also aired publicly his differences with the private sector and others with whom he was not in agreement." Rachel M. McCleary, *Dictating Democracy: Guatemala and the End of Violent Revolution* (Gainesville, FL: University Press of Florida, 1999), 55.

44. Francisco Beltranena was a founder and board member of the military's *Centro de Estudios Estratégicos para la Estabilidad Nacional* (Centro ESTNA, Strategic Studies Center for National Security).

45. This account relies on Rachel McCleary's detailed examination of CACIF, although it disagrees with the normative nature of her assessment that capitalism promoted "democratization," given the elitist definition of

democracy that it relies upon. Nonetheless, such claims expose the influence of the private sector, which is illuminating. McCleary, *Dictating Democracy*. For a discussion of how such elite-oriented theories rely on the separation of the political and the economic to justify economic inequalities, only to later reunite them with claims about the affinities between capitalism and democracy, see William I. Robinson, *Promoting Polyarchy: Globalization, US Intervention, and Hegemony*, vol. 48, *Cambridge Studies in International Relations* (Cambridge: Cambridge University Press, 1996), 52–56.

46. Indeed at this point CACIF was able to consolidate virtually all of the "organized private sector, incorporating previously independent USAID organizations." McCleary, *Dictating Democracy*, 58. The Commerce Commission was a public-private forum called at the behest of CACIF. The suspension of the IMF agreement, among other consequences, led to an acrimonious debate about the source of inflation in Guatemala: the government blaming it on capital flight and the private sector blaming it on corrupt government and debt. McCleary, *Dictating Democracy*, 61.

47. It is interesting to note the other places Lodge established/oversaw management schools: Philippines, India, Turkey, and later Iran.

48. Gustavo Rodriguez, interview, 4 April 2001. See also Michael E. Porter, "Competitiveness in Central America," in *Competitiveness in Central America: Preparing Companies for Globalization*, ed. INCAE (San Jose, Costa Rica: Latin American Center for Competitiveness and Sustainable Development, 1996).

49. See also Asociación Gremial de Exportadores de Productos No Tradicionales, ([cited 21 March 2002]); available from http://www.agexpront.com/ingles.htm.

4   The Peace Process

1. The dominant interpretation is expressed in Guillermo O'Donnell, Phillippe C. Schmitter, and Laurence Whitehead, eds., *Transitions from Authoritarian Rule: Prospects for Democracy* (Baltimore: Johns Hopkins University Press, 1986); Larry Diamond, Jonathan Hartlyn, Juan Linz , and Seymour Martin Lipset, eds., *Democracy in Developing Countries: Latin America*, 2nd ed. (Boulder: Lynne Rienner, 1999). Robinson describes the intellectual and moral leadership involved in the construction of these volumes: "Both were commissioned with the intent of informing US policy and policymakers, and are considered standard references in government and academia on 'transitions to democracy.'" William I. Robinson, "Globalization, the World System, and 'Democracy Promotion' in U. S. Foreign Policy," *Theory and Society 25*, no. 5 (1996): 45. "Democracy" in this context is in fact "polyarchy," the endorsement of elite-chosen options through elections.

2. See also Adolofo Aguilar Zinser, "Negotiation in Conflict: Central America and Contadora," in *Crisis in Central America: Regional Dynamics and US Policy in the 1980s*, ed. Nora Hamilton, Jeffry A. Frieden, Linda Fuller, and

Manuel Pastor Jr. (Boulder: Westview Press, 1988), and Dario Moreno, *The Struggle for Peace in Central America* (Gainsville: University of Florida Press, 1994), Chapter 3. Moreno contains the main Contadora texts (communiqués and agreements) in English.

3. The initiative remained, as Bruce Michael Bagley has observed, within distinctly "moderate" parameters: "the Contadora countries were also unanimous in their desire to moderate and contain the revolutionaries in Nicaragua and El Salvador." Bruce Michael Bagley, "Contadora: The Failure of Diplomacy," *Journal of Interamerican Studies and World Affairs* 28, no. 3 (1986): 3.

4. The Contadora process has been compared to a cat with nine lives because of its resilience despite what seemed like impossible set backs. Bagley, "Contadora," 4. What seems clear is that at different points both the Sandinistas and the Reagan administration renewed their involvement in the process for diplomatically strategic reasons, in the Nicaraguan case to put Washington on the defensive and in the latter case often to appear to be working in good faith to the U.S. Congress and thus justify greater aid to the contras.

5. Similarly references to foreign bases could imply either the United States in Honduras and El Salvador or concerns about a Cuban/Soviet presence in Nicaragua. Aguilar Zinser, "Negotiation in Conflict," 108.

6. In addition to its continued support for the contras throughout the Contadora process, an oft-cited example is the 1984 report of a commission chaired by Henry Kissinger that argued that Contadora was not necessarily in the U.S. national interest and that "'force remains an ultimate recourse' of US policy." Bagley, "Contadora," 7. See also James Dunkerley, *The Pacification of Central America* (London: Institute of Latin American Studies, 1993), 37.

7. The purpose here is to describe the international dynamic of the regional peace processes, not to assess the Sandinista revolution per se. However, it bears observation that even by conventional, "institutional" measures—such as a constitution protecting freedom of speech, assembly, movement, and the right to due process; the separation of powers; and regular elections—the Sandinistas had as strong a claim to democracy as several of its neighbours. William I. Robinson, *Promoting Polyarchy: Globalization, US Intervention, and Hegemony*, vol. 48, *Cambridge Studies in International Relations* (Cambridge: Cambridge University Press, 1996), 216.

8. Several Social Democratic governments, including Spain, Sweden, West Germany, and France, responded to a call by the Socialist International for such support.

9. According to Biekart, "Although exact figures are difficult to acquire, in 1987 the forty largest European private aid agencies channelled approximately US$ 130 million to Central America, a figure that increased to almost US$200 million in 1992. In relative terms this was about ten percent of total bilateral and multilateral aid flows to the region and more than forty percent of total bilateral aid flows to Central America of all the European governments combined." Kees Biekart, *The Politics of Civil Soceity Building: European Private Aid Agencies and Democratic Transitions in Central America* (Utrecht: International Books, 1999), 182.

10. European bilateral aid includes contributions from the following countries: Austria, Belgium, Denmark, Finland, France, Germany, Greece, Ireland, Italy, Luxembourg, the Netherlands, Norway, Portugal, Spain, Sweden, Switzerland, and the UK. Graphs 4.1 and 4.2 were calculated based on total net receipts.

11. For an explanation of the domestic factors behind Arias's election and regional peace initiative, see Moreno, *The Struggle for Peace in Central America*, Chapter 4.

12. This and the next two citations in this paragraph refer to the text of the agreement, which can be found in Moreno, *The Struggle for Peace in Central America*, Appendix 5.

13. Indeed Adolofo Aguilar Zinser argues that the Contadora process failed in part from its lack of initiative in lobbying the U.S. Congress against the Reagan administration's policies. Aguilar Zinser, "Negotiation in Conflict," 109–110.

14. The process included agreements between various parties, not necessarily exclusively the government and the guerrilla (URNG); thus the number varies according to what criteria are used. Further, not all of the agreements between the government and the URNG are substantive agreements; several are procedural. The substantive agreements between the URNG and the government are commonly understood as Framework Agreement for the Resumption of the Negotiating Process (Mexico, 10 January 1994), Comprehensive Agreement Human Rights (Mexico, 29 March 1994), Agreement on Resettlement of the Population Groups Uprooted by the Armed Conflict (Oslo, 17 June 1994), Agreement on the Historical Clarification (Oslo, 23 June 1994), Agreement on Identity and Rights of Indigenous Peoples (Mexico, 31 March 1995), Agreement on Social and Economic Aspects and Agrarian Situation (Mexico, 6 May 1996), Agreement on the Strengthening of Civilian Power and on the Role of the Armed Forces in a Democratic Society (Mexico, 19 September 1996), Agreement on the Basis for the Legal Integration of the Unidad Revolucionaria Nacional Guatemalteca (Madrid, 12 December 1996), and Agreement on a Firm and Lasting Peace (Guatemala, 29 December 1996). The Agreement on Constitutional Reforms and the Electoral Regime (Estocolmo [Sweden], 7 December 1996) was considered procedural, although it has significant implications for the fate of several substantive accords, as discussed below.

15. The URNG and CACIF accounts of this meeting differ significantly: the URNG describes it as very combative, tense, and aggressive, while the private sector described it as the occasion where the private sector communicated its good will toward open communication. Arnoldo Noriega, interview, 25 April 2001; Eduardo Gonzalez, interview, 24 April 2001.

16. Serrano's *auto-golpe* has been compared to that of Fujimori in Peru. See Rachel M McCleary, *Dictating Democracy: Guatemala and the End of Violent Revolution* (Gainesville, FL: University Press of Florida, 1999), for how the similarity may have pressured international actors to respond.

17. Rodrigo Asturias argues the URNG requested the United States as a "friend" government, given its sense that U.S. foreign policy had changed and it

would have the influence to ensure the Guatemalan government lived up to its commitments. Rodrigo Asturias, interview, 6 April 2001.

18. For a discussion of the resources CACIF was able to bring to the negotiations, see McCleary, *Dictating Democracy*.

19. As Roman Krznaric has pointed out, analyses that examine the empowerment of "civil" groups "informal" political processes should not neglect the power that "uncivil" groups may wield in these processes as well. He considers CACIF an "uncivil" group because of "its historical propensity to support non-democratic politics and, more broadly, . . . its attempts to limit citizenship rights in order to preserve economic privileges." Roman Krznaric, "Civil and Uncivil Actors in the Guatemalan Peace Process," *Bulletin of Latin American Studies Research* 18, no. 1 (1999): 15.

20. It should be noted that the ASC did successfully keep out "army front-organisations." Krznaric, "Civil and Uncivil Actors in the Guatemalan Peace Process," 9.

21. "Many sectors consider that Atlixco has tried to monopolise the Asamblea. The Atlixco group take the position that is was an 'open minority' in ASC and that the Asamblea is plagued by 'sectarianism, hegemony and dirigismo,' with some individuals and groups having disproportionate influence in ASC and its various committees, such as the organising committee." Krznaric, "Civil and Uncivil Actors in the Guatemalan Peace Process," 10.

22. In fact, participation reached its lowest point of the period 1950–1999 in 1990, with only 14.1 percent of those eligible voting. The figure was 14.5 percent in 1994 and 33.3 percent in 1995. Horacio Boneo and Edelberto Torres-Rivas, "¿Por Qué No Votan Los Guatemaltecos? Estudio De Participación Y Abstención Electoral" (Guatemala: Tribunal Supremo Electoral, 2001).

23. Another concern is that "institutional strengthening could modernise and legitimise institutions which are inherently unwilling to protect human rights by enforcing the law." Stephen Baranyi, "The Challenge in Guatemala: Verifying Human Rights, Strengthening National Institutions and Enhancing an Integrated UN Approach to Peace" (London: The Centre for the Study of Global Governance [London School of Economics], 1995), 19.

24. Although by any measure an enormous problem in humanitarian terms and by proportion of the population, estimates regarding the magnitude of the displaced population vary significantly. According to Diana Pritchard, the counterinsurgency resulted in 500,000 internally displaced people, 44,000 recognised and an estimated 110,000 undocumented Guatemalan refugees throughout Mexico. Diana Pritchard, "Refugee Repatriation and Reintegration," in *Central America: Fragile Transition*, ed. Rachel Sieder (London: Macmillan, 1996), 122. Finn Stepputat provides higher figures: one million internally displaced people and on the order of 350,000–400,000 refugees abroad, primarily in Mexico and the United States. Finn Stepputat, "Politics of Displacement in Guatemala," *Journal of Historical Sociology* 12, no. 1 (1999): 55.

25. The language of the Resettlement Accord understands land as a question of title, underscoring property rights, and reiterates the constitution as the

basis for participation in agrarian development; see the discussion of the texts of the Socio-Economic Accord below as well.

26. Many indigenous groups are satisfied with the accord, but not that it relied upon a package of constitutional reforms that failed, as discussed further below. Francisco Raymundo, interview, 2 April 2001.

27. Even representatives of such prominent organizations as the widow's association CONAVIGUA express the sentiment that the negotiations took place in a context "very isolated form the population." T. Macahio, interview, 23 April 2001.

28. Unfortunately Torres-Rivas does not provide a citation and I have been unable to acquire a copy of this statement; the date of issue of which would, of course, be very interesting. It does not appear explicitly in the URNG's 1992 proposals to the government. URNG, "Una Paz Justa Y Democratica: Contenido De La Negociacion," (Guatemala: URNG, 1992).

29. The ASC called for the reorientation of the military to external defense, its subordination to civil power, a 50 percent reduction in military personnel, equipment and troops, constitutional changes including allowing the minister of defense to be a civilian, the security of citizens to be the function of civilian security forces divorced from the military, the dismantlement of all the counterinsurgency structure including military intelligence and the dissolution of the PACs, and the definition of military service as voluntary with the possibility of conscientious objection. Asemblea de la Sociedad Civil, *Propuesta De La Asamblea De La Sociedad Civil—El Ejercito En Democracia* ([cited 10 June 2002]); available from http://www.us.net/cip/dialogue/1203.htm.

30. The reduction in the budget involves a 33 percent reduction in spending as a proportion of GDP from 1995 to 1999. Thus the proposed reduction would be somewhat offset by the then projected economic growth. Raúl Molina Mejía, "The Struggle against Impunity in Guatemala," *Social Justice* 26, no. 4 (1999): 65.

31. For details, see Central America Report, "Orpa Kidnapping Revealed; Peace Talks on Hold," *Central America Report*, 31 October 1996; Central America Report, "Peace Negotiations Still in Limbo," *Central America Report*, 7 November 1996.

5   The Post-Conflict State

1. There is much good evidence that growth does not lead automatically to development. For diverse but compelling arguments, see Victor Bulmer-Thomas, *The New Economic Model in Latin American and Its Impact on Income Distribution and Poverty* (London: Institute for Latin American Studies, 1996); Elmar Altvater, "The Growth Obsession," *Socialist Register* (2002); Sharachchandra Lélé, "Sustainable Development: A Critical Review," *World Development* 19, no. 6 (1991); see esp. p. 614. Furthermore, as de Janvry argues, growth does not automatically lead to articulation, de Janvry, *The Agrarian Question and Reformism in Latin America*, 49.

2. In fact, the annual percent increase in real GDP in Guatemala from 1995 to 2000 was 4.9 (1995) 3.0 (1996) 4.4 (1997) 5.0 (1998) 3.6 (1999) 3.3 (2000). Quest Economics Database: Americas Review World of Information, *Guatemala: Key Inidcators* (Janet Matthews Information Services, 2001 [cited 1 July 2002]); available from Lexis-Nexis.; Alex Tanzi, IMF's Annual GDP Percent Change Forecasts (2001 [cited 1 July 2002]); available from Lexis-Nexis.

3. For a discussion of women's rights as the "missing accord," see Susanne Jonas, *Of Centaurs and Doves: Guatemala's Peace Process* (Oxford: Westview Press, 2000), 86.

4. MINUGUA wrote numerous reports on the implementation of the accords: 16 specifically on the accords, 14 on its human rights missions, and approximately 18 others on related issues. This section relies significantly on the more recent MINUGUA reports on indigenous rights (MINUGUA, "The Indigenous Peoples of Guatemala: Overcoming Discrimination in the Framework of the Peace Agreements" [Guatemala: 2001]), on the armed forces agreement (MINUGUA, "Status of the Commitments of the Peace Agreements Relating to the Armed Forces" [Guatemala: 2002]), and its reports for the Consultative Group meetings (discussed further below) MINUGUA, "Report for the Consultative Group Meeting for Guatemala," (Guatemala: 2002); MINUGUA, "Executive Summary: MINUGUA Report to the Consultative Group Meeting for Guatemala." Susanne Jonas provides the most extensive discussion of the defeat of the constitutional reforms and is therefore relied upon heavily in that discussion. Jonas, *Of Centaurs and Doves*. The URNG has also created its own reports on implementation: URNG, "Balance Del Processo De Paz 1997–1999" (Guatemala: URNG, 1999).

5. The agreement required that the government propose draft constitutional amendments to congress within 60 days of its entry into force (which occurred with the final agreement on a Firm and Lasting Peace on 29 December 1996). The proposals were finally forwarded to congress in May 1997, subject to negotiation in congress until October 1998, and then put to a national referendum in May 1999, an election year.

6. Among these new elements were proposals regarding the incorporation of indigenous customary law into the new constitution, which were negotiated between the PAN and the Permanent Land Commission of the Coordinating Office of Organizations of the Maya People of Guatemala (COPMAGUA, Coordinadóra de Organizaciones del Pueblo Maya de Guatemala), the latter supported by the FDNG Jonas, *Of Centaurs and Doves*, 191–192. They passed congress with the necessary 2/3 majority, without the support of the FRG Jonas, *Of Centaurs and Doves*, 192.

7. According to the military's strategy in 2000, deployments in the Ixil area were to be dismantled in two stages in 2001, but neither stage was carried out. The chief of general staff in charge of the operation, who subsequently became minister of defence in the FRG/Portillo government, "spoke of the existence of a five-year plan for compliance with the commitments Peace Agreements [*sic*], including those concerning military redeployment. The Mission [MINUGUA] repeatedly requested a copy of this plan without receiving a

response..." MINUGUA, "Status of the Commitments of the Peace Agreements Relating to the Armed Forces," 17. MINUGUA describes the replacement of counterinsurgency operations handbook by "the comprehensive cooperation handbook" as a change "in name only . . . there have been few changes to the substantive content." MINUGUA, "Status of the Commitments of the Peace Agreements Relating to the Armed Forces," 21. Although some human rights and international humanitarian law themes have been incorporated, "a lack of coherence persists in the way they are approached." MINUGUA, "Status of the Commitments of the Peace Agreements Relating to the Armed Forces," 21.

8. Such monitoring is manifest internationally both in public, multilateral institutions such as the IFIs as well as in private institutions such as bond-rating agencies. Stephen Gill, *Power and Resistance in the New World Order* (Basingstoke: Palgrave Macmillan, 2003), 136–137. For how this surveillance has evolved since the Asian financial crises, see Susanne Soederberg, "On the Contradictions of the New International Financial Architecture: Another Procrustean Bed for Emerging Markets?" *Third World Quarterly* 23, no. 4 (2002).

Bibliography

Official Documents

Acuerdo de El Escorial [cited 3 May 2001]. Available from http://minugua. guate.net.

Acuerdo de Oslo [cited 5 June 2001]. Available from http://www.minugua.guate. net/negociacion/73a76.htm.

Agreement on Constitutional Reforms and the Electoral Regime 7 December 1996 [cited 3 May 2001]. Available from http://www.minugua.guate.net/.

Agreement on Resettlement of the Population Groups Uprooted by the Armed Conflict 17 June 1994 [cited 3 May 2001]. Available from http://www. minugua.guate.net/.

Agreement on the Identity and Rights of Indigenous Peoples 31 March 1995 [cited 3 May 2001]. Available from http://www.un.org.Depts/minugua.

Agreement on the Social and Economic Aspects and Agrarian Situation 6 May 1996 [cited 3 May 2001]. Available from http://www.un.org.Depts/minugua.

Agreement on the Strengthening of Civilian Power and the Role of the Armed Forces in a Democratic Society 19 September 1996 [cited 3 May 2001]. Available from http://www.un.org.Depts/minugua.

The Comprehensive Agreement on Human Rights 29 March 1994 [cited 3 May 2001]. Available from http://www.minugua.guate.net/.

Comunicado del CACIF en Ottawa [cited 3 May 2001]. Available from http:// www.minugua.guate.net/negociacion/83a84.htm.

Declaración de Atlixco [cited 31 May 2001]. Available from http://www. minugua.guate.net/negociacion/95a100.htm.

Declaración de Metepec [cited 31 May 2001]. Available from http://www. minugua.guate.net/negociacion/89a94.htm.

Declaración de Quito [cited 31 May 2001]. Available from http://www.minugua. guate.net/negociacion/85a88.htm.

Statement of the Delegation of Guatemala in the Security Council on Disarmament, Demobilization and Reintegration 23 March 2000 [cited 3 May 2001]. Available from www.un.int/guatemala/english/speeches/ pysd/2000/english.html.

Interviews

Arnault, Jean. Oxford, 16 November 2001.
Asturias, Rodrigo. Guatemala, 6 April 2001.
Briz, Jorge. Guatemala, April 2001.
Castillo, Rolando. Guatemala, 16 April 2001.
Corlazzoli, Juan Pablo. Guatemala, 18 April 2001.
Coxil, Enrique. Guatemala, 2 April 2001.
Fuentes, Juan Alberto. Guatemala, 4 April 2001.
González, Eduardo. Guatemala, 24 April 2001.
Macahio, T. Guatemala, 23 April 2001.
Noriega, Arnoldo. Guatemala, 25 April 2001.
Pivaral, José. Guatemala, 3 April 2001.
Porras, Gustavo. Guatemala, 24 April 2001.
Raymundo, Francisco. Guatemala, 2 April 2001.
Rodriguez, Gustavo. Guatemala, 4 April 2001.
Rosende, Raúl. Guatemala, 17 April 2001.
Stein, Ricardo. Guatemala, 24 April 2001.
Tiney, Juan. Guatemala, 5 April 2001.
Tiu, Romeo. Guatemala, 19 April 2001.
Wohlers, Patricia. Guatemala, 17 April 2001.
Zelaya, Raquel. Guatemala, 3 April 2001.

Articles, Books, and Other Sources

Adams, Richard. *Crucifixion by Power: Essays on Guatemalan National Social Structure, 1944–1966.* Austin: University of Texas Press, 1970.

Adamson, Walter L. *Hegemony and Revolution: A Study of Antonio Gramsci's Political and Cultural Theory.* Berkeley: University of California Press, 1980.

Adler, John H. *Public Finance and Economic Development in Guatemala.* Westport, CT: Greenwood Press, 1970.

Aguilar Zinser, Adolofo. "Negotiation in Conflict: Central America and Contadora." In *Crisis in Central America: Regional Dynamics and US Policy in the 1980s,* edited by Nora Hamilton, Jeffery A. Frieden, Linda Fuller, and Jr. Manuel Pastor, 97–119. Boulder: Westview Press, 1988.

Aguilera, Gabriel, Rosalinda Bran, and Claudinne Ogaldes. *Buscando La Paz: El Bienio 1994–1995.* Vol. 32, *Debate.* Guatemala: FLACSO, 1996.

Althusser, Louis. *Lenin and Philosophy, and Other Essays.* New York: Monthly Review Press, 1971.

Altvater, Elmar. "The Growth Obsession." *Socialist Register* (2002).

Andersen, Robert B. "Unilateralism and Multilateralism in a Transitional World: Lessons of the Arias Peace Plan." *Peace and Change* 17, no. 4 (1992): 434–457.

Anderson, Perry. "The Antinomies of Antonio Gramsci." *New Left Review* no. 100 (1976–1977): 5–78.

Annis, Sheldon. *God and Production in a Guatemalan Town.* Austin: University of Texas Press, 1987.

Arias, Arturo. "Changing Indian Identity: Guatemala's Violent Transition to Modernity." In *Guatemalan Indians and the State, 1540 to 1988,* edited by Carol Smith, 230–258. Austin: University of Texas Press, 1990.

———, ed. *The Rigoberta Menchú Controversy.* Minneapolis: University of Minnesota Press, 2001.

"Arias's Central American Peace Plan Gains European Support." *Latin America Weekly Report,* 28 May 1987, 1.

Armon, Jeremy, Rachel Sieder, and Richard Wilson, eds. *Negotiating Rights: The Guatemalan Peace Process.* 2nd ed. London: Conciliation Resources, 1997.

Asamblea de la Sociedad Civil. Propuesta De La Asamblea De La Sociedad Civil—El Ejercito En Democracia. In http://www.us.net/cip/dialogue/1203. htm. (accessed 10 June 2002).

Asociación Gremial de Exportadores de Productos No Tradicionales. In http:// www.agexpront.com/ingles.htm. (accessed 21 March 2002).

Azpuru, Dinorah. "Peace and Democratization in Guatemala." In *Comparative Peace Processes in Latin America,* edited by Cynthia Arnson, 97–126. Stanford: Stanford University Press, 1999.

Bagley, Bruce Michael. "Contadora: The Failure of Diplomacy." *Journal of Interamerican Studies and World Affairs* 28, no. 3 (1986): 1–32.

Banuri, Tariq. "Development and the Politics of Knowledge: A Critical Interpretation of the Social Role of Modernization Theories in the Development of the Third World." In *Dominating Knowledge: Development, Culture and Resistance,* edited by Federique Apffel Marglin and Stephen A. Marglin, 29–72. Oxford: Oxford University Press, 1990.

Baranyi, Stephen. "The Challenge in Guatemala: Verifying Human Rights, Strengthening National Institutions and Enhancing an Integrated UN Approach to Peace." 31. London: The Centre for the Study of Global Governance (London School of Economics), 1995.

———. "UN Verification: Achievements, Limitations and Prospects." In *Central America: Fragile Transition,* edited by Rachel Sieder, 247–270. London: Macmillan, 1996.

Barrett, Michèle. *The Politics of Truth: From Marx to Foucault.* Stanford: Stanford University Press, 1991.

Bates, Thomas R. "Gramsci and the Theory of Hegemony." *Journal of the History of Ideas* 36, no. 2 (1975): 351–366.

Bello, Walden. "Prospects for Good Global Governance: A View from the South." Focus on the Global South, 2002.

Biekart, Kees. *The Politics of Civil Society Building: European Private Aid Agencies and Democratic Transitions in Central America.* Utrecht: International Books, 1999.

Blaufarb, Douglas S. *The Counterinsurgency Era: US Doctrine and Performance, 1950 to the Present.* New York: Free Press, 1977.

Boggs, Carl. *The Two Revolutions: Antonio Gramsci and the Dilemmas of Western Marxism.* Boston: South End Press, 1984.

174   Bibliography

Boneo, Horacio, and Edelberto Torres-Rivas. "¿Por Qué No Votan Los Guatemaltecos? Estudio De Participación Y Abstención Electoral." 210. Guatemala: Tribunal Supremo Electoral, 2001.

Boyce, James K. "Aid Conditionality as a Toll for Peacebuilding: Opportunities and Constraints." *Development and Change* 33, no. 5 (2002): 1025–1084.

Broadhead, Lee-Anne. "Beyond the Traditions: Casting a Critical Light on Peace Research." In *Issues in Peace Research 1997–98*, edited by Lee-Anne Broadhead, 1–18. Bradford: University of Bradford Department of Peace Studies, 1997.

Brockett, Charles D. *Land, Power and Poverty: Agrarian Transformation and Political Conflict in Central America*. Edited by Gilbert W. Merkx, *Thematic Studies in Latin America*. Boston: Unwin Hyman, 1988.

Buchanan, James. "Guatemala under the FRG: Peace at a Crossroads." 11. Ottawa: Canadian Foundation for the Americas, 2000.

Bulmer-Thomas, Victor. *The New Economic Model in Latin American and Its Impact on Income Distribution and Poverty*. London: Institute for Latin American Studies, 1996.

Burgerman, Susan D. "Building the Peace by Mandating Reform: United Nations–Mediated Human Rights Agreements in El Salvador and Guatemala." *Latin American Perspectives* 27, no. 3 (2000): 63–87.

Buttigieg, Joseph A. "The Contemporary Discourse on Civil Society: A Gramscian Critique." *boundary 2* 32, no. 1 (2005): 33–52.

Byrne, Hugh. "The First Nine Months of the Guatemalan Peace Process High Expectations and Daunting Challenges." 15. Washington, DC: Washington Office on Latin America, 1997.

Cambranes, Julio Castellanos. *Coffee and Peasants: The Origins of the Modern Plantation Economy in Guatemala, 1853–1897*. Stockholm: Institute of Latin American Studies, 1985.

Carmack, Robert M., ed. *Harvest of Violence: The Maya Indians and the Guatemalan Crisis*. Norman: University of Oklahoma Press, 1988.

Cavalcati, Pedro, and Paul Piccone, eds. *History, Philosophy and Culture in the Young Gramsci*. St. Louis: Telos Press, 1975.

Central America Report. "International Community Rejects, Condemns and Isolates Serrano." *Central America Report*, 4 June 1993, 158–159.

———. "Last Minute Consensus." *Central America Report*, 11 June 1993, 165–166.

———. "Orpa Kidnapping Revealed; Peace Talks on Hold." *Central America Report*, 31 October 1996, 1–3.

———. "Peace Negotiations Still in Limbo." *Central America Report*, 7 November 1996, 4–5.

Chase-Dunn, Christopher. "Guatemala in the Gobal System." *Journal of Interamerican Studies and World Affairs* 42, no. 2 (2000): 109–126.

Colburn, Forrest D., and Fernando F. Sánchez. *Empresarios Centroamericanos Y Apertura Económica*. San José, Costa Rica: Educa, 2000.

Cox, Robert W. "Ideologies and the New International Economic Order: Reflections on Some Recent Literature." *International Organization* 33, no. 2 (1979): 257–302.

————. "Social Forces, States and World Orders: Beyond International Relations Theory." *Millennium* 10, no. 2 (1981): 126–155.

————. *Production, Power and World Order: Social Forces in the Making of History.* 4 vols. Vol. 1, *Power and Production.* New York: Columbia University Press, 1987.

————. "Gramsci, Hegemony and International Relations: An Essay in Method." In *Gramsci, Historical Materialism and International Relations,* edited by Stephen Gill, 49–67. Cambridge: Cambridge University Press, 1993.

Croce, Benedetto. *Etica E Politica.* Bari: Laterza, 1931.

————. *Politics and Morals.* Translated by Salvatore J. Castiglione. New York: Philosophical Library, 1945.

Cullather, Nick. *Secret History: The Cia's Classified Account of Its Operations in Guatemala, 1952–1954.* Stanford: Stanford University Press, 1999.

Davidson, Alastair. *Antonio Gramsci: Towards an Intellectual Biography.* London: Merlin Press, 1977.

de Janvry, Alain. *The Agrarian Question and Reformism in Latin America.* Baltimore: Johns Hopkins University Press, 1981.

de Soto, Alvaro, and Graciana del Castillo. "Obstacles to Peacebuilding." *Foreign Policy* 94 (1994): 69–83.

Debray, Régis. *The Revolution on Trial: A Critique of Arms.* Translated by Rosemary Sheed. 2 vols. Vol. 2. New York: Penguin Books, 1978.

Diamond, Larry, Jonathan Hartlyn, Juan J. Linz, and Seymour Martin Lipset, eds. *Democracy in Developing Countries: Latin America.* 2nd ed. Boulder: Lynne Rienner, 1999.

Dosal, Paul J. *Doing Business with the Dictators: A Political History of United Fruit in Guatemala 1899–1944.* Wilmington, DE: Scholarly Resources, 1993.

————. *Power in Transition: The Rise of Guatemala's Industrial Oligarchy, 1871–1994.* Westport, CT: Praeger, 1995.

Dunkerley, James. *Power in the Isthmus: A Political History of Modern Central America.* London: Verso, 1988.

————. "Guatemala since 1930." In *Cambridge History of Latin America,* edited by Leslie Bethell, 211–249. Cambridge: Cambridge University Press, 1990.

————. *The Pacification of Central America.* London: Institute of Latin American Studies, 1993.

Dunkerley, James, and Rachel Sieder. "The Military: The Challenge of Transition." In *Central America: Fragile Transition,* edited by Rachel Sieder, 55–102. London: Macmillan, 1996.

Equipo de Antropoloígia Forense de Guatemala. *Las Masacres En Rabinal.* 2nd ed. Guatemala: EAFG, 1997.

Falla, Ricardo. *Massacres in the Jungle: Ixcán, Guatemala, 1975–1982.* Translated by Julia Howland. Boulder: Westview Press, 1994.

Feinberg, Richard E. "The Changing Relationship between the World Bank and the International Monetary Fund." *International Organization* 42, no. 3 (1988): 545–560.

Femia, Joseph. "Hegemony and Consciousness in the Thought of Antonio Gramsci." *Political Studies* 23, no. 1 (1975): 75–93.

Fine, Ben. "The Developmental State Is Dead—Long Live Social Capital?" *Development and Change* 30 (1999): 1–19.

Fiori, Guiseppe. *Antonio Gramsci: Life of a Revolutionary.* Translated by Tom Narin. New York: E.P. Dutton & Co., 1971.

Forgacs, David, ed. *A Gramsci Reader: Selected Writings 1916–1935.* London: Lawrence and Wishart, 1988.

Forster, Cindy. *The Time of Freedom: Campesino Workers in Guatemala's October Revolution.* Pittsburgh: University of Pittsburgh Press, 2001.

FRG. 2001. 1995 Election Platform. In http://www.agora.stm.it/elections/election/guatemal.htm. (accessed April, 2001).

Gamboa M. Nuria, and Barbara Trentavizi. *La Guatemala Posible: La Senda Del Pacto Fiscal.* Guatemala: Asociación Centroamericana Hombres de Maíz, 2001.

Gendzier, Irene L. *Managing Political Change: Social Scientists and the Third World.* Boulder: Westview Press, 1985.

Ghosh, Peter. "Gramscian Hegemony: An Absolutely Historicist Aproach." *History of European Ideas* 27, no. 1 (2001): 1–43.

Gill, Stephen. *American Hegemony and the Trilateral Commission.* Cambridge: Cambridge University Press, 1990.

———. "Epistemology, Ontology, and the 'Italian School.'" In *Gramsci, Historical Materialism and International Relations*, edited by Stephen Gill, 21–48. Cambridge: Cambridge University Press, 1993a.

———. "Gramsci and Global Politics: Towards a Post-hegemonic Research Agenda." In *Gramsci, Historical Materialism and International Relations*, edited by Stephen Gill, 1–18. Cambridge: Cambridge University Press, 1993b.

———. "Globalisation, Market Civilisation, and Disciplenary Neoliberalism." *Millennium: Journal of International Studies* 23, no. 3 (1995): 399–423.

———. *Power and Resistance in the New World Order.* Basingstoke: Palgrave Macmillan, 2003.

Gleijeses, Piero. *Shattered Hope: The Guatemalan Revolution and the United States, 1944–1954.* Princeton: Princeton University Press, 1991.

Godoy, Julio. "Duarte, Arias Visits End Year of Diplomatic Successes." *Inter Press Service*, 4 December 1987.

Gordon, Colin. "Introduction." In *Power: Essential Works of Foucault 1954–1984*, edited by James D. Faubion, xi–xli. New York: The New Press, 2000.

Goulding, Sir Marrack. "Preface." In *Of Centaurs and Doves: Guatemala's Peace Process*, edited by Susanne Jonas, xiii–xvi. Oxford: Westview Press, 2000.

Gramsci, Antonio. *Selections from the Political Writings 1910–1920.* Translated by John Mathews. Edited by Quintin Hoare. London: Lawrence and Wishart, 1977.

———. *Selections from the Political Writings 1921–1926.* Translated and edited by Quintin Hoare. London: Lawrence and Wishart, 1978.

———. *Selections from Cultural Writings.* Translated by William Boelhower. Edited by David Forgacs and Geoffrey Nowell-Smith. London: Lawrence and Wishart, 1985.

————. *Selections from the Prison Notebooks of Antonio Gramsci.* Translated and edited by Quintin Hoare and Geoffrey Nowell Smith. London: Lawrence and Wishart, 1991.

————. *Further Selections from the Prison Notebooks of Antonio Gramsci.* Translated and edited by Derek Bootham. London: Lawrence and Wishart, 1995.

Grandin, Greg. "To End with All These Evils: Ethnic Transformation and Community Mobilisation in Guatemala's Western Highlands, 1954–1980." *Latin American Perspectives* 24, no. 93 (1997): 7–34.

————. *The Blood of Guatemala.* Edited by Walter D. Minggnolo, Irene Silverblatt, and Sonia Saldívar-Hull, *Latin America Otherwise: Languages, Empires, Nations.* Durham: Duke University Press, 2000.

Green, Marcus E. "Gramsci's Concept of Subaltern Social Groups." York University, Toronto, 2006.

Grieb, Kenneth J. *Guatemalan Caudillo, the Regime of Jorge Ubico: Guatemala, 1931–1944.* Athens: Ohio University Press, 1979.

Hall, Stuart. "Race, Articulation and Societies Structured in Dominance." In *Sociological Theories: Race and Colonialism,* edited by UNESCO, 305–345. Paris: UNESCO, 1980.

————. "Gramsci's Relevance for the Study of Race and Ethnicity." In *Stuart Hall: Critical Dialogues in Cultural Studies,* edited by David Morley and Kuan-Hsing Chen, 411–440. London: Routledge, 1996.

Handy, Jim. *Gift of the Devil: A History of Guatemala.* Toronto: Between the Lines, 1984.

————. *Revolution in the Countryside: Rural Conflict and Agrarian Reform in Guatemala, 1944–1954.* Chapel Hill: University of North Carolina Press, 1994.

Harvey, David. *A Brief History of Neoliberalism.* Oxford: Oxford University Press, 2005.

Hindess, Barry. "On Three-Dimensional Power." *Political Studies* 24, no. 3 (1976): 329–333.

Hirst, Paul. "The Eighty Years' Crisis, 1919–1999—Power." *Review of International Studies* 24, no. 5 (1998): 133–148.

Hobsbawm, E.J. "The Great Gramsci." *The New York Review of Books,* 4 April 1974, 39–44.

Holden, Robert H. "The Real Diplomacy of Violence: United States Military Power in Central America, 1950–1990." *The International History Review* 15, no. 2 (1993): 283–322.

Human Rights Office of the Archdiocese of Guatemala. *Guatemala: Never Again!* Translated by Gretta Tovar Siebentritt. London: Catholic Institute for International Relations, 1999.

IMF. "Guatemala: Recent Economic Developments." Washington, DC: International Monetary Fund, 1995.

————. "Guatemala: Recent Economic Developments." Washington, DC: International Monetary Fund, 1998.

Immerman, Richard H. *The Cia in Guatemala: The Foreign Policy of Intervention.* Austin: University of Texas Press, 1982.

Inter-American Development Bank. "Summary of Internationally Financed Projects: Document Presented to the Members of the Consultative Group of Guatemala." Washington, DC: Inter-American Development Bank, 2002.

James, Martin, ed. *Antonio Gramsci: Critical Assessments of Leading Political Philosophers*. 4 vols. London: Routledge, 2002.

Jonas, Susanne. "Showcase; for Counterrevolution." In *Guatemala*, edited by Susanne Jonas and David Tobis, 74–81. Berkeley, CA: North American Congress on Latin America, 1974.

————— *Of Centaurs and Doves: Guatemala's Peace Process*. Oxford: Westview Press, 2000a.

—————. "Democratization through Peace: The Difficult Case of Guatemala." *Journal of Interamerican Studies and World Affairs* 42, no. 2 (2000b): 9–38.

—————. "Democratization through Peace." In *Globalization on the Ground: Postbellum Guatemalan Democracy and Development*, edited by Christopher Chase-Dunn, Susanne Jonas, and Nelson Amaro. Lanham, MD: Rowman and Littlefield, 2001.

Kepner, Charles David. *The Banana Empire: A Case Study of Economic Imperialism*. New York: Russell and Russell, 1967.

Krugman, Paul. "Dutch Tulips and Emerging Markets: Another Bubble Bursts." *Foreign Affairs* 74, no. 4 (1995): 28–44.

Krznaric, Roman. "Civil and Uncivil Actors in the Guatemalan Peace Process." *Bulletin of Latin American Studies Research* 18, no. 1 (1999): 1–16.

Laclau, Ernesto, and Chantal Mouffe. *Hegemony and Socialist Strategy: Towards a Radical Democratic Politics*. 2nd ed. London: Verso, 2001.

LaFeber, Walter. *Inevitable Revolutions: The United States in Central America*. 2nd ed. New York: W.W. Norton & Company, 1993.

Lehman, Kenneth. "Revolutions and Attributions: Making Sense of Eisenhower Administration Policies in Bolivia and Guatemala." *Diplomatic History* 21, no. 2 (1997): 185–213.

Lélé, Sharachchandra. "Sustainable Development: A Critical Review." *World Development* 19, no. 6 (1991): 607–621.

Lemke, Thomas. "'the Birth of Bio-Politics': Michel Foucault's Lecture at the Collège De France on Neo-liberal Governmentality." *Economy and Society* 30, no. 2 (2001): 190–207.

LeoGrande, William. "Deciding to Intervene: The Reagan Doctrine and American Foreign Policy; Promoting Polyarchy: Globalization, US Intervention, and Hegemony." *The Journal of Politics* 60, no. 1 (1998): 306–310.

Leys, Colin. *The Rise and Fall of Development Theory*. London: James Currey Ltd., 1996.

Lodge, George Cabot. "The Birth of Incae (1963–1965): A View from Harvard." *ReVista* (Fall 1999). Available online at http://drclas.fas.harvard.edu/revista/articles/view/486 (accessed 25 June 2007).

Loomba, Ania. *Colonialism/Postcolonialism, The New Critical Idiom*. London: Routledge, 1998.

Louise, Christopher. "Minugua's Peacebuilding Mandate in Western Guatemala." *International Peacekeeping* 4, no. 2 (1997): 50–73.

Lukes, Steven. *Power: A Radical View.* London: Macmillan, 1974.

MacLachlan, Colin M. *Spain's Empire in the New World: The Role of Ideas in Institutional and Social Change.* Berkeley: University of California Press, 1988.

Macpherson, C.B. *The Political Theory of Possessive Individualism.* Oxford: Clarendon Press, 1962.

Manz, Beatriz. *Refugees of a Hidden War.* Albany: State University of New York Press, 1988.

McCleary, Rachel M. *Dictating Democracy: Guatemala and the End of Violent Revolution.* Gainesville, FL: University Press of Florida, 1999.

McClintock, Michael. *The American Connection, Vol. Ii: State Terror and Popular Resistance in Guatemala.* London: Zed Books, 1985.

McCreery, David. " 'An Odious Feudalism': Mandamiento Labor and Commercial Agriculture in Guatemala, 1858–1920." *Latin American Perspectives* 13, no. 1 (1986): 99–117.

———. *Rural Guatemala 1760–1940.* Stanford: Stanford University Press, 1994.

———. "Wage Labor, Free Labor, and Vagrancy Laws: The Transition to Capitalism in Guatemala, 1920–1945." In *Coffee, Society, and Power in Latin America,* edited by William Roseberry, Lowell Gudmundson, and Mario Samper Kutschbach, 206–231. Baltimore: Johns Hopkins University Press, 1995.

McCuen, John J. *The Art of Counter-revolutionary War: The Strategy of Counter-Insurgency.* Harrisburg, PA: Stackpole Books, 1966.

Menchú, Rigoberta. *I, Rigoberta Menchú: An Indian Woman in Guatemala.* Translated by Ann Wright. London: Verson, 1984.

MINUGUA. "The Indigenous Peoples of Guatemala: Overcoming Discrimination in the Framework of the Peace Agreements." Guatemala: MINUGUA, 2001.

———. "Report for the Consultative Group Meeting for Guatemala." 21. Guatemala: MINUGUA, 2002a.

———. "Status of the Commitments of the Peace Agreements Relating to the Armed Forces." Guatemala, MINUGUA, 2002b.

———. "Executive Summary: MINUGUA Report to the Consultative Group Meeting for Guatemala." 5. Guatemala: MINUGUA, 2003.

Molina Mejía, Raúl. "The Struggle against Impunity in Guatemala." *Social Justice* 26, no. 4 (1999): 55–83.

Monsanto, Pablo. "Discurso Pronunciado Por El Comandante Pablo Monsanto En Nobre De La Comandancia General De La URNG, En El Acto De Firma Del Acuerdo "Aspectos Socioeconomicos Y Situacion Agraria." In *Acuerdos De Paz: Aspectos Socioeconomicos Y Situacion Agraria,* edited by Asociacion de Investigacion y Estudios Sociales, 7–10. Guatemala: Asociacion de Investigacion y Estudios Sociales, 1996.

Moreno, Dario. *The Struggle for Peace in Central America.* Gainsville: University of Florida Press, 1994.

Mouffe, Chantal, ed. *Gramsci and Marxist Theory.* London: Routledge and Kegan Paul, 1979.

Nordquist, Joan, ed. *Antonio Gramsci: A Bibliography, Social Theory: A Bibliographic Series.* Santa Cruz, CA: Reference Research Services, 1987.

O'Donnell, Guillermo, Phillippe C. Schmitter, and Laurence Whitehead, eds. *Transitions from Authoritarian Rule: Prospects for Democracy.* Baltimore: Johns Hopkins University Press, 1986.

OECD. Aid Activity Database of the Dac. In www.oecd.org/dac/stats. (accessed 6 August 2003).

Palencia Prado, Tania. "Peace in the Making: Civil Groups in Guatemala." 44. London: Catholic Institute for International Relations, 1996.

Palma Murga, Gustavo. "Promised the Earth: Agrarian Reform in the Socio-Economic Agreement." In *Negotiating Rights: The Guatemalan Peace Process*, edited by Jeremy Armon, Rachel Sieder, and Richard Wilson, 74–80. London: Conciliation Resources, 1997.

Paris, Roland. *At War's End.* Cambridge: Cambridge University Press, 2004.

Pásara, Luis. "The Guatemalan Peace Process: The Accords and Their Accomplishments." In *Kroc Institute Occasional Paper #21: OP:3*, 33. South Bend, 2001.

Pearce, Jenny. "From Civil War to 'Civil Society': Has the End of the Cold War Brought Peace to Central America?" *International Affairs* 74, no. 3 (1998): 587–615.

Pérez Sáinz, Juan Pablo. *De La Finca a La Maquila.* San José, Costa Rica: FLACSO, 1996.

Polanyi, Karl. *The Great Transformation.* Boston: Beacon Press, 1957.

Porter, Michael E. *The Competitive Advantage of Nations.* New York: Free Press, 1990.

———. "The Competitive Advantage of Nations." *Harvard Business Review* 65, no. 2 (1990): 73–93.

———. "Competitiveness in Central America." In *Competitiveness in Central America: Preparing Companies for Globalization*, edited by INCAE, 63–119. San Jose, Costa Rica: Latin American Center for Competitiveness and Sustainable Development, 1996.

Pritchard, Diana. "Refugee Repatriation and Reintegration." In *Central America: Fragile Transition*, edited by Rachel Sieder, 103–136. London: Macmillan, 1996.

Quest Economics Database: Americas Review World of Information. 2001. Guatemala: Key Indicators. In Janet Matthews Information Services, Lexis-Nexis. (accessed 1 July 2002).

Ramsbotham, Oliver, Tom Woodhouse, and Hugh Miall. *Contemporary Conflict Resolution.* 2nd ed. Cambridge: Polity Press, 2005.

Razeto Migliaro, Luis, and Pasquale Misuraca. "The Theory of Modern Bureaucracy." In *Approaches to Gramsci*, edited by Anne Showstack Sassoon, 70–91. London: Writers and Readers, 1982.

Reid, Herbert, and Ernest J. Yanarella. "Toward a Critical Theory of Peace Research in the United States: The Search for an 'Intelligible Core.'" *Journal of Peace Research* 13, no. 4 (1976): 315–341.

Robinson, William I. "Globalization, the World System, and 'Democracy Promotion' in U.S. Foreign Policy." *Theory and Society* 25, no. 5 (1996a): 615–665.

————. *Promoting Polyarchy: Globalization, US Intervention, and Hegemony.* Vol. 48, *Cambridge Studies in International Relations.* Cambridge: Cambridge University Press, 1996b.

————. "Neoliberalism, the Global Elite, and the Guatemalan Transition: A Critical Macrosocial Analysis." *Journal of Interamerican Studies and World Affairs* 42, no. 4 (2000): 89–107.

Rojas, Paz. "Impunity and the Inner History of Life." *Social Justice* 26, no. 4 (1999): 13–29.

Rose, Susan D., and Steve Brouwer. "The Export of Fundamentalist Americanism: US Evangelical Education in Guatemala." *Latin American Perspectives* 17, no. 4 (1990): 42–56.

Rostow, W.W. *The Stages of Economic Growth: A Non-communist Manifesto.* 3rd ed. Cambridge: Cambridge University Press, 1990.

Roxborough, Ian. "Modernization Theory Revisited: A Review Article." *Comparative Studies in Society and History* 30, no. 4 (1988): 753–761.

Ruggie, John Gerard. "International Regimes, Transactions, and Change: Embedded Liberalism in the Postwar Economic Order." *International Organization* 36, no. 2 (1982): 379–415.

Salvesen, Hilde. "Guatemala: Five Years after the Peace Accords, the Challenges of Implementing Peace." Oslo: Peace Research Institute, 2002.

Sassoon, Anne Showstack, ed. *Approaches to Gramsci.* London: Writers and Readers, 1982.

————. *Gramsci's Politics.* Minneapolis: University of Minnesota Press, 1987.

Schirmer, Jennifer G. *The Guatemalan Military Project: A Violence Called Democracy.* Philadelphia: University of Pennsylvania Press, 1998.

Schlesinger, Stephen, and Stephen Kinzer. *Bitter Fruit: The Untold Story of the American Coup in Guatemala.* New York: Anchor Books, 1983.

Scott, James C. *Weapons of the Weak: Everyday Forms of Peasant Resistance.* New Haven: Yale University Press, 1985.

Shafer, D. Michael. *Deadly Paradigms: The Failure of US Counterinsurgency Policy.* Princeton: Princeton University Press, 1988.

Sharckman, Howard. "The Vietnamization of Guatemala: US Counterinsurgency Programs." In *Guatemala*, edited by Susanne Jonas and David Tobis, 193–203. Berkeley, CA: North American Congress on Latin America, 1974.

Sieder, Rachel. "Reframing Citizenship: Indigenous Rights, Local Power and the Peace Process." In *Negotiating Rights: The Guatemalan Peace Process*, edited by Jeremy Armon, Rachel Sieder, and Richard Wilson, 66–73. London: Conciliation Resources, 1997.

Simon, Roger. *Gramsci's Political Thought.* London: Lawrence and Wishart, 1991.

Smart, Barry. *Foucault, Marxism and Critique.* London: Routledge and Kegan Paul, 1983.

Smith, Anna Marie. *Laclau and Mouffe: The Radical Democratic Imaginary.* London: Routledge, 1998.

Smith, Carol A., ed. *Guatemalan Indians and the State, 1540 to 1988.* Austin: University of Texas Press, 1990a.

Smith, Carol A. ed. "Origins of the National Question in Guatemala: A Hypothesis." In *Guatemalan Indians and the State, 1540 to 1988*, edited by Carol A. Smith, 72–95. Austin: University of Texas Press, 1990b.

Soederberg, Susanne. "On the Contradictions of the New International Financial Architecture: Another Procrustean Bed for Emerging Markets?" *Third World Quarterly* 23, no. 4 (2002): 607–620.

Sollis, Peter. "Partners in Development? The State, Nongovernmental Organisations and the UN in Central America." *Third World Quarterly* 16, no. 3 (1995): 526–542.

Steele, Johnathan. "Europeans Back Arias Peace Plan for Central America." *The Guardian*, 22 May 1987.

Stepputat, Finn. "Politics of Displacement in Guatemala." *Journal of Historical Sociology* 12, no. 1 (1999): 54–80.

Stoll, David. *Is Latin America Turning Protestant? The Politics of Evangelical Growth*. Berkeley: University of California Press, 1990.

Szakolczai, Arpád. "From Governmentality to the Genealogy of Subjectivity: On Foucault's Path in the 1980s." Florence: European University Institute, 1993.

Tanzi, Alex. 2001. IMF's Annual GDP Percent Change Forecasts. In *Bloomberg News*, Lexis-Nexis. (accessed 1 July 2002).

Tobis, David. "The US Investment Bubble in Guatemala." In *Guatemala*, edited by Susanne Jonas and David Tobis, 132–142. Berkeley, CA: North American Congress on Latin America, 1974.

Torres-Rivas, Edelberto. *History and Society in Central America*. Translated by Douglass Sullivan-González. Austin: University of Texas Press, 1993.

———. *Negociando El Futuro: La Paz En Una Sociedad Violenta*. Vol. 36, *Debate*. Guatemala: FLACSO, 1997.

Trudeau, Robert H. *Guatemalan Politics: The Popular Struggle for Democracy*. Boulder: Lynne Rienner, 1993.

URNG. "Una Paz Justa Y Democratica: Contenido De La Negociacion." Guatemala: URNG, 1992a.

———. "Una Paz Justa Y Democrática: Contenido De La Negociación." May. Guatemala, 1992b.

———. "Balance Del Processo De Paz 1997–1999." 36. Guatemala: URNG, 1999.

Vitalis, Robert. "The Graceful and Generous Liberal Gesture: Making Racism Invisible in American International Relations." *Millennium* 29, no. 2 (2000): 331–356.

Warren, Kay B. *Indigenous Movements and Their Critics: Pan-Mayan Activism in Guatemala*. Princeton, NJ: Princeton University Press, 1998.

Weaver, Frederick Stirton. "Reform and (Counter)Revolution in Post-independence Guatemala: Liberalism, Conservatism and Postmodern Controversies." *Latin American Perspectives* 26, no. 2 (1999): 129–158.

White, Stuart, 'Macpherson, Crawford Brough'. In *The Concise Oxford Dictionary of Politics*, edited by Iain McLean and Alistair McMillan. Oxrford: Oxford University Press, 2003. http://www.oxfordreference.com.

ezproxy.library.yorku.ca/views/ENTRY.html?subview=Main&entry=t86. e771. (accessed 19 February 2007).

Whitehead, Laurence. "Pacification and Reconstruction in Central America: The International Components." In *Central America: Fragile Transition*, edited by Rachel Sieder, 215–246. London: Macmillan, 1996.

Whitfield, Teresa. "The Role of the United Nations in El Salvador and Guatemala: A Preliminary Comparison." In *Comparative Peace Processes in Latin America*, edited by Cynthia Arnson, 257–290. Stanford: Stanford University Press, 1999.

Wilson, Richard. "Violent Truths: The Politics of Memory in Guatemala." In *Negotiating Rights: The Guatemalan Peace Process*, edited by Jeremy Armon, Rachel Sieder, and Richard Wilson, 18–27. London: Conciliation Resources, 1997.

Woolcock, Joseph A. "Politics, Ideology and Hegemony in Gramsci's Theory." *Social and Economic Studies* 34, no. 3 (1985): 199–210.

Yashar, Deborah. "The Quetzal Is Red: Military States, Popular Movements, and Political Violence in Guatemala." In *The New Politics of Inequality in Latin America*, edited by Douglas Chalmers, Carlos M. Vilas, Katherine Hite, Scott B. Martin, Kerianne Piester, and Monique Segarra, 239–260. Oxford: Oxford University Press, 1997.

Zur, Judith. "The Psychological Effects of Impunity: The Language of Denial." In *Impunity in Latin America*, edited by Rachel Sieder, 57–72. London: University of London, Institute of Latin American Studies, 1995.

Index

Acción Católica 48, 52
Arbenz, Jacobo 39–42, 112, 159, 161
Archdiocese of Guatemala 50–1, 53
Arévalo, Juan José 38–9, 112, 159
ASC (Asamblea de Sociedad Civil) 75–7, 79, 80, 82–5, 89, 113, 115–16, 167–8
Auto-golpe (Serranazo) 74–5, 80, 113

CACIF (Coodinador de Asociaciones Agricolas, Comericiales, Industriales y Financieras) 46, 54, 56–7, 64, 72–5, 81–2, 84, 86, 92, 103, 158, 163–4, 167
CIA 42, 46, 160–1
Civil society (see also ASC; NGOs) 2, 5, 6, 9, 15–18, 28, 63–4, 66, 68, 71–2, 74, 80, 84, 86, 102–3, 108, 115–16
Clusters 54, 57, 98
CNR (Comisión Nacional de Reconciliación) 72–3
Cold War 3, 24–5, 31
Commissions 75, 78, 80–1, 102, 113, 128, 165
Contadora process 65–6, 68–70, 165–6
Counterinsurgency 6, 24, 43, 49, 51, 53–5, 60, 66, 81, 87–8, 101, 103, 162, 167

and modernization 60, 81, 99, 106, 108
trauma of 87–8
Counterinsurgent state 5, 6, 32, 43, 54, 59, 63
Cox, Robert 4, 5, 11–12, 20–2, 25–6, 155–7
CUC (Comité de Unidad Campesina) 48–9, 52, 162

De Janvry, Alain 23, 31, 156, 168
Demobilization 77, 80, 84–6, 88, 100
Democratization 66, 69–71, 93, 118–19, 163
Disarticulation 23–4, 31–2, 38, 41–3, 54, 60, 64
Dunkerley, James 41, 159–60

EGP (Ejercito Guerrillero de los Pobres) 47, 112
Electoral
reform 73, 82
system 72–3, 86, 96, 100, 166
Ensemble of Social Relations 5, 14, 16–17, 20–1, 30–2, 41, 54, 60, 63, 155
Esquípulas 65–6, 69, 70, 72, 113
Ethnicity 34, 52, see also indigenous peoples
ladino 34, 49, 52, 159
European Union, European Community 66, 69, 71, 89, 104

Evangelical Christianity   43, 51–2,
    55, 81, 163
Evangelical movement   43

FAR (Fuerzas Armadas
    Rebeldes)   46–7
FDNG (Frente Democratico de Nueva
    Guatemala)   77, 82, 86, 88
Financial services   57, 140
Fiscal policy   55, 93–4, 102–3,
    145–6
FRG (Frente Republicano
    Guatemalteco)   81–2, 86,
    100–1, 103

Gill, Stephen   12, 14, 20, 26–7, 30,
    103, 155
Gramsci, Antonio   5, 6, 9–20, 64,
    106–9, 151–7
Guerrilla (see also EGP; FAR;
    URNG)   49–51, 63, 77, 82–6,
    89, 100, 103, 162, 166

Hall, Stuart   5, 13, 18–19
Hegemony   5, 9–11, 13, 15–16, 22,
    152–4, 164–5, 167
Historical blocs   5, 17–20, 22, 25,
    30–1, 154–5
Human rights   2, 43–4, 63–4, 66,
    77–8, 86–7, 96, 102, 116,
    126–7, 136, 143, 147, 167, 170
Human Rights Office   50–1, 53
Human Rights Ombudsman   55,
    74–5

IDB (Inter-American Development
    Bank)   57, 104–5
IFIs (International Financial
    Institutions)   3, 27–8, 71, 84,
    92, 94, 103–4, 170
IMF (International Monetary
    Fund)   22, 26–7, 58, 71, 82, 156
Impunity   64, 84, 86–9, 116, 168
INCAE 56–7, 164

Indigenous
    peoples   2, 33–4, 37–8, 43, 46,
        49–54, 63, 79, 80, 94, 96,
        98–9, 121, 127–30, 135–6,
        141–4, 158
    organizations of/for   80, 86,
        102, 121, 137
    rights   2, 4, 53, 64, 77, 79, 82,
        169, see also peace
        agreements, indigenous
        rights
Integral state   17, 20, 99
International community (see also
    IDB; IFIs; IMF; World
    Bank)   1–3, 30, 48, 63, 65, 70,
    74–5, 82, 86, 90, 108, 139
Group of Friend states   75, 86,
    89, 166
Investment   29, 37, 43, 45, 92,
    124–5, 134, 139, 147
    foreign   34–6, 43, 45, 73

Jonas, Susanne   76

K&S (Klein and Saks)   45

Labor   19, 22–4, 34, 37, 59, 73,
    92, 94, 97, 120, 123, 133–4,
    136, 140, 146, 158
    code   39, 41
    relations   133–4, 136, 144
Land   37, 40–1, 52, 75, 83, 92–4,
    98–9, 118, 133, 135–8, 142–3,
    145, 158–9, 163, 167
    conflicts   83, 94, 142–3
    ownership   82, 92, 122, 136–8,
        142
    reform   39, 40, 42, 56, 73, 82–3,
        94, 99
Liberalization   27, 107

Maquila   57–9
Market mechanisms   27, 29, 30,
    92, 108

Massacres   76, 162–3
Maya, *see* indigenous peoples
Menchú, Rigoberta   52, 162
MINUGUA (UN verification
   mission)   2, 78, 80, 102,
   116–17, 169–70
Model villages   49, 55, 162
Modernization theory   5, 23–4,
   32, 36, 42, 60, 156

Neoliberalism   25–30, 32, 54, 61,
   63, 91, 96, 99, 103–4, 108,
   153, 155–7
NGOs (non-governmental
   organizations)   68, 129, 137,
   140, *see also* civil society
ORPA (Organización
   Revolucionaria del Pueblo en
   Armas)   47, 49, 85, 161

PACs (Patrullas de Autodefensa
   Civil)   50, 55, 85, 168
Pacto Fiscal   100, 103–4
Paris, Roland   3, 107
Passive revolution   6, 15, 54, 63,
   89, 107
Peace
   agreements: armed forces   76,
      85, 88, 100, 103;
      constitutional reforms   86,
      96, 100, 166; framework
      accord   75, 77, 149, 166;
      historical
      clarification   77–8, 166;
      indigenous rights   2, 79, 80,
      96, 100, 102–3, 113, 127–9,
      142, 166; operational   80,
      86, 100; Oslo   72–3;
      procedural   75;
      socioeconomic   2, 75, 77–8,
      82–3, 90–3, 95–6, 99, 100,
      102–3, 105, 115, 168
   conditionality   3, 6, 91, 104–7

PGT (Partido Guatemalteco de
   Trabajo)   40, 46, 112
Porter, Michael E.   29, 57, 98
Post-conflict state   3, 4, 6, 7, 25,
   30, 83, 91, 93, 95, 97, 99, 101,
   103, 105–7, 109, 168
Power   10–12, 14–16, 20–1, 23, 25,
   153–4
Privatization   27, 81, 94, 98–9, 156

Regional peace processes   63, 65,
   69–71, 89, 165
Resettlement   77–8, 96, 119, 129,
   136, 142, 166
Ríos Montt, José Efraín   51, 55,
   81, 113, 163
Robinson, William I.   12, 14, 20,
   64, 84, 108, 153–5, 164–5

Sieder, Rachel   79
Smith, Carol A.   34, 158
Social bases of conflict   1, 4, 71–2,
   90–1, 99, 107–8
Social security   39, 93, 123, 129,
   131
Subjectivity   16, 19, 20, 22, 99,
   108, 157
Surveillance   28, 102–4, 106,
   170
Sustainable development   115, 124,
   144, 146, 164, 168

Taxation   45, 57, 73, 92, 94, 100,
   102–6, 160
Taxes   25, 59, 94, 102–3, 106, 145,
   147–9
Tax evasion   147–8
Tourism   57, 59, 72, 81, 98–9, 135,
   139
Trade unions   130, 136–7, 154
Trasformismo   64, 76, 84, 89, 107

UFCO (United Fruit
   Company)   36–8, 41–2, 160

United Nations   3, 70, 75–6,
   116–17, 149, *see also*
   MINUGUA
United States   22–3, 25–6, 32,
   36–7, 39–42, 44, 51, 58, 65–6,
   70–1, 75, 104–5, 108, 155,
   161–2, 166–7
URNG (Unidad Revolucionaria
   Nacional Guatemalteca)   72–7,
   79, 82–7, 100, 113, 115–18,
   166, 168–9
USAID   44–5, 48, 162

Women   59, 93, 96, 122–3, 130,
   134, 137, 169
World Bank   27, 40, 42, 45,
   71, 82, 104–5, 156, 160,
   162

The Institute of World Politics
1521 16th Street, NW
Washington, DC 20036